CHILDREN COMMUNICATING

SAGE ANNUAL REVIEWS OF COMMUNICATION RESEARCH

SERIES EDITORS

F. Gerald Kline, *University of Minnesota*
Peter Clarke, *University of Michigan*

ADVISORY BOARD

Other Books in this Series:

Volume 1—   *Current Perspectives in Mass Communication Research*
F. Gerald Kline and Phillip J. Tichenor, Editors

Volume 2—   *New Models for Communication Research*
Peter Clarke, Editor

Volume 3—   *The Uses of Mass Communications:*
Current Perspectives on Gratifications Research
Jay G. Blumler and Elihu Katz, Editors

Volume 4—   *Political Communication:*
Issues and Strategies for Research
Steven H. Chaffee, Editor

Volume 5—   *Explorations in Interpersonal Communication*
Gerald R. Miller, Editor

Volume 6—   *Strategies for Communication Research*
Paul M. Hirsch, Peter V. Miller, and
F. Gerald Kline, Editors

Volume 7

SAGE ANNUAL REVIEWS OF COMMUNICATION RESEARCH

Children Communicating:

Media and Development of Thought, Speech, Understanding

ELLEN WARTELLA

Editor

SAGE PUBLICATIONS Beverly Hills / London

HQ
784
.T4
C5

For information address:

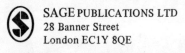

SAGE PUBLICATIONS, INC.
275 South Beverly Drive
Beverly Hills, California 90212

SAGE PUBLICATIONS LTD
28 Banner Street
London EC1Y 8QE

Printed in the United States of America

Library of Congress Cataloging in Publication Data

Main entry under title:

Children communicating.

   (Sage annual reviews of communication research ; v. 7)
   Bibliographic references throughout volume.
   1. Television and children—Addresses, essays, lectures.   2. Child development—addresses, essays, lectures.   3. Cognition (Child psychology)—addresses, essays, lectures.
4. Interpersonal communication—Addresses, essays, lectures.
I. Wartella, Ellen.
HQ784.T4C5   155.4'18   78-25867
ISBN 0-8039-1171-8
ISBN 0-8039-1172-6 pbk.

FIRST PRINTING

CONTENTS

Chapter 1

THE DEVELOPMENTAL PERSPECTIVE

Ellen Wartella

ADULTS' PERCEPTIONS OF CHILDREN have changed radically since the court of Louis XIV where children were dressed and regarded as miniature adults. Anyone who has observed a five year old and his 10-year-old sibling talking while watching television can intuitively recognize that children think differently and communicate differently. The "adjustment" of most adults in the way we talk to children reflects our strong intuition that they are not miniature adults. Indeed, as parents consistently confirm, "children" are different from adults, and a four year old is also different from a six year old who is different from a 10 or 12 year old. However, these strong intuitive notions of development have not always been built into research on children communicating.

This volume presents research studies which attempt to move away from wholesale adoption of adult models to describe how children communicate. These are studies of children's communicative behavior grounded in a "developmental perspective." This perspective seeks to describe and explain the nature of the communicative differences between four year olds, six year olds, 10 year olds, etc., and adults.

Two themes recur in the volume. First, all of the chapters are developmental research studies in the sense that they examine how communication activities change as children grow older. Implicit in the notion of abilities or behavior "developing" is the concept of time. Accordingly, the concern here is how children make sense of and communicate about their worlds as they grow older.

Second, all of the research studies presented here are strongly interested in cognitive aspects of communication. Because children's cognitive abilities change greatly through the course of development, the studies are influenced by such cognitive theorists as Jean Piaget, John Flavell, Joachim Wohlwill, Jerome Bruner and Heinz Werner. Specific reference to these and other scholars is made throughout the chapters.

This interest in cognitive factors of communication is not particular to research on children. Current communication research (both media related and interpersonally focused research) has shown new interest in the cognitive, interpretive activities of communication. For instance, two earlier volumes of this series, Clarke's *New Models for Communication Research* (1973) and Miller's *Explorations in Interpersonal Communication* (1976), are innovative approaches to examining the influence of these interpretive activities in communication.

This volume contains investigations of the growth of communicative behavior and ability both in terms of children's interaction with media and their communication with others around them. The common interest in associating qualitative change with age, while recognizing the involvement of cognition in these changes, serves as a consistent framing for both the interpersonal and the mass communication studies of development in this book.

The media related studies of children's communicative development diverge from the preponderance of research on children and television. Even a cursory bibliographic search of the area indicates that social learning theory is the predominant theoretical paradigm, while questions of children's modeling of televised behavior has been the major focus of experimental and survey research in this area (Surgeon General's Report on Television and Social Behavior, 1972). This is *not* the case for the studies in this volume. New questions and different sorts of communication issues regarding children's learning from television and use of television are dealt with in the following chapters. Of concern here are such issues as Collins' questions regarding children's interpretation and understanding of television narrative messages. His chapter reports the findings of several research studies which focus on children's abilities to make sense of the plotlines of entertainment programs.

In contrast, Salomon examines the nature of audio-visual media symbols or filmic attributes and their impact on the development of children's cognitive skills. Reeves is concerned with the nature of children's perceptions of television characters. He argues that while most television research with children has centered on children's "modeling" or learning of televised behaviors, potential modifiers of behavior learning may be children's interpretations and evaluations of the television people who perform the behaviors.

Krull and Husson focus their research interest on the question of children's attention behavior in front of the television set. They ask whether there are cycles in children's attention. What factors are important in developing a model of attention behavior?

Faber, Brown, and McLeod present a conceptualization for studying the impact of television entertainment programs on adolescents. Their model starts from the premise that adolescents are faced with certain developmental tasks, such as career planning and the development of sexual identity. The authors go on to identify the variables of interest in examining how media portrayals of these developmental tasks may have an impact on the adolescents' own resolutions of these tasks.

Lastly, Wartella, Wackman, Ward, Shamir, and Alexander are interested in the impact of television advertising on young children's consumer behavior. They adopt an information-processing perspective both to probe the extent of young children's memory for discrete elements in advertisements and to interpret the gist of the advertising message. They also examine how children use information such as that presented in television advertisements in reaching product choices.

Two studies focus on interpersonal communicative processes, the study by Delia and O'Keefe and that by Elliott. Delia and O'Keefe outline and review their research on the development of communicative competencies in children. This piece, which focuses on children's developing abilities to understand and communicate with other people, serves as a good companion piece to the Reeves essay on children's understanding of TV people.

Elliott tackles a major issue in communicative development: the general relationship between language development and cognitive development. Based on his assessment of the dominant theoretical positions regarding the developmental relationship of language to cognition, he systematically examines whether changes in language development occur prior to, follow, or are reciprocal with changes in general cognitive development. His piece is of particular interest both for its delineation of theoretical positions and as an examplar of analysis of distinctions between cognitive processes and linguistic abilities.

With this brief overview of each of the individual chapters, it is useful to examine the notion of developmental research generally. It is my intent to set the stage for the studies that follow by placing their contributions into a developmental perspective that considers alternative approaches to scrutinizing development. Specifically, this discussion considers three issues fundamental to such a perspective. First, the nature of developmental research will be examined in terms of the research treatment of the "age" variable. Second, varying ways of accounting for developmental changes in communicative behavior will be discussed. Finally, consideration will be given to the concept of "stages" in models of communicative development. The aim here is to identify important general issues of developmental research, but with the selectivity that focuses on communication research. For the scholar interested in more elaborated discussions of this sort, such sources as Baltes and Goulet (1971), Mussen (1970), and Wohlwill (1973) are recommended.

DEVELOPMENTAL RESEARCH AND THE AGE VARIABLE

The major objective of developmental research is "the description and explanation of age related behavioral change" (Baltes and Goulet, 1971). To talk about developing abilities then necessitates dealing with the concept of change over time. One cannot talk about developmental communication research without including in the discussion a notion of how children's communicative activities vary ontogenetically. The first step for studying a phenomenon developmentally then is to identify the phenomenon—to describe how it is manifested through the course of development (Flavell, 1977). How can communication researchers describe the nature of the communication processes for children of various ages? Diagnosis of communicative activities, or descriptions of how children of different ages communicate, is the predominant focus of the ensuing research studies.

Each chapter attempts to grapple with this first developmental research task of diagnosing the communication phenomenon of interest. As Flavell (1977) points out, diagnoses of age changes are not so easily demonstrated. As he notes in his distinction between production and performance deficiencies, sometimes children do not perform at their operative best in experimental research tasks; sometimes they can perform better than our tools can diagnose. A discussion of the impact of the problem of performance versus production can be seen in the chapters by Collins and Wartella et al. In the latter, for example, direct manipulation of experimental stimuli is used to examine kindergarten and third grade children's optimal ability in reaching product choices.

A second problem in diagnosing developmental aspects of children's communicative behavior is the inadequacy of our research tools. Central to this issue of conducting developmental studies of communication is the general problem posed by the relationship of language development to other aspects of communication. When we use verbal measures of communicative performance or thought, whether it be measuring children's comprehension of television content or interpersonal persuasive strategies, are we confounding verbal ability or limited verbal skills with more general communication skills? The issue is a thorny one. Elliott confronts this issue by examining language development per se. For most of the research studies in this volume, researchers attempt to use multiple measures, both verbal and nonverbal. The problem nevertheless remains one of the adequacy of our tools.

A third aspect of diagnosing communicative phenomenon is how to describe a variable through the course of development. Obviously, longitudinal studies would be most useful. While none of the current studies relies on longitudinal data to chart the course of developmental communicative activity (all are cross-sectional), each does rely on the convenience of studying children at different ages in the course of development to maximize the opportunity to examine ontogenetic changes in behavior. Sampling plans that judiciously take into account ages at which major differences in developmental growth are likely can maximize the researchers' ability to find age-related change. Collins' work on children's understanding of televised social portrayals, for instance, includes a wide age range of subjects from second grade through high school. Similarly, Delia and O'Keefe report data on communicative competencies in subjects from grade school through college. On the other hand, Krull and Husson, Wartella et al., Reeves, and Elliott are interested primarily in grade-school-aged children's communicative activities. Faber, Brown, and McLeod, furthermore, focus solely on adolescents. Thus, the researchers represented in this volume examine aspects of communicative processes in children spanning the developmental range from young preschoolers through adolescence.

Descriptions of how a communicative activity may or may not vary as children grow older do not constitute explanations for the communicative activity, however. The literature of developmental psychology is replete with discussions of the status of "age" as a developmental variable of interest (see, for example, Goulet and Baltes, 1970). Is age an independent variable? Is it part of the dependent variable? As Flavell (1977) notes, "Age is a vehicle and not a cause in itself."

This understanding implies certain problems associated with age as a variable of interest in conducting developmental research: (1) Age is an assigned variable; it cannot be manipulated or varied while holding other age-related variables constant. (2) In as much as some researchers argue that chronological age has no inherent psychological meaning (e.g., Wohlwill, 1973), age may only serve to help locate developmental aspects of behavior, not account for them. (3) Charting behavioral change across age levels is only *descriptive.* Explanations of age-related behavioral changes must of necessity derive from more than recourse to age alone because age does not have the status of an explanatory variable. Explanations of age-related behavior change must rely on other environmental or psychological variables (Baltes and Goulet, 1971).

Yet, we cannot discount the fact that children's cognitive, communicative, and social interaction abilities change radically as they grow older. Age, at least, is a good descriptive, blocking variable. Furthermore, through judicious sampling procedures, researchers can maximize their search for age-related changes in communicative activities. Particularly, cognitive and communicative activities seem to change dramatically around middle childhood (about seven or eight years of age). By sampling children for study from those younger and older than middle childhood, the researcher, using a cross-sectional study, can maximize his ability to discover age-related changes in a communicative activity where there are ontogenetic changes to be found. However, not all communicative activities may change with age. Reeves, for instance, argues that the underlying dimensions grade-school-aged children use to describe television characters are stable.

If the first step in conducting a developmental research study is to describe the developing phenomenon, that is to describe the phenomenon for children of different ages, then what constitutes explanation of a developmentally changing behavior? If age is not an explanatory variable, then how can communication researchers account for or explain age-related communicative processes? This brings us to the second major issue in developmental research, that of explanation.

SEEKING EXPLANATIONS OF
DEVELOPMENTAL ASPECTS OF COMMUNICATION

Where the current authors have sought to go beyond descriptions of age-related changes in communicative activities of children, several kinds of factors seem to emerge in explaining developmental change. Two such classes of variables are cognitive abilities of children and environmental/experiential factors, such as socialization variables or specific situational characteristics of communication tasks. For the interpersonal communication studies, a third class of variables, those relating to language development, should be noted. These classes of variables represent the major sources for explanation of age-related changes in children's communicative development. Recourse to one or more of them are found in the current studies.

First, consider how an understanding of cognitive growth in children might be used to account for, or at least identify, changing communicative activities. On the one hand, the researcher can posit certain differences in cognitive ability among the children under study based on some previous theoretical account of cognitive growth (e.g., Piaget's theory of intellectual development). In this case, the researcher might reason that, because children between four and seven vary along certain cognitive dimensions, children between these ages may resultantly differ in their communicative activities. In this case, the researcher does not directly measure cognitive growth, but rather reasons that given the age range of children under study, certain levels of cognitive abilities have been reached by these children.

On the other hand, the researcher may attempt to measure directly specific cognitive abilities, such as role-taking skills, to examine their impact on the communicative activity under study. Moreover, the more a researcher is interested in "explaining" rather than solely "describing" age-related changes in communicative activities, the more likely he or she is to measure directly the cognitive skills deemed important in the child's performance of a communicative task. Examples of both of these research strategies are present in this volume.

An illustration of the former strategy is that of Wartella et al. They examine whether changing memorial abilities in children are manifested in differences between kindergarteners and third graders' understanding of television advertisements. While they do not directly measure underlying aspects of memory development in their subjects, they rely on the general course of memory development as charted from other research studies to predict age-related differences in children's memory for an advertisement. Exemplifying the latter approach, Delia and O'Keefe measure the organization of cognitive constructs used by children in forming impressions of others to predict interpersonal communication activities such as children's ability to adapt messages to their listeners. In addition, Delia and O'Keefe also examine linguistic factors of communication.

In several of the other chapters in this volume, both cognitive factors and experiential variables are included in the researchers' accounts of communicative development. Collins, for example, starts from the assumption that children of different ages bring varying cognitive and experiential skills to the television viewing situation. These experiential skills vary in terms of children's understanding of media as a stimulus, understanding of how stories are constructed, and their general knowledge of the social world. He then attempts to describe how these factors result in differing interpretations of the same television narrative for children of different ages.

Similarly, Faber, Brown, and McLeod in conceptualizing the kinds of effects television presentations may have on adolescents include in their model such cognitive abilities as the ability to think abstractly and role-taking skills which may have an impact on how the adolescent interprets the media message. Furthermore, they also include several socialization variables such as family communication patterns and peer group interaction as potential environmental variables which also may mediate television effects on adolescent viewers.

There are other factors also cited in the various studies to account for age-related changes in communicative development, such as the child's motivation to make sense of a television plotline, situational contraints in the communicative task, affective factors, and individual differences in intelligence. The importance of these factors vary from one chapter to the next.

Thus far, we have noted research studies in this volume which have examined cognitive and environmental factors to explain communicative development. However, two authors *reverse* the causal relationship to examine the impact of communicative activities on the growth of cognitive abilities. Elliott, in his scrutiny of the relationship of cognition and language considers how development of linguistic factors may result in cognitive change. Salomon asks specifically how media, television in particular, as an environmental stimulus children encounter in the course of development, might have an impact on the growth of more general cognitive or mental skills. He is interested in how the symbol system of television, rather than the message content, may cultivate such mental skills as the ability to relate parts to the whole. So while some studies in this volume manifest the common presumption that cognitive abilities will have an impact on communicative activities, others entertain the notion of reverse causality.

THE CONCEPT OF "STAGE" IN
MODELS OF COMMUNICATIVE DEVELOPMENT

In two of the articles, Reeves and Delia and O'Keefe, the authors posit developmental stages in the growth of communicative activities in children. A brief introduction to the notion of "stages" and their use as a theoretical strategy would be useful.

Piaget's theory of intellectual development may be the best known "stage" theory. He posits that children from infancy through adolescence undergo qualitative changes in the cognitive skills available to them. His work attempts to describe and characterize the major dimensions of the child's thought from the sensorimotor (approximately ages 0-2), to preoperational (ages 2-7), to concrete operational (ages 7-12), to formal operational (12) stages of development. While Piaget's stage theory may be the best known, other developmental psychologists have also posited stage theories in the development of children's thought about both the phsyical and social worlds, e.g., Bruner's cognitive stages of enactive, iconic, and symbolic though processes (Bruner et al., 1966), Selman's (1971) stages of role-taking ability, and Kohlberg's (1969a) stage theory of moral development.

While the age ranges typically associated with, let's say, a Piagetian stage of development are not hard and fast, the crucial concept of stage serves as a convenient construct for summarizing and describing the child's available abilities. The notion of stage, as Kohlberg (1969b) points out, has certain theoretical implications. First, stages imply distinct, qualitative differences in children's modes of thinking or performance at each stage of development. Second, stages in development are typically posited to refer to activities which form an invariant sequence in individual development, such that while environmental or heredity factors may alter the rate of growth from one stage to another, they do not change the sequence of stage development. Third, activities or abilities associated with a given stage of development form a structured, interrelated whole. Fourth, stages are thought to be hierarchical and integrative: higher stages become increasingly differentiated while at the same time integrating lower stages to a new level of organization; in short, one stage "melds" into another.

The concept of stage thus serves the theoretical function of organizing sequentially and wholistically integrated characteristics of children's thought and behavior. With this conception, however, problems also arise. For example, critics of Piaget's theory (Pascual-Leone, 1970) point out that all abilities Piaget characterizes as available to a child at a particular stage may not be consistently available or developed. The posited relationship between a set of cognitive skills simply may not hold for all children at a given stage level.

Furthermore, in order to account for or explain developmental growth, it is often necessary for the theorist to specify what constitutes transition from one stage of development to the next. Here as well, critics of Piaget and other stage theorists dispute the validity of various transition rules (see, for example, Pinard and Laurendeau, 1969; Flavell and Wohlwill, 1969; Pascual-Leone, 1970).

Stage theories, however, do offer a succinct and convenient description of the manner in which the activity in question is manifested as children grow older. The facility of "stages" for describing developmental change is well-demonstrated by two chapters in this volume.

In his chapter, Reeves posits that a developmental account of television effects on children of different ages requires a more general theoretical model of the stages of children's understanding of television as a phenomenon. He argues, what is it that children understand about television and television people? When and how do children come to know that television is make believe? When do children begin to have notions of television as an economic industry? Similarly, Delia and O'Keefe sketch a model of the possible stages which describe the development of interpersonal communication skills in children, how children come to "manage meaning" through communicative interaction with others. Both of these contributions offer, through their attempts to construct stage models of communicative development, a host of research questions for future research.

AN INTRODUCTORY NOTE

With this brief overview, this chapter has attempted to introduce the reader to the developmental research perspective which characterizes the volume's studies. Rather than present any one "theory" of children's communicative behavior, this chapter has sought to identify some conceptual and methodological issues fundamental to studying how children communicate as they grow older. In the remaining chapters of this book, far richer theoretical accounts of children's communicative activities will be offered. It is the hope that this volume will encourage other researchers to adopt a developmental perspective by illustrating its heuristic value for studying how children communicate in both media and interpersonal communication situations.

REFERENCES

BALTES, P.B., and GOULET, L.R. (1970). "Status and issues of life-span developmental psychology." Pp. 4-23 in L.R. Goulet and P.B. Baltes (eds.), Life span developmental psychology. New York: Academic Press.

––– (1971). "Explanation of developmental variables by manipulation and simulation of age differences in behavior." Human Development, 14:149-170.

BRUNER, J.S., OLVER, R.R. and GREENFIELD, P.M. (1966). Studies in cognitive growth. New York: Wiley.

CLARKE, P. (ed.) (1973). New models for communication research, Vol. 2. Beverly Hills, Cal.: Sage.

FLAVELL, J.H. (1977). Cognitive development. Englewood Cliffs, N.J.: Prentice-Hall.

––– and WOHLWILL, J.F. (1969). "Formal and functional aspects of cognitive development." Pp. 67-120 in D. Elkins and J.H. Flavell (eds.), Studies in cognitive development. New York: Oxford University Press.

GOULET, L.R., and BALTES, P.B. (1970). Life span developmental psychology. New York: Academic Press.

KOHLBERG, L. (1969a) Stages in the development of moral thought and action. New York: Holt, Rinehart and Winston.

––– (1969b). "The cognitive developmental approach to socialization." In D. Goslin (ed.), Handbook of socialization theory and research. Chicago: Rand-McNally.

MILLER, G.R. (ed.) (1976). Explorations in interpersonal communication, Vol. 5. Beverly Hills, Cal.: Sage.

MUSSEN, P.H. (ed.) (1970). Carmichael's manual of child psychology, Vols. 1 & 2. New York: Wiley.

PASCUAL-LEONE, J. (1970). "A mathematical model for the transition rule in Piaget's developmental stages." Acta Psychologica, 63:301-345.

PINARD, A., and LAURENDEAU, M. (1969). "Stage in Piaget's cognitive developmental theory: Exigesis of a concept." Pp. 121-170 in D. Elkind and J.H. Flavell (eds.), Studies in cognitive development. New York: Oxford University Press.

SELMAN, R. (1971). "Taking another perspective: Role-taking development in early childhood." Child Development, 42:439-453.

Surgeon General's Scientific Advisory Committee on Television and Social Behavior (1972). Television and growing up: The impact of televised violence. Washington, D.C.: U.S. Government Printing Office.

WOHLWILL, J.F. (1970). "Methodology and research strategy in the study of developmental change." Pp. 4-23 in L.R. Goulet and P.B. Balter (eds.), Life span developmental psychology. New York: Academic Press.

––– (1973). The Study of Behavioral Development. New York: Academic Press.

Chapter 2

CHILDREN'S COMPREHENSION
OF TELEVISION CONTENT

W. Andrew Collins

The chief part television plays in the lives of children depends at least as much on what the child brings to television as on what television brings to the child (Schramm, Lyle, and Parker, 1961:74).

MASS MEDIA EFFECTS ON CHILDREN have been studied for more than a half-century; but Schramm, Lyle, and Parker's well known appraisal notwithstanding, most researchers have concerned themselves with *whether* and *in what ways* children are affected by what television brings to them (Stein and Friedrich, 1975). Much less attention has been given to the wide-ranging cognitive and predispositional characteristics that the child brings to television.

This is particularly true with regard to the questions of what skills children possess for comprehending portrayals of social roles, attitudes, and behaviors in adult entertainment programs. Such fare as action-adventure shows, family dramas, and situa-

AUTHOR'S NOTE: The preparation of this chapter was supported by Grant No. 24197 from the National Institute of Mental Health.

tion comedies attracts a large audience of children and adolescents, but they are produced primarily with the predilections and capabilities of adult viewers in mind. Their portrayals of social roles and behaviors are embedded in plots that are often subtle, inexplicit, and interspersed with extraneous or tangentially relevant material. The ways in which children understand these widely disseminated depictions of social reality are likely to be determined as much by the varying levels of cognitive capabilities that children bring to television as by the manifest content of the shows.

A brief example may clarify the pertinence of children's comprehension skills to the potential social impact of typical programs. Television dramas often involve one or more distinctive and salient social acts—say, aggression—along with some information that is relevant to evaluations of those acts and the characters who perform them. If violent fighting or shooting is perpetrated by a character who clearly wishes to harm his victim and who is obviously punished for what he does, the character and his behavior are likely to be evaluated negatively; on the other hand, aggression for the purpose of freeing a hostage, for which the perpetrator earns a medal of bravery, would probably be viewed much more positively. This contrast is familiar from laboratory studies (e.g., Berndt and Berndt, 1975; Costanzo et al., 1973; King, 1971; Piaget, 1965) in which characters are judged to be naughty or nice, or good or bad, because of the motives or consequences that are described along with their actions; and the same factors have been shown to affect observers' social behavior after watching aggressive models in observational-learning experiments (e.g., Bandura, 1965; Berkowitz and Geen, 1967; Berkowitz and Rawlings, 1963). However, in the stimuli for these laboratory studies, motives and consequences are explicitly portrayed and related to the action; while in television narratives, cues like motives and consequences are often portrayed subtly and inexplicitly and are frequently separated in time from each other and from the act to which they pertain. The viewer must *infer* that an action occurred because of the actor's motive that was portrayed some minutes earlier and that the consequences were, indeed, the result of the action.

Although adults commonly use their perceptions of emotions, motives, and outcomes as the bases for evaluations of others and their behavior (Jones, et al., 1971), children use such cues unreliably, depending heavily on concreteness, salience, and other characteristics of the portrayals (Chandler et al., 1973; Swann and Collins, 1978). In a complex presentation like the hypothetical ones in this example, their evaluations of social portrayals may be exacerbated by the need to infer interrelationships of important social cues, with the result that models affect them in ways that would not be readily predicted.

CHILDREN'S PROCESSING OF TELEVISION NARRATIVES

This chapter describes a program of research into children's comprehension of the complex events that occur in typical television dramas. In particular, their understanding of information such as the motives and consequences associated with a character's social actions and role behaviors has been examined. Of special interest is the fact that, if children of different ages perceive such information to different degrees or in different ways, the attitudinal and behavioral effects of television programs might well vary correspondingly.

Although it is not yet possible to give a complete account of the cognitive activities necessary for understanding a televised dramatic plot, it seems likely that mature comprehension involves at least three tasks or phases. First, the viewer *selects* essential pieces of information from the presentation, ignoring or paying less attention to extraneous detail. Second, these essential scenes or actions are *ordered* according to some scheme. Third, the viewer *makes certain inferences* that go beyond what has been explicitly presented in the stimulus. At its most efficient, the process may well involve continuous efforts during viewing not only to choose from the large amount of available information, but also to infer the relatedness among discretely presented units of information across time.

PARSING PROGRAMS

This analysis of processing activities suggests that children's comprehension should be examined with respect to two types of content in typical television plots: (1) *explicit* events that occur discretely in single scenes of a show, and (2) *implicit* information that is not explicitly mentioned or depicted, but is implied by the relations between scenes. For example, consider the following two hypothetical explicit events: Character A observes character B kill an old woman; later B jumps A from behind as A enters a room. The causal relation between these two events (that B jumped A because A had witnessed the assault he committed) is only implicit in the program and must be inferred by the viewer. The *because* connector is not explicitly mentioned, as it might well be in a written or orally presented story, but it is essential to understanding the nature of B's action. In short, in order to comprehend the social roles, behaviors, and attitudes portrayed in typical television dramas, children must not only select judiciously among the large number of single happenings or events that are shown, but they also must infer the relations among these discretely presented units of information across time.

Several steps are involved in assessing whether children understand explicit and implicit content. First, the content of the program must be specified. In the research being described here, this has been accomplished in a multiphase, overlapping process. Groups of naive adult raters are asked to view a program and list the essential information, the content "without which the plot cannot understandably be retold." The information they identify is then compiled into a master list along with "distractor" events that are portrayed but are not judged essential to understanding. This list of propositions about the program is then submitted to a second group of adults, who are asked to indicate the items they consider essential to comprehension. Information that is independently selected by a large proportion of the adult raters then becomes the focal content for study. Second, the terms in which children describe the plot must be identified. In the present research program stimulus programs were shown to pretest groups of children, who were then asked detailed open-ended questions about thy plot. This procedure uncovers possible differences between children's and adults' understanding of the program that deserve further study and also elicits words and phrases that are likely to be understandable to children when referring to the programs. Finally, measurement procedures must be devised to cover the essential content of the program. In the present work structured recognition measures, as well as open-ended interview measures of recall and explanation, were used. The multiple-choice recognition items dealt both with the explicit central scenes identified by the adult judges and the implicit antecedent and consequent circumstances relevant to them in the program. The working of questions and the correct and incorrect alternatives were based on the responses of children who had been interviewed in the development phases of projects (see phase 2 above).

One example may clarify the nature of the recognition measure. An explicit content item might concern a violent act ("When Luke was walking in the alley, he . . . saw a man kill an old woman"). Another might concern a later act of violence ("When Luke walked into the office, another man . . . jumped on him from behind"). A subsequent question concerns the cause of the fight ("Someone jumped on Luke . . . "because Luke knew they had killed an old woman"). The first two questions deal with central-scene comprehension; the third with inference. Children get one point for each correct answer in each category. Responses to open-ended questions and requests for explanations about the relations among program events provide within-subject checks on responses to recognition items.

COMPREHENSION OF EXPLICIT AND IMPLICIT CONTENT

The value of parsing the content of televised dramatic plots in this way can be seen in a recent investigation of children's comprehension by Collins et al. (1978). The design of this research enabled comparisons of children's comprehension of programs that differed in amount of information and in the difficulty of inferring relatedness among the essential events.

The program in question was an hour-long action-adventure show that was edited into four different versions. One version, the *Simple* version, portrays the murder of an elderly pan-handler who has inadvertently come upon the scene when a young man is committing a robbery. The police tie the killer to a series of forged checks written with a check protector stolen in the robbery and eventually track him down. The second, *Complex* version of the program contains this same plot, but in addition intermingles it with an extraneous subplot from the original show. This subplot is the story of an ex-detective who is rehabilitated back to the police force from skid row in the course of helping with the investigation and is not necessary for comprehension of the basic story line. The third and fourth versions are *Jumbled* renderings, in which the scenes from the Simple and Complex versions are randomly ordered rather than appearing in the original narrative sequence. Thus, there were four versions of the stimulus program: simple-ordered, simple-jumbled, complex-ordered, and complex-jumbled.

In the experiment, second, fifth, and eighth grade children watched one or another of the four versions and then answered recognition items about discrete scenes in the show and about the causal relationships that exist among scenes. These tests were constructed according to the procedure outlined above, which involved extensive work with samples of college under-graduates and children of the ages to be included in the study. These participants viewed the program and then selected scenes they considered crucial to understanding the plot and answered interview questions about various events, their causes and conse-quences. Adult judges (N=21) showed 89% average agreement on which scenes were central to the plot. Their answers, rephrased in terms readily understandable to the children, were used to formulate the questions and correct answers were the basis for incorrect alternative answers in the final item set; thus, these response options can be viewed as common misunderstandings of program events by children of the age groups included in the study.

Comprehension of Explicit Content

Comparison of performance on these recognition items across different age groups of children indicates that comprehension of story material presented in typical television programs is surprisingly more limited and more fragmentary than might be predicted for children as old as second and third graders. It is *limited* in the obvious sense that these grade-school children seem to remember a significantly smaller proportion of the essential, or central, information that is explicitly presented in single scenes than do older children, adolescents, and adults. On items dealing with the essential information in the program, second graders recalled an average of only 66% of the scenes that adults had judged as essential to the plot; fifth graders recalled 84% of these scenes, and eighth graders recalled 92%—nearly all of them. These age differences occur across the different versions of this program, organized in different ways and containing different numbers of scenes as Figure 1 shows. Furthermore, they parallel age trends reported in a different study in which the stimulus was a situation comedy (Collins, 1970).

A striking perspective on the limited comprehension of the younger children can be seen in the comparison between their knowledge of essential information and of nonessential informa-

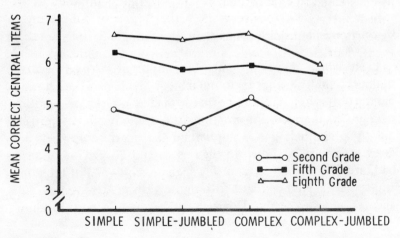

Figure 1

tion, on which they were also tested. The proportion of non-essential, or peripheral, detail increases just as the essential-content memory does during most of the early years. However, at the junior-high level, children either begin to decline in their knowledge of the incidental details or their rate of increase slows, while their knowledge of central content continues to improve. This pattern has also been found with other types of televised stimuli (Collins, 1970) and in studies of incidental learning in a variety of tasks (e.g., Hagen and Hale, 1973).

What do these results imply about young viewers' abilities for comprehending the central events in a television drama? It may be that, at the older ages tested in our studies, there is greater ability both to know what is important in the plot and to focus on that important information while ignoring nonessential content. Clearly, young grade-school children are less likely than older children to remember program content that adults consider essential to understanding a plot—that is why we call their understanding "limited." But it is also the case that a larger proportion of what they do recall is only peripheral to the sense of the portrayal. Thus, it is possible that second and third graders take away not only a less complete understanding of the program than fifth and eighth graders do, they may also be perceiving the content of the program somewhat differently because they retain a different set of cues. This possibility will be considered further in a later section of this chapter.

Comprehension of Implicit Content

Even when they do remember important explicit events, younger children appear to remember them in a rather fragmentary fashion. Children's performance on the recognition measure of implicit information—the content that is not explicitly presented, but is implicit in the relationships between discrete scenes—is shown in Figures 2a and 2b. Second graders had an overall mean score of fewer than half (47%) of the items adults had agreed on, and fifth and eighth graders scored 67% and 77%, respectively. However, as Figures 2a and 2b show, children's ability to make the inferences required for understanding implicit information varied with the particular version of the stimulus program they watched. It is clear from both boys' (Figure 2a) and girls' (Figure 2b) data that fifth and eighth graders comprehended best in the two ordered conditions. This also appears to be true for girls at the second-grade level, although not for second-grade boys. Indeed, second-grade boys appear to be performing at about chance level on this measure of inferences in all four conditions. The data are plotted for the sexes separately to show this difference in pattern among second graders. Since these younger girls were found to perform significantly better overall on the inference items than second-grade boys, with no sex differences at the older ages, the contrasting patterns in Figures 2a and 2b may simply reflect some verbal-memory advantages for second-grade girls (Maccoby and Jacklin, 1974) that are less apparent at older ages. In any case, contrasts between second-grade and older

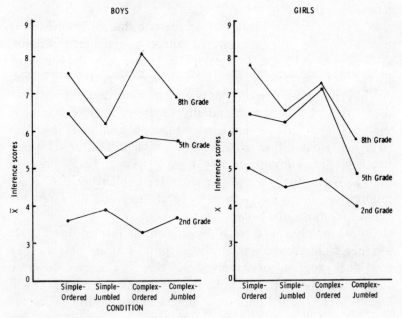

Figure 2a and 2b

viewers are apparent, both in terms of the extent of inferences and the likelihood of correct inferences from different stimulus programs.

Why these differences between young grade-school children and pre-adolescents and adolescents in the extent to which they have inferred information across temporally separate scenes? One possibility is that second-grade boys' poor performance on the recognition inference items is simply an artifact of their poor knowledge of individual scenes. Fortunately, it could be determined from questionnaire measures and interviews whether individual children knew the two discrete scenes or *premises* on which each of the inference items was based. Thus, the conditional probability could be computed that each child would make correct inferences, given that both of the relevant premise scenes, or only one of them, or neither one, were known at the time the children were tested. This kind of analysis reveals the extent to which children of different ages have inferred the relationships among discrete pieces of information from the program.

In Figure 3, the black bars represent the probability that inference items will be answered correctly, given that children have shown evidence in testing of knowing both pieces of discrete information on which the inference is based. Clearly, the likelihood of correctly integrating important information about the plot across temporally separate discrete scenes is relatively small for second graders; the probability is less than 50%, just greater than chance. The probabilities for fifth and eighth graders are considerably higher (68% and 75%, respectively). When they know the discrete, explicit scenes, older children are more likely to go beyond them and draw out the implied relationships between them.

Unfortunately, it is not possible to tell from these data whether children spontaneously integrate information as they view the program or simply draw the conclusions they are questioned about at the time the questions are presented. In Figure 3, the shaded bars show the mean probability of correct inferences at each age, given that only one piece or none of the premise information was known at time of testing. The likelihood of correct inferences when there is evidence at testing that children know only one, or neither, of the premise scenes is just greater than chance at all three grade levels. This might be taken as an indication that inferences are made and stored in memory during viewing, since premises might be forgotten once higher order integration of information is established. However, fifth and eighth graders were significantly more likely to infer cor- rectly when *both* premises were known; and the possibility

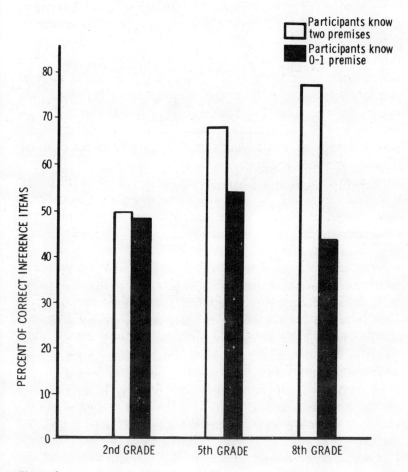

Figure 3

exists that since they know the premises, they may often be making inferences at the time of testing, rather than spontaneously during viewing. This problem is an important one, because it would be pertinent to know how likely children of different ages are to infer spontaneously the relations among cues that are potentially relevant to behavioral effects—even when they are not being questioned about them. If the testing procedure leads to an overestimate of children's comprehension, of course, the implication is that young viewers may actually understand even less about television portrayals than the present data indicate.

THE NATURE OF COMPREHENSION DIFFICULTIES

The apparently limited fragmentary knowledge of television plots shown by children as old as second and third graders raises two provocative questions: (1) Why do younger children infer so few relationships among scenes in dramas? and (2) what do they retain from programs, if not the array of occurrences and relationships that adults define as essential to adequate understanding?

STIMULUS ORGANIZATION AND COMPREHENSION

Some clues to the first of these questions emerge from the fact that, in the study by Collins et al. (1978), a number of the second-grade children were relatively unaffected by the varied ways in which the content of the television program was organized. Second-grade boys were not reliably worse on the comprehension measures when the scenes in the program were randomly scrambled than when they were presented in the chronological order in which they were outlined in the plot; but the older children and adolescents inferred the relations among scenes considerably better when the scenes were in the proper order.

In what ways did order of information seem to be important? Effects appeared both in facilitating selection and recall of explicitly presented information and in imputing inferences about their implicit relations. Knowledge of explicit content declined notably in the complex-jumbled condition at all grade levels; and distinctions between central and peripheral content were generally less marked in the jumbled, than in the ordered, conditions. As far as inference of implicit information are concerned, children at all these grade levels knew the explicit information required for making the inferences better in the ordered than in the jumbled conditions; moreover, even when they knew the requisite information, correct inferences were less likely in the complex-jumbled condition at all ages. Organization, then, seems important not only for inferring information that is not explicitly presented, but also for recognition of the explicit events that undergird these inferences. Apparently, the older children and the possibly more verbally mature second graders made better use of the information conveyed by order than younger children and, thus, more readily extracted the information implied by the temporal relation of scenes to one another.

In short, younger children's difficulties in comprehending complex audiovisual narratives seem to involve not only poor memory for explicitly portrayed content; they also involve relatively little likelihood that remembered information will be integrated to relate these explicit events across time. Furthermore, the order of scenes and their importance to understanding, as adults define it, make relatively little difference to preschool and grade-school viewers. From the perspective of an interest in television effects, the low power of these two predictors—order of events and importance of scenes—raises questions about whether merely portraying certain cues (e.g., the antecedent events for an antisocial act) necessarily means that the effect of the antisocial model will be moderated for younger viewers. It may be that these children will not ordinarily comprehend the causal relationship between action and antecedents—particularly if the two events occur in temporally disparate scenes and other cues about the link between them are absent or obscure.

AGE DIFFERENCES IN INFERENTIAL "ACTIVITY"

Results from the recognition measures discussed above emphasize that younger viewers' knowledge *accuracy* is often poor. However, further analyses and additional data supplement the findings of age differences in accuracy by showing parallel age differences in viewers' *activity* with respect to program content. Several procedures have been employed to extract indicators of cognitive activity in viewing (Collins & Wellman, forthcoming).

One such procedure involved interrupting each of the four stimulus versions at one or the other of two standard points that had been selected with the help of 21 adult judges. These adults agreed unanimously that the two scenes after which interruption occurred were points after which "something important might be expected to happen." Approximately two-thirds of the children in each condition at each grade level were interrupted at one of the two points. The remaining one-third of the children were not interrupted during viewing.[1] In the procedure the videotape was stopped at the designated interruption point, and children were asked to predict what they thought was going to happen next. Their predictions were coded, without regard to the accuracy of the predictions, according to whether they mentioned previous events from the program in explaining their answers.

Grade level markedly affected the relevance of predictions. The majority of the fifth and eighth graders (78% and 68%, respectively) predicted events that invoked, or followed from, plot occurrences prior to interruption. For example, following a scene in which the protagonist met a panhandler who resembled the man he had killed, *relevant* predictions often involved the likelihood that the confused murderer would react as though the man were his earlier victim ("He'll think he didn't kill the wino and will go after this guy"). Second graders rarely (28% of the cases) predicted events that followed from the pre-interruption scenes, but tended to rely on arbitrary or stereotypical action sequences (such as suggesting that the protagonist would

"grab him [the panhandler] and flip him or something").
Neither viewing condition nor sex affected predictions.

Related findings emerged in children's open-ended descriptions of the plot. Following viewing of the complete program
and completion of the recognition measure, the participants
were also asked to retell the story so that "someone who has
not seen it would know what happened." Transcripts of the
plot descriptions of children who were not interrupted during
viewing were coded by two independent coders for the extent
to which explicit or inferred relationships among events were
specified (interrater reliability = .74). Typically, second graders
simply strung together isolated events from the program, in the
manner described by Piaget's term, juxtaposition (Piaget, 1955);
whereas older children specified causal relations more explicitly
(and mostly correctly). Proportions of responses assigned to
higher-level categories (those in which causal relations are mentioned explicitly) increased significantly as a function of grade.
It should be noted that, in further analysis of the sequences
children described, younger children's retellings were found to
consist of virtually random orderings of scenes. That is, there
was no reliable order in which they cited the events, nor did it
appear that the children were specifying or implying relations
among events that would indicate age-characteristic reconstruc-
tions of what they saw.

All children were further presented with a randomly ordered
sequence of still pictures of the nine central scenes from the
primary plot (as identified by the panel of adult raters) and
were asked to reconstruct the order of occurrence of these
scenes in the program they had viewed. That is, they were asked
to choose the picture that showed what happened first, then the
one that showed what happened next, and so on to the end of
the sequence. No feedback was given about the choices they
made at each juncture. They were also asked to describe what
was happening in each of the nine pictures after they had
completed their ordering. Each child's ordering was compared
to the actual order of these events in the version of the program
that the child watched (i.e., ordered-condition participants'

orderings were compared to the sequence of scenes in those versions; jumbled-condition participants' to the order of scenes in the jumbled versions). One point was assigned to each possible pair of pictures that retained the correct order of scenes, and points were summed across all pairs. Correct recall of scene order was a linear function of grade level. Participants in the two ordered conditions matched the correct sequence of scenes in their versions more often than jumbled-condition errors were essentially random across subjects. No distinctive ordering emerged that was characteristic of younger, compared to older participants, or of jumbled-condition children compared to those in the ordered conditions.

QUALITATIVE VERSUS QUANTITATIVE DIFFERENCES

These results, taken together with the age-related changes in recognition of explicit and implicit program content, point to pronounced changes from second to fifth grade in children's understanding of a complex audiovisual narrative. Changes after fifth grade, while meaningful, are less dramatic. However, we can point to few differences in these grade-related trends that can be described as qualitative in the usual sense of that term. The observed age changes did not reflect *different* integration of cues, but simply the fact that younger viewers were less consistent and thorough in inferring relationships among portrayed depicted cues.

What accounts for their less reliable inference-making? To answer this question, post-hoc analyses were conducted of the inferences required by each item on the recognition test of inferences. All of these implicit-content items were rated independently within three different taxonomic frameworks: (1) types of content involved (i.e., did the inferences involve cues about motives, action, goals, or consequences, etc.?); (2) relations among the separate events that were involved in the inferences (e.g., did one event *cause* another, and was the cause psychological or physical?; did one event enable another one to happen?); and (3) number and abstruseness of inferential steps required to answer each item. Interrater reliabilities for the three sets of ratings were .92, .96, and .88, respectively. Independently, difficult items were arbitrarily identified as those that fewer than 45% of the second-grade children answered correctly. The item categorizations were then compared to the difficulty ratings.

Neither content category nor nature of the relation among events were related to item difficulty for the second graders. However, items rated as notably complex, in terms of number and abstruseness of intermediate inferential steps, overlapped significantly (80%) with the set of items that were difficult for second graders.

It is conceivable, of course, that important qualitative changes occur earlier in development and that the second graders in the study by Collins et al. represent a transition from earlier developmental states. This hypothesis cannot be evaluated without data from younger children, who have not been included in the research program thus far because the markedly different procedures needed to test them would make comparison with older groups difficult. However, since there was little evidence of age-characteristic regularities in second graders' responses, an appropriate working hypothesis is that younger children's comprehension and inference would simply be more severely constrained by even more inefficient processing activities and poorer selective abilities than appear to characterize young grade-school children.

EFFECTS OF PROGRAM CHARACTERISTICS

The less completely developed skills of younger children may be further taxed in much television viewing by the greater unfamiliarity of young viewers with a variety of characters, settings, and situations than more mature viewers are likely to suffer. Studies of information processing in memory tasks indicates that some prior experience with or knowledge of basic information about the material to be remembered facilitates memory for additional related content (Chi, 1977; Trabasso and

Foellinger, forthcoming). Perhaps the ease with which certain key information in a new task can be assimilated when there has been prior experience with similar materials reflects deeper processing (Craik and Lockhart, 1972) than occurs with relatively unfamiliar tasks, with the result that relationships among events, as well as the events themselves, are retained. Thus, when young children are generally familiar with the types of characters and settings in a program, they may find it relatively easier to accomplish the additional mental steps required to move from explicit portrayal to the implicit interrelationships carried by the plot.

In one study (Newcomb and Collins, 1977) designed to test this reasoning, socioeconomic status (SES) and ethnic-group membership served as the summary variables for the different information sets that may result from varying socialization experiences. Children who have been socialized in certain socioeconomic and/or ethnic subcultures were expected to show relatively better comprehension of television plots featuring characters and settings similar to their own backgrounds, compared to shows portraying relatively different social-class characters and settings. The design involved two replication studies in which equal numbers of black and white children from both lower- and middle-socioeconomic samples at second-, fifth-, and eighth-grade levels participated. One set of children including all of these subgroups viewed an edited version of a network situation comedy featuring white, middle-class characters; the second set of participants saw the same type of show featuring a similar plot line, but with black, working-class characters. In both narratives, the father is offered a better job in another city; his accpeting it would mean that members of the family would be separated. Both programs concluded with the father declining the job offer so that the family could stay together. In an earlier phase of the study, 14 white and black adults independently judged that the content of the middle-class, white family show would be more familiar to middle-class and white children, while the scenes in the working-class, black family show would be more familiar to working-class and black children. Composition of the two families and the complexity of the two narratives were similar.

After viewing these programs, the participants completed a recognition measure of comprehension similar to the instrument used by Collins et al. (1978). The items were based on the results of a series of open-ended interviews with samples of adults and children who independently indicated which information in the program was essential to understanding the plot. As in earlier studies children's answers were used in wording questions appropriately for child respondents and in formulating incorrect alternatives that reflected common types of misunderstandings of the plot. Four types of items were included about each of the scenes in which a plot-essential event had been judged to occur: a *central-content* item, dealing with the specific occurrence that was essential to remember about the plot; an *inferred-cause* item, about the reason or motive relevant to the action; an item about *inferred emotions*, or feelings of the actor during the scene; and a *peripheral-content* item, about some plot-irrelevant aspect of the scene. Incorrect alternatives to the central, peripheral, and inferred cause items were categorized as either *arbitrary* (a stereo-typical answer that had no basis in fact in the depicted occurrences) or *confusion* (an alternative based on an actual event occurring in another scene of the show, but that was not pertinent to the particular question). Each correct answer was given one point, and points were summed within categories of items to get subscores (e.g., for central-score memory or inferred-cause memory) and across all items to get a general recognition-memory score.

The data from the two programs were analyzed separately because of the differences in content, but the results of the replications parallel each other to a striking degree. Regardless of which program they viewed, second graders remembered all content categories more poorly than fifth graders, who in turn remembered significantly more poorly than eighth graders. The more pertinent data for the familiarity hypothesis, however, are the significant SES differences at the second-grade level, but not at the fifth and eighth grades in both replications (see Figure 4).

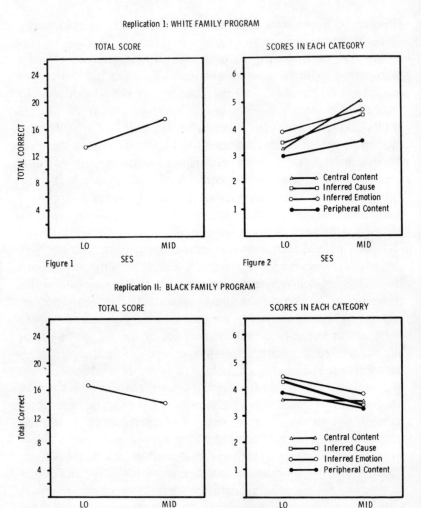

Replication I: WHITE FAMILY PROGRAM

TOTAL SCORE

SCORES IN EACH CATEGORY

Figure 1

Figure 2

Replication II: BLACK FAMILY PROGRAM

TOTAL SCORE

SCORES IN EACH CATEGORY

Figure 3

Figure 4

Figure 4

Among children who viewed the middle-class family program, middle-SES second graders remembered significantly more content overall and in the central and inferred-cause categories than lower-SES second graders. Among children who viewed the working-class family program, the reverse was true: compared to middle-SES second graders, lower-SES second graders knew significantly more overall, in the inferred-cause category, and in the inferred emotion and peripheral-content categories. These significantly higher scores did not, however, eliminate the comprehension differences between the best-performing second-grade groups and the fifth-grade viewers of the same program. There were no effects on ethnicity, nor was this variable involved in any noteworthy interactions with other variables.

These findings reiterate second graders' difficulties in comprehending typical television content, compared to preadolescents' and adolescents' understanding of similar programs. However, they also suggest that the comprehension difficulties of young grade-school children may reside partly in their lack of familiarity with the types of roles, characters, and setting portrayed in many adult entertainment programs. This is seen in second graders' improved performance when their own social-class background was watched with the social-class setting and characters being portrayed in a situation comedy. The fact that SES is, at the least, a rather gross indicator of what might be familiar to children underscores the striking nature of this finding.

Nevertheless, the generally better comprehension of fifth and eighth graders, compared to even the best-performing second graders, can probably not be fully explained by the fact that these older participants generally have more extensive and varied knowledge. Further examination of Newcomb and Collins' data yielded relevant evidence on this point. In one analysis, the nature of children's errors was determined by computing for each child the conditional probability of selecting a confusion, as opposed to an arbitrary, alternative when an incorrect response was made. The error patterns were similar for the two programs the children watched. When errors were made in the central-content items, second graders were equally likely to choose confusion and arbitrary alternatives; but for fifth and eighth graders, the confusion response was predominant in both the middle-class and working-class programs. This pattern suggests that when older children answer items about essential content incorrectly, it is likely to be because they incorrectly related pieces of information within the program. In contrast, second graders' errors resulted from their reliance on stereotypes of action sequences that had little to do with the implicit content of the stimulus shows.

The effect of knowing the central, or plot-essential, information in the program on knowledge of other content was also pertinent to processing the differences between older and younger children. Conditional probabilities were computed for correct associated content answers, given that the central-content answer was correct. Three conditional probabilities were computed for each participant: (1) probability that cause would be inferred if the central occurrence was known; (2) probability that the emotional state of the actor would be recognized if the central event was known; and (3) probability that peripheral or incidental details would be remembered if the central event was known. There were major increases in the conditional probabilities between second and fifth grades in all instances. Only in the middle-class family program did SES affect conditional probabilities, however. Particularly at the second-grade level in this replication, middle-SES children had significantly higher probabilities of all three types than lower-SES children.

Thus, the older participants in the study again appeared to employ selective and inferential strategies more effectively than the younger subjects, regardless of the presumed familiarity of the type of program they watched. This conclusion is supported by the two conditional probabilities analyses, and it is consistent with the extensive data on age-related comprehension differences in the study described above. In both cases, the fifth and eighth graders appeared to actively organize and infer relations among program occurrences; but second graders' perceptions of the programs were more random and fragmentary. Thus, age-related differences appear important, although younger viewers may be more likely than they otherwise would to appreciate the social and emotional concomitants of the central actions portrayed in televised social portrayals when there is some degree of familiarity with the general settings and types of characters being portrayed. One implication, which warrants further research, may be that this better comprehension is associated with more astute evaluations of the persons and events portrayed on television.

IMPLICATION OF COMPREHENSION DIFFERENCES
FOR TELEVISION EFFECTS

It is obviously too early to estimate what part of the variance in the social impact of television should be attributed to incomplete or distorted comprehension of what children see. Certainly, comprehension is only one age-related factor in a very complex equation for television effects. Other age-related discounting and self-control factors must also be considered. For example, younger children are less aware of the fictional nature of television and film dramas (Dysinger and Ruckmick, 1933); they have had less time to internalize social knowledge and social and moral values contrary to those depicted on television (cf. Feshback, 1970; Hoffman, 1970); they are perhaps less likely to use fantasy rather than overt behavior as a way of coping with social suggestions from television and real-life aggressive opportunities (Feshback and Singer, 1971; Singer, 1971); and so on.

At the same time, there is suggestive evidence of comprehension difficulties that may affect which program cues are retained by children and are, therefore, available to moderate the impact of socially relevant portrayals like antisocial violence. For example, Collins, Berndt, and Hess (1974) showed an edited version of an action-adventure program that is heavily viewed by children to kindergarten, second, fifth, and eighth graders and then interviewed them to assess their memory for the plot and their understanding of the motives of the main characters and the consequences of their actions. The focal variable was the extent to which violence was construed in terms of its relevant context—the aggressor's motives for committing the violence and the consequences to him. Kindergarteners typically recalled only the aggressive action; but the older subjects associated, first, consequences, then motives, and finally, the full complex of motives *and* consequences with retelling the aggressive action. The older viewers, but not the younger ones, understood that A had killed B for a certain reason and, as a result, had been arrested and tried. They had less difficulty comprehending the portrayal in its social, causal context. In laboratory studies of imitation (Bandura, 1965; Berkowitz and Rawlings, 1963), information about an aggressive model's motives and the consequences to him has been found to moderate the likelihood that viewers will be affected by what they see; but in this study with television, kindergarteners and second graders primarily remembered the aggressive action and only infrequently knew its links with the motives and consequences that were potential moderators of it.

Although Collins, Berndt, and Hess did not go on to measure effects on behavior, behavioral differences after watching violent TV have been reported (Collins, 1973) that appear to be related to age differences in comprehension and evaluation. In this work, real television programs were edited to vary the ease with which the action of an aggressive model could be related to cues about the actor's motives and the consequences to him. Third, sixth, and tenth graders either saw a television program in which negative motives and consequences scenes were separated from aggression by commercials (separation condition), or they saw the negative modifying cues in contiguity with the aggression (no separation). The measure of aggression was a self-report instrument, in which children were asked to indicate how they would behave in response to a series of hypothetical situations.

This increase in separation among important scenes had a dramatic effect on the behavior of third graders. The separation group subsequently became significantly more aggressive than the no-separation group at the third-grade level. These differences were not statistically significant for the sixth and tenth graders in the study. Apparently, for the separation third graders, the separating commercials interfered with comprehension of aggression in terms of negative motives and consequences, so that the aggression stood alone—unmodified—as a model for behavior. But having the three scenes close together in time seemed to make the comprehension task easier for the other group of third graders. Older viewers apparently could handle the cognitive difficulties caused by separation, so that their comprehensions of the act when commercials were inserted were essentially the same as those formed when the important scenes were close together in time. Presumably, these cognitive differences are similar to the kinds of age-related differences in comprehension and evaluation that have been found in the research described in earlier sections of this chapter. Taken together, those data and this evidence of differences in behavioral effects suggest that variations in comprehension may mediate variations in the effects of observing social interaction.

CONCLUSIONS AND PROSPECTS

The findings on children's comprehension of televised narratives presented here, like the results of other research on understanding of content (e.g., Flapan, 1968; Leifer et al., 1971; Leifer and Roberts, 1972), are dominated by age-related trends. Children as old as second and third graders have repeatedly been found to know significantly less of the information in portrayals that mature raters have characterized as central to comprehension of the plot. Further, these younger viewers' inferences about the meaningful interrelationships among the central events is typically poor. It appears that, compared to more mature viewers, young grade-school children are much less likely to "go beyond the information given" when viewing audiovisually presented narratives, a tendency that becomes more marked as the difficulty and unfamiliarity of the information to be comprehended increases. Thus, comprehension of television content appears to involve skills that are strongly age-related and also pronounced effects of the nature and difficulty of the tasks required by different programs. Both aspects deserve further discussion.

Age-related effects in comprehending audiovisually presented narratives parallel comprehension patterns that have emerged in recent years in studies of memory and still pictures. These latter findings have frequently been attributed to less spontaneous "straining for meaning" among less mature children (Paris, 1975)—a characterization that is completely appropriate for the results described in this chapter. More specific explanations have also been suggested. In recent research on prose stories (e.g., Mandler and Johnson, 1977; Poulsen et al., 1978; Stein and Glenn, 1975), preschool and young grade-school children's relatively poor recall of story details has been attributed to their possessing "grammars of meaning" (e.g., Rumelhart, 1975) that are less adequate for parsing story details than the grammars of more mature individuals. A somewhat different perspective has been emphasized by Sedlak (1977) and others (Bower, 1977; Schank and Abelson, 1975; Schmidt, 1976; Worth and Gross, 1974), who assume that inferences about connections among an actor's behaviors require that the observers recognize a *plan* or a point of view behind the action. Thus, Sedlak suggests that young children fail to comprehend observed actions and events in an adult-like way because they arrive at different interpretations of the various actors' plans or intentions. Both approaches specify types of constraints that older children appear to impose on the processing of narratives, but that younger children employ less reliably.

These approaches suggest important factors in comprehension of narratives generally, including televised dramas like the ones used in the present research. However, it seems likely that younger children's difficulties with television plots often involve additional factors beyond the sources of difficulty that occur in comprehension of prose stories that are somewhat peculiar to the audiovisual medium. In fact, Berndt and Berndt (1975), in their comparison of verbal-narrative and filmed versions of stories, found that audiovisual treatments facilitate comprehension of some details of events and hamper comprehension of other cues.

The implications of such differences are not yet clear, but must be examined in the future research on television comprehension. Several aspects of audiovisual portrayals undoubtedly deserve attention. One is the implicit or ambiguous nature of portrayed cues. In studies of prose narratives, the explictness with which story elements are stated can be relatively easily controlled; but control is less feasible in audiovisual narratives, because of certain dramatic and cinematic techniques. For example, Tada (1969), working with Japanese children, documented notable difficulties in comprehension of audiovisually presented material in which symbolism and filmic devices compress time and content. Another factor in audiovisual comprehension is the presence of formal features such as pacing, activity level, and music (Huston-Stein, 1977; Krull, Watt, and Lichty, 1977; Watt and Krull, 1974). Characteristics like these have been previously found to be associated with movie content that is especially well remembered by children (Holaday and Stoddard, 1933), but it is difficult to specify their effects on comprehension of complex plots. Consider a possible comparison between an aggressive resolution of conflict and a negotiated resolution of the same situation (e.g., Collins and Getz, 1976). Clearly, the aggressive portrayal would contrast markedly with the negotiation model in formal features like activity level and pacing and probably cannot realistically be constructed to be more comparable to it in these respects. Prose descriptions of the two events could be more closely matched at a formal level, but comparison between children's comprehension of the two different types of televised content would be confounded by the concomitant variation in presentation characteristics.

The effect of presentation factors is particularly pertinent to the question of children's understanding of social cues like motives and consequences associated with a character's actions. The research discussed in this chapter demonstrated both the frequent inadequacy of younger children's comprehension of the causal interrelationships associated with televised events and the possible pertinence of poor comprehension to the behavioral effects of television portrayals. Besides these apparently age-related difficulties in inferring implied connections, however, there is ample evidence that for younger children, the impact of motives and consequences also depends heavily on the ways in which the cues are portrayed separately. In recent studies, the following content and presentation characteristics have been found to affect young children's ability to employ motive information making evaluations: intensity (Gutkin, 1972) and valence of the consequences (Costanzo et al., 1973); perceptual salience and explicitness of motives and consequences (Chandler et al., 1973); and order effects and memory requirements (Austin et al., 1977; Feldman et al., 1976). Similar presentation characteristics have been found to affect the extent to which young children can successfully perform other types of social inference tasks (e.g., Kun et al., 1976; Shultz and Butkowsky, 1977; Swann and Collins, 1978). In one sense, such effects of presentation characteristics are unsurprising; but where television comprehension is concerned, they suggest that some consideration should be given to what is required when a viewer—particularly a cognitively immature one—attempts to understand varying portrayals of social cues.

The finding that young viewers are relatively unlikely to infer relationships among cues like motives and consequences even when they are apparently well understood separately suggests two other implications for further reflection and investigation. One question is whether the nature of children's errors can provide a basis for helping younger viewers understand complex programs on television better than they would on their own. For instance, parents might deliberately attempt to induce children to infer the interrelationships among important scenes in the program that the children often do not infer spontaneously, and these attempts might take account of the tendency for younger viewers' errors to resort to stereotyped social sequences for their understanding of what is portrayed, rather than spontaneously seeking the relevant information within the program. School curricula might be developed to teach viewing strategies, with an emphasis on inducing children to ask themselves the implicit questions that appear to be spontaneous in older children's viewing behavior (Collins, 1978). Research is needed on the effectiveness of such interventions and on the possible remediating value for behavioral effects such as those described in this chapter (Collins, 1973).

A second, more general implication of the present research is that the primary risk of possible deleterious effects of age-related comprehension differences accrues to younger viewers in the child audience. Although the extent of this risk cannot be accurately estimated, there is little doubt that it is relatively greater for them than for adolescents and adults. For a more complete understanding of the role of comprehension, however, it will be necessary to consider children's comprehension of television content in interaction with a number of age-related and individual differences in children's responses. For example, possible age-related increases in discrimination between fantasy and reality, the effects of individual variables like arousal thresholds and aggression anxiety, and the variance due to the situations that comprise children's everyday experiences are all relevant to the way in which age variation in television content may be expected to enter the complex equation for television effects. This more elaborated approach to the nature and importance of what the child brings to television is basic to a more complete appreciation of the significance of this medium in child development.

NOTE

1. All children, regardless of whether they were interrupted during viewing, were tested in the same manner at the end of the program. Four-way ANOVAs (grade x sex x viewing condition x interrupted-not interrupted) indicated no effect of interruption on recognition-memory scores.

REFERENCES

AUSTIN, V., RUBLE, D., and TRABASSO, T. (1977). "Recall and order effects as factors in children's moral judgements." Child Development, 48:470-474.

BANDURA, A. (1965). "Influence of models' reinforcement contingencies on the acquisition of imitative responses." Journal of Personality and Social Psychology, 1(6):589-595.

BERKOWITZ, L., and GEEN, R. (1967). "The stimulus qualities of the target of aggression: A further study." Journal of Abnormal and Social Psychology, 5:364-368.

BERKOWITZ, L., and RAWLINGS, E. (1963). "Effects of film violence on inhibitions against subsequent aggression." Journal of Abnormal and Social Psychology, 66(5):405-412.

BERNDT, T., and BERNDT, E. (1975). "Children's use of motives and intentionality in person perception and moral judgment." Child Development, 46:904-912.

BOWER, G. H. (1977). "On injecting life into deadly prose." Invited address at the meeting of the Western Psychological Association, Seattle, Washington, April.

CHANDLER, M., GREENSPAŃ, S., and BARENBOIM, C. (1973). "Judgments of intentionality in response to videotaped and verbally presented moral dilemmas: The medium is the message." Child Development, 44:315-320.

CHI, M. (1977). "Knowledge structure and memory development." Paper presented at the Carnegie Symposium on Cognition, Carnegie-Mellon University, May.

COLLINS, W. A. (1970). "Learning of media content: A developmental study." Child Development, 41:1133-1142.

––– (1973). "Effect of temporal separation between motivation, aggression, and consequences: A developmental study." Developmental Psychology, 8(2):215-221.

––– (1978). "Developmental aspects of literacy: Communication skills and the specter of television." In R. Beach and P. D. Pearson (eds.), Perspectives on literacy. Minneapolis: University of Minnesota College of Education (in press).

–––, BERNDT, T., and HESS, V. (1974). "Observational learning of motives and consequences for television aggression: A developmental study." Child Development, 45:799-802.

COLLINS, W. A., and GETZ, S. (1976). "Children's social responses following modeled reactions to provocation: Prosocial effects of a television drama." Journal of personality, 44:488-500.

COLLINS, W. A., and WELLMAN, H. (forthcoming). Developmental characteristics of comprehension and inference from a televised dramatic narrative. Unpublished manuscript.

COLLINS, W. A., WELLMAN, H., KENISTON, A., and WESTBY, S. (1978). "Age-related aspects of comprehension and inferences from a televised dramatic narrative." Child Development, 49:389-399.

COSTANZO, P. R., COIE, J. D., GRUMENT, J. F., and FARNILL, D. (1973). "A reexamination of the effects of intent and consequence on children's moral judgments." Child Development, 44:154-161.

CRAIK, F., and LOCKHART, R. (1972). "Levels of processing: A framework for memory research." Journal of Verbal Learning and Verbal Behavior, 11:671-684.

DYSINGER, W., and RUCKMICK, C. (1933). The emotional responses of children to the motion picture situation. New York: Macmillan.

FELDMAN, N.S., KLOSSON, E.C., PARSONS, J.E., RHOLES, W.S., and RUBLE, D.N. (1976). "Order of information presentation and children's moral judgments." Child Development, 47:556-559.

FESHBACH, S. (1970). "Aggression." In P. Mussen (ed.), Carmichael's manual of child psychology (Vol. 2, 3rd ed.). New York: John Wiley.

―――, and SINGER, R. (1971). Television and aggression: An experimental field study. San Francisco: Jossey-Bass.

FLAPAN, D. (1968). Children's understanding of social interaction. New York: Teacher's College Press, Columbia University.

GUTKIN, D. (1972). "The effect of systematic story changes on intentionality in children's moral judgments." Child Development, 43(1):187-196.

HAGEN, J., and HALE, G. (1973). "The development of attention in children." In A. Pick (ed.), Minnesota symposia on child psychology (Vol. 7). Minneapolis: University of Minnesota Press.

HOFFMAN, M.L. (1970). "Moral development." In P. Mussen (ed.), Carmichael's manual of child psychology (Vol. 2, 3rd ed.). New York: John Wiley.

HOLADAY, P., and STODDARD, G. (1933). Getting ideas from the movies. New York: Macmillan.

HUSTON-STEIN, A. (1977). "Television and growing up: The medium gets equal time." Invited address presented to Divisions 9 and 15 of the American Psychological Association, San Francisco, August.

JONES, E.E., KANOUSE, D.E., KELLEY, H.H., NISBETT, R.E., VALINS, S., and WEINER, B. (eds.) (1971). Attribution: Perceiving the causes of behavior. Morristown, N.J.: General Learning Press.

KING, M. (1971). "The development of some intention concepts in young children." Child Development, 42(4):1145-1152.

KRULL, R., WATT, J., and LICHTY, L. (1977). "Entropy and structure: Two measures of complexity in television programs." Communication Research, 4:61-85.

KUN, A., PARSONS, J.E., and RUBLE, D. (1976). "Development of integration processes using ability and effort information to predict outcome." Developmental Psychology, 10:721-732.

LEIFER, A.D., COLLINS, W.A., GROSS, B., TAYLOR, P., ANDREWS, L., and BLACKMER, E. (1971). "Developmental aspects of variables relevant to observational learning." Child Development, 42:1509-1516.

LEIFER, A., and ROBERTS, D. (1972). "Children's responses to television violence." In J. Murray, C. Rubinstein, and G. Comstock (eds.), Television and social behavior (Vol. 2). Washington, D.C.: U.S. Government Printing Office.

MACCOBY, E., and JACKLIN, C. (1974). The psychology of sex differences. Stanford, Cal.: Stanford University Press.

MANDLER, J., and JOHNSON, N. (1977). "Remembrance of things parsed: Story structure and recall." Cognitive Psychology, 9:111-151.

NEWCOMB, A., and COLLINS, W.A. (1977). "Children's processing of television portrayals of black and white families." Paper presented at the biennial meeting of the Society for Research in Child Development, New Orleans, Louisiana, March.

PARIS, S. (1975). "Integration and inference in children's comprehension and memory." In F. Restle, R. Shiffrin, J. Castellan, H. Lindman, and D. Pisoni (eds.), Cognitive theory (Vol. 1). Potomac, Md.: Erlbaum and Associates.

PAULSEN, D., KINTSCH, E., KINTSCH, W., and PREMACK, D. (1978). Children's comprehension and memory for stories. Unpublished manuscript, University of Colorado.

PIAGET, J. (1955). The language and thought of the child. Cleveland, Ohio: Meridian.

——— (1965). The moral judgment of the child. New York: Free Press.

RUMELHART, D. (1975). "Notes on a schema for stories." In D. Bobrow and A. Collins (eds.), Studies in cognitive science. New York: Academic Press.

SCHANK, R., and ABELSON, R. (1975). "Scripts, plans and knowledge." In Advance papers of the Fourth International Joint Conference on Artificial Intelligence, Tbilisi, Georgia, U.S.S.R.

SCHMIDT, C. (1976). "Understanding human action: Recognizing the plans and motives of other persons." In J. Carroll and J. Payne (eds.), Cognition and social behavior. Potomac, Md.: Erlbaum and Associates.

SCHRAMM, W., LYLE, J., and PARKER, E. (1961). Television in the lives of our children. Stanford, Cal.: Stanford University Press.

SEDLAK, A. (1977). "Understanding an actor's behavior: Developmental differences in plan interpretation." Paper presented as part of a symposium entitled Cognitive Processing of Television Content: Perspectives on the Effects of Television on Children at the biennial meeting of the Society for Research in Child Development, New Orleans, Louisiana, March.

SHULTZ, T., and BUTKOWSKY, I. (1977). "Young children's use of the scheme for multiple sufficient causes in the attribution of real and hypothetical behavior." Child Development, 48:464-469.

SINGER, J. (1971). The control of aggression and violence: Cognitive and physiological factors. New York: Academic Press.

STEIN, A., and FRIEDRICH, L. (1975). "Impact of television on children and youth." Pp. 183-268 in E.M. Hetherington (ed.), Review of child development research (Vol. 5). Chicago: University of Chicago Press.

STEIN, N., and GLENN, C. (1975). "A developmental study of children's recall of story material." Paper presented at the biennial meeting of the Society for Research in Child Developmental, Denver, Colorado, April.

SWANN, W., and COLLINS, W.A. (1978). When persons become causes: Age and consensus as moderators of causal attribution. Unpublished manuscript, University of Minnesota.

TADA, T. (1969). "Image-cognition: A developmental approach." Pp. 105-173 in Studies of broadcasting. Tokyo: Nippon Hoso Kyokai.

TRABASSO, T., and FOELLINGER, D. (forthcoming). "The growth of information processing capacity in children: A critical test of Pascual-Leone's model." Journal of Experimental Child Psychology.

WATT, J., and KRULL, R. (1974). "An information theory measure for television programming." Communication Research, 1:44-68.

WORTH, S., and GROSS, L. (1974). "Symbolic strategies." Journal of Communication, 24(4):27-39.

Chapter 3

SHAPE, NOT ONLY CONTENT:
HOW MEDIA SYMBOLS PARTAKE IN
THE DEVELOPMENT OF ABILITIES

Gavriel Salomon

TRADITIONALLY, MEDIA HAVE BEEN ATTACKED, praised, and researched for their *contents*. Starting perhaps with Plato's criticism of stories which he feared might cultivate undesirable ideas in youngsters, through the feared horrors of Grimm's tales, the rejected immorality of films, and the violence on television, media's *contents* were the focus of attention. Also most research of child development vis-a-vis the media has focused mainly on children's comprehension of plots, attribution of credibility to specific messages, acceptance of stereotypes, learning of sex roles, and the like. The effects of other

AUTHOR'S NOTE: Preparation of this chapter was supported by a grant from the Spencer Foundation. Some of the ideas presented here were developed to a large measure as a result of discussions with Drs. Howard Gardner of Harvard University, David Feldman of Tufts University, and David Olson of the Ontario Institute for the Study of Education. I am thankful for their important help.

I also wish to thank Dennis Cronin, Andrea Lash, and Dorothy Piantkofsky for their assistance in preparing this chapter.

attributes of media, notably their modes of presenting messages, were until recently not seriously studied.

Without diminishing for a moment the great importance of studying the effects of media contents on children, it seems important to ask what effects modes of presentation may have because, for example, "television is a representational system, not little people behaving in a box" (Dorr, 1977). Recognizing this aspect of media, Katz, Blumler and Gurevitch (1974) argue that focusing only on the content of media messages may, on occasion, be misleading. If social science would have proliferated in opera-loving Italy of the 19th century, they claim, researchers would have addressed themselves to the medium's "grammar" or functions and gratifications, not on its effects on opinions and attitudes (although operas contained political messages).

Very often content and form have been confounded by researchers. For instance, Huston-Stein and Wright (1977) show that televised violence is usually seen within rapid action, fast-paced changes of scenes, whereas prosaic behaviors are set within slow-paced, low-action programs. They find that television programs aimed at different ages differ more in formal modes of presentation than in violent contents. Programs for preschoolers have higher levels of actions, pace, variability, and special visual effects than programs designed for older children. Looking at such formal features, Singer et al. (1977) have found that preschoolers are more attentive to the rapid-paced structure of *Sesame Street* but appear to learn more from the slow-paced *Mister Rogers.*

Research such as the work done on the effects of story structures (e.g., Bower, 1976) suggests that media modes of presentation, aside from their typical contents, deserve the attention of researchers. It may illuminate the ways children learn to cope with different modes of information packagings, beyond what they acquire in terms of knowledge.

But what does it mean to study the effects of media modes of presentation to complement those of their contents, and why should it be undertaken? A medium per se does not interact with individuals, nor does it partake in any simple way in a child's development. Rather, some attributes—sometimes unique to a medium and sometimes shared by a number of media—differentially interact with children's knowledge, beliefs, abilities, and the like. The effects of the social situations created by, or correlated with the use of a medium are not to be confused with those of, say, the contents of its typical messages, nor should the effects of the latter be confused with those of the mode of presentation (Salomon and Cohen, 1978).

When a medium's messages are encountered, knowledge of two different kinds are acquired: information about the *represented world* and information about the *mental activity* used in gaining it. Thus, while the *contents* of messages and experiences address themselves to one's knowledge and map upon one's knowledge base, the *ways* they are structured and presented, address themselves to one's mental skills or abilities (Olson and Bruner, 1974). Assuming that the major media of communication differ—to a smaller or larger extent—in their modes of gathering, selecting, packaging, and presenting information, it becomes important to examine the psychological consequences of these differences. Also, because there is reason to assume that differences in modes of presentation are associated mainly with the differential employment of mental skills (e.g., Olson, 1974; Gardner, 1977), their effects on the *cultivation* of such skills can become a focal point for research.

In what follows a line of research is described that focuses on the cultivation of mental skills as a function of exposure to specific modes of presentation, particularly the symbolic elements employed by film and television. Although film and television served as the pool from which the sample of symbolic elements was chosen, the purpose was to investigate the extent to which this *class* of media-attributes partakes in knowledge acquisiton, and (more importantly) in the cultivation of mental skills in children of different ages.

MEDIA MODES OF PRESENTATION

The term "mode of presentation" while intuitively different from "content" is quite vague because it is too broad. Take a particular observation and describe it in a journalistic and then in a narrative way. Assuming you did a fair job, two "modes of presentation" would emerge. But a filmed version of the same observation would also be considered a different "mode" of presentation than the linguistic narrative. So would a cartoon-like presentation or a scientific treatise.

Indeed, there are numerous classes of "representational modes," which may cut across each other. One class may entail elements such as "story," "journalistic description," "metaphor," and "scientific treatise." Each element would have its own unique mode of structuring information, which affects the kind of mental operations employed and the kinds of meanings accrued.

Another class of "representational modes" would entail elements such as "structuredness," "complexity," and "redundancy." This class of "modes" cuts across the previous one. It exerts its influences on one's states of uncertainty and epistemic behavior, on perceived novelty, exploratory and information search behaviors, and the like.

A third class of elements deals with the symbol systems by which messages are coded. Such messages can be narrative or scientific, complex or simple. They differ from each other in terms of the codes into which they are "dressed": a story in print versus the same story in cartoon form versus the story made into a television show. Briefly stated, a symbol system, according to Goodman (1976), is a set of elements, such as words, numbers, shapes, or musical scores, that are interrelated within each system by syntactic rules or conventions, and are used in specifiable ways in relation to fields of reference. Some systems are more "notational" (e.g., musical scores) because they entail discrete and unambiguous elements which can be organized in lawful ways. They are syntactically articulate, because they have readily identifiable and discrete inscriptions (e.g., alphabet), and they may be semantically unambiguous with regard to their referents. Other systems are "non-notational" as is the case with pictures. They are both syntactically and semantically "dense" because they allow "for infinitely many characters so ordered that between each two there is a third," and there is no unambiguous relationship between symbol and referent.

It is difficult sometimes to conceive of non-notational systems, such as artistic painting, film, or caricatures, as entailing symbols. It is less difficult to see how they serve in representational capacities. However, what makes them representational, and what differentiates between them, is their symbolic nature, i.e., the way the represented relates to the presented, and the way the presented, as a whole, is organized and structured. Thus, some symbol systems emphasize denotation (e.g., the Morse code, the number system), while other systems (e.g., ballet) emphasize expressive reference. Still others (language, pictures) can vary from instances of denotation to expression and imitative exemplification. The greater the variability of a symbol system in terms of its emphasis on denotation, expression, and exemplification, and the "denser" it is, the more levels of meanings it can potentially carry. Thus, for instance, one can read graphs for a relatively narrow range of denotative meanings, but a picture can be "read" for literal, denotative, expressional, and metaphoric meanings.

Yet, whether highlighting denotational, expressive, or exemplicatory powers, all symbol systems correlate with fields of reference. Such a correlation (which may be a low or a high correlation) involves not only a correspondence between symbol and event, object, relation or feeling, but also a relationship between combinational modes (e.g., syntax) and relations among the referents. For instance, the left-right succession of letters and words in script is correlated with the temporal succession of sounds, while the spatial arrangement of cartographic symbols corresponds to the spaces maps represent. No wonder, therefore, that the quality of "suspense" is probably better rendered by music than by sculpture as the latter symbol system correlates only poorly with the temporal qualities entailed in "suspense" (Eisner, 1978).

When dealing with media modes of presentation, any one of the three classes of elements could be selected. And because they are more or less independent of each other, one should not have advantages for research on media over the others. However, it appears that of the three classes only the third—symbol systems—is the most *generic* to media. Stories, jokes, metaphors, and scientific or journalistic accounts can be presented through most, if not all media. For that reason the study of children's comprehension of *televised* stories can follow the research done on comprehension of verbally presented stories (Dorr, 1977). The same applies to our second class of representational modes. Redundancy, structure, ambiguity, and the like are not associated with any medium in particular. Hence, for instance, the study of stimuli that affect children's exploratory and search behavior is medium, or modality independent.

Symbol systems are correlated with media, however, although in complex ways. It is true that hardly any medium of communication is associated with one and only one symbol system. Indeed, language serves many media, while the medium of television is served by a number of symbol systems. However, it is equally true that each medium, *generically at least,* develops its own unique *blend* of symbol systems, some of the elements of which may have been adopted from other media (e.g., natural language in film), while others have been stimulated by the medium's own technology (e.g., certain montages in film). Remove cartography from maps, the "dense" nature of the image from paintings, and "spatialization of time" from film, the movement from ballet, and language from texts, and little is left.

One often tends to associate a symbol system with a collection of equally complex elements which can be strung together (e.g., traffic lights or genealogical trees). However, most symbol systems entail a whole range of symbolic elements that vary in complexity. The black hat of the villain, the flashback, and the overall structure of temporal sequences in film are symbolic elements that vary in complexity. It is the more complex elements that make the arrangement of the simple ones more medium-specific. Film and television share numerous simple symbolic elements, but they differ generically when time, space, causality, and the like are to be rendered (e.g., Kjorup, 1977).

Space limitations make it impossible to do justice to the issue of representational modes and symbol systems. Detailed discussions can be found, for instance, in Langer (1942), Goodman (1976), Perkins and Leondar (1977), and others. The question of immediate interest here is the extent to which children's encounters with media's symbol systems have any significant developmental consequences. Also, because the issue pertains to children's mental abilities (rather than their knowledge), we might consider the cultivation of mental skills by media's symbol systems as our focal point.

A DEVELOPMENTAL PARADIGM

Symbol systems are among the most important carriers of human knowledge and communications. They constitute a class of cultural entities to be examined side by side with the contents of cultures, their technologies and techniques of using technology. The possible interplay between culture's symbol systems and those used by the individual for internal representation has lead Bruner (1966:2), among others, to argue that: "Where internal presentation of the environment is concerned it . . . depends upon techniques that are *learned*—and these are *precisely the techniques* that serve to amplify our motor acts, our perception, and our ratiocinative activities" [Emphasis added]. Working within the Brunerian framework, Greenfield (1972) has argued that the use of written language cultivates abstract thought. Olson (1977), similarly, maintains that the development of general logic is based in part on literacy. However, as Scribner and Cole (1978) show, literacy (and by extension—perhaps learning to cope also with other symbol systems) may have much more specific cognitive effects. While not contradictory, such claims predict cognitive achievements of variable magnitudes. This suggests that a more general "map" to aid in the generation of hypotheses is needed.

Feldman (1979) has advanced a theory according to which intellectual achievements can be arranged from the *universal* through the *cultural, disciplined, idiosyncratic* to the *unique.* All developmental achievements follow specific sequences of acquisition and are hierarchically ordered; but only some (e.g., object permanence, conservation, speech) are also universal and spontaneous. That is, they are generally achieved by most children and their attainment needs no specific kind of environmental input in the form of tutoring or deliberate arrangement of stimuli.

Cultural achievements, although sequentially ordered and hierarchically organized (within specific domains of knowledge and performance!), are neither universal nor spontaneous. The expectation *within* a culture is that "every child who is a member of the cultural group should be able to reach a certain level [of achievement]." Thus, domains chosen for mastery differ from culture to culture, as well as the level of mastery expected from each individual. For instance, most cultures expect literacy from their members, but only a few emphasize navigational skills. And while some level of map reading may be common to many cultures, some expect higher levels of proficiency than others.

Cultural achievements (let alone discipline-based ones such as mathematics, and unique ones such as artistic painting) are highly dependent on tutoring as well as on specific tools, techniques, and symbol systems which are part of the culture. Tools and techniques call for the employment of specific skills and thus cultivate them. For instance (Feldman, 1979:23),

> A ruler is a tool that permits extraction of information about heights, sizes, distances, and so forth. Learning to use a ruler, however, is likely to contribute to the *understanding* of these concepts; it may also enhance understanding of certain mathematical rules and logical operations.

Hatano, Miyake and Binks (1977) show in their study of expert abacus users how the techniques associated with the use of an abacus become internalized as mental skills, which thus develops computational skills.

Symbol systems similarly call upon different sets of mental skills in the service of information extraction (Perkins and

Leondar, 1977; Salomon and Cohen, 1977), thereby cultivating better mastery of these skills. Hence, as Olson (1974) claims, "intelligence is skill in a cultural medium."

A hypothetical matrix of achievements and environments that cultivate them seems to emerge from this conception. Environmental elements which exist universally and entail little direct tutoring give rise to universal achievements of perhaps the Piagetian kind, while increasingly more specific environmental elements (book reading, traveling, studying math, or watching television) facilitate the development of increasingly more specific achievements. The latter require tutoring; also not every individual attains them to the same extent. Although only a heuristic matrix, some empirical findings could be placed in it.

Luria (1976) has studied the psychological consequences in Central Asia of introducing schooling, planning, and collectivization. He found very profound effects on logical thinking and abstract thinking. His findings, it seems, can be placed relatively close to the universal, Piagetian-like achievements.

Scribner and Cole (1973) have studied the cognitive effects of formal schooling and found that it involves "the process of becoming competent in the use of various symbol systems" such that schooled children are distinctive in their ability to generalize and transfer solutions of problems. Such effects, although general within schooled cultures, are less universal than the ones reported by Luria. Also the inputs that stimulated these achievements were somewhat more specific.

When only literacy *without* schooling was studied (Scribner and Cole, 1978), its effects were found to be even more specific and limited. As suggested by Feldman's matrix, more focused and specific inputs cultivate more specific achievements. Indeed, Scribner and Cole (1978:24) suggest that:

> carrying out critical analyses of text might promote certain analytic operations with language; rote learning from the same text, or reading it for some other purpose, is not likely to do so. Writing poetry is likely to have different consequences for language skills than preparing a letter to a department store requesting a refund for damaged goods.

The paradigm sketched above allows us to subsume different kinds of developmental achievements, from the Piagetian to the highly artistic, under one framework. Such a paradigm suggests, for instance, how the different clusters of achievements—the universal, cultural, unique—interrelate. The more universal achievements of, say, the Piagetian kind, are needed *partly* for cultural and other achievements to occur. It may be necessary to know that symbols stand for something (a universal achievement) before reading can be learned, but it is not necessary to have mastery of *Piagetian* formal operations to begin to learn to read. Thus, Feldman (1979) suggests that "achievements of at least certain aspects of universal domains must precede initial mastery of any aspect of cultural domains."

The use of this heuristic paradigm also allows us to map the cognitive effects of media symbol systems on a wider developmental terrain. For one thing, media symbol systems can be considered as relatively general inputs, thus their effects need not be of only limited generalizability. For another, children's exposure to them is hardly ever accompanied by any tutoring and hence—tutoring would enhance their possible effects. Finally, as media symbol systems would be located within the cultural portion of the continuum, skill cultivation which is facilitated by them would depend on some previous universal achievements.

Three kinds of questions suggest themselves. One kind of question pertains to the meanings children learn to secure from differently coded messages. It is exemplified by the work of Meringoff (1978) on how children of varying ages comprehend stories which are either read or shown to them on television.

A second kind of question pertains to the development of symbolic capacities in children, the development of their abilities to extract information from differently coded messages, and the development of their symbolic expressive capacities. The work by Gardner et al. (1977) on early symbolic developments and that of Feldman (1979) on map drawing exemplify this thrust.

The third kind of question deals with the *effects* of media symbol systems on cognition. Obviously, the cognitive effects of symbol system are related to the development of a child's ability to cope with coded messages, and vice versa. Yet, the two types of questions are somewhat different. Studying, for instance, how reading is learned is not the same as studying the effects of literacy on development of the cognitive skills. But then, these may be no more than two ways to examine the same phenomenon.

The research to be described below and the discussion that follows pertain to the third kind of question. Thus, it pertains to the hypothesis that exposure to symbolic elements utilized by media (particularly film and television), affects children's mastery of specific mental skills in interaction with age, abilities, SES, and other factors.

We have presently only very limited understanding of the specific structures of those symbol systems which are most generic to the major audio-visual media of communication. Furthermore, these symbol systems (unlike those of, say, chemistry, mathematics, or cartography) are still under constant change, while other systems, such as heat photography, are only now being developed. It would be too pretentious to offer any "psycholinguistics" of film, television, or cartoons. However, it is possible to examine in *principle* the general ways in which symbol systems can affect the development of cognitive skills.

TWO MECHANISMS OF CULTIVATING SKILLS IN INTERACTION WITH INDIVIDUAL DIFFERENCES

The expectation that different symbol systems have the potential of differentially cultivating mental skills is based on the assumption that symbol systems *require* the employment of different sets of mental skills. This assumption has been stated by Olson (1974) and Olson and Bruner (1974) who argued that while the information in messages converges on a common knowledge base, the symbolic modes of the messages diverge as to the skills they call on. Thus, it follows that, say, reading a map requires different skills than reading the same information off a printed page. Perkins and Leondar (1977) state that: "Symbol systems are neither better nor worse but are simply different as the degree of notationality varies and as they differ in the styles of information processing they require of the maker or reader."

There are also claims to the contrary, arguing that all kinds of incoming information are transformed into "internal propositions" *regardless* of symbol systems (e.g., Norman and Rumelhart, 1975). However, these assertions can be questioned in light of neuropsychological evidence pertaining to the lateralization of brain functions and the differential effects of hemispheric damage (e.g., Gardner, 1974, 1977; Singer, 1978). On a more specific level, there is also evidence to show that when the same television program is produced to emphasize alternative symbolic elements, different kinds of mental skills are called into play (Salomon and Cohen, 1977).

This does not mean that each and every symbolic element requires "its" skill, and that every symbol system corresponds to "its" set of mental skills. Yet, it is possible to postulate that more similar symbol systems require more similar skills, while less similar ones require more diversified skills. Moreover, as different contents lend themselves better to one symbol system than another, one is likely to transform coded messages from one code into another which "fits" it more conveniently. Thus, one quite often tends to process spatial information by means of the internal "analog" systems of representation; and, if the spatial information is provided by means of a verbal code, a transformation would tend to take place (Huttenlocher, 1973).

More importantly, the world does not seem to be comprehended as it presents itself to a child, but rather it is comprehended in terms of the mental schemata and mental operations which a child applies to it. A child (as well as an adult) thus transforms the externally coded messages into internal ones that, given a particular content and task, are the most appropriate ones for the child. As Huttenlocher (1973) puts it, thought does not duplicate reality, but represents it through internal symbol systems which pertain to different domains, such as logic, space, and the like. The elements of one symbol system can represent those of another domain. First, however, the former must be systematically mapped on the latter. Furthermore, the symbol systems by means of which one can best represent and process incoming information are not identical to those through which a given message is conveyed. *Thus, the symbolic codes of a message need to be converted or transformed from external to internal modes of representation.*

Although it is extremely difficult to follow, let alone observe, the occurrence of such transformations, their existence can be inferred from studies in which modes of presentation are experimentally provided to "save" some transformation. Black et al. (1977) found that college students adopt, so to speak, a *spatial* point of view when listening to a story. When a change in the point of view is introduced into the story ("Terry worked in the yard and *came* into the house"), comprehension is slower. A transformation is added when the consistency of points of view is being violated.

The findings that children's comprehension of text is facilitated by pictorial illustrations (Pressley, 1977) suggest that their presence "saves" children's efforts to transform verbal descriptions into imagery. Similarly, we have found in one of our studies (Salomon and Cohen, 1977) that extraction of knowledge from a television film saturated with close-ups correlates .67 with mastery of relating parts to wholes; however, using zooms (which simulate the relations between parts to wholes) reduces the correlation to .27, suggesting that a crucial transformation was done for the children, freeing them from applying it themselves.

Mental skills that are called upon to transform external into internal representations serve a definite purpose: the extraction of knowledge from coded messages. The successful extraction of knowledge is, in effect, a reinforcing event which could, hypothetically at least, partake in the cultivation of the skills involved in the process. Thus, the mastery of skills that are called upon for transformational purposes can be expected to *improve* as the result of their successful employment. *To the extent that the symbol systems of the media vary as to the skills they require, they can be expected to also cultivate different skills.*

In a series a five experiments, children ranging in age from eight to 14 years were experimentally exposed to symbolic elements generic to film, that, when combined with specific task requirements, called upon a number of measurable skills. These codes were of varied kinds, such as close ups, changes of points of view, and animated assemblance. The skills measured varied similarly, such as ability to relate parts to wholes, ability to change points of view, and field independence (for details, see Salomon, 1974).

As expected, experimental exposure to the skill-activating elements significantly improved children's mastery of those skills. However, the children who were most affected by exposure to these elements were the ones who *initially* had a fair mastery of the skills. Those with poorer initial mastery of the relevant skills were not so significantly affected by such *skill-activating* symbolic elements. (However, they were affected by another type of elements, namely, elements which offered them a transformation they could imitate, as will be described below).

The consistent finding that media skill-activating elements, when accompanied by proper tutoring (experimentally provided problems to be solved), improve the mastery of the relevant skills in partly skilled children should come as no surprise. As Scribner and Cole (1978) argue, specific uses promote specific skills when they invoke (or in our case—are *made* to invoke) these skills. This should be true whether it is writing or film-viewing which is the skill-invoking activity.

Of greater interest is what happened to the initially unskilled children. While media skill-activating elements had hardly any effect on them, other media elements did. What are these elements? Some symbol systems, including some of those used in film and television, do not *require* a transformation (as when two points of view are juxtaposed and require coordination), but rather the symbols themselves perform at least part of the transformation *for* the viewer. Thus, for instance, the zoom *models* or *supplants* the operation of relating parts to whole, an operation one has to apply internally when shown a close-up and long-shot. Similarly, the movement of the camera around an object supplants the process of coordinating points of view.

By assuming that such elements supplant or model an operation (an assumption borne out by the data), it is implied that they can, under some conditions at least, serve as *models* for observational learning. Indeed, there is nothing in the observational learning literature which would exclude the possibility that children might learn (by imitation, perhaps) the "behavior" of operations which model, or overtly supplant, those skills which they would have to employ on their own. Little wonder, then, that children, who do not master the needed mental skills and are still required to extract the coded information, learn the skill-supplanting element and use it covertly on new test material.

Whether these children *"internalize"* the symbolic element in the Vigotzkian or Brunerian sense, or whether the *application* of skill they already possess is improved, as Cole and Scribner (1974) would claim, is of course open to debate. Yet, the

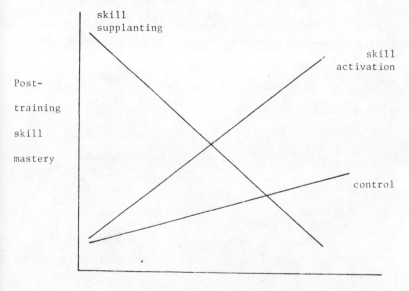

Figure 1

consistent findings, schematically summarized in Figure 1, clearly suggest that under tutorial conditions, specific symbolic elements of film can improve observable skill mastery by either activating skills or supplanting them. Children's initial levels of mastery strongly interact with these treatments.

CULTIVATION OF SKILLS ACROSS AGES

The experimental findings described above lend credence to the possibility that symbolic elements of a medium *can be made* to demand *or* supplant mental skills and thus cultivate their mastery. But while these findings are of great educational interest, they do not shed much light on the developmental issues involved. The skills and the experimentally designed tasks were selected to match the children's general level of development: eight-year-olders participated in the experiment in which changes of points of view were invoked, while 14-year-olders participated when figure-assemblance was involved.

The introduction of *Sesame Street* into Israel provided an opportunity to study the skill-cultivating effects of the program's symbolic elements, whether specific (e.g., changes of points of view) or more complex (e.g., the mosaic-like overall structure), under more natural conditions. It should be noted that the unique structure and symbolic elements of the program were extremely novel to the then television-naive Israeli children. Thus, there was reason to expect these elements, due to their novelty, would require the application of skills which were only rarely demanded before. Also, there was reason to expect that a number of particular symbolic elements would overtly supplant mental skills and because of their novelty they would be learned by the less skilled children.

About 90 preschoolers and 224 second and third graders of lower and middle class background participated in three studies (for details, see Salomon, 1976). Using a variety of statistical methods, and continuous observations and testing over a six-month period, very strong effects were observed. By and large, exposure to the program's relatively novel symbol elements affected children's mastery of those skills which were initially hypothesized to be called upon by some elements or supplanted by others. Exposure to the program accounted for up to 13.3% of the post-viewing variance of skill measures, such as relating parts to wholes, in the preschool sample, and up to 21% on classification in the school age sample. Furthermore, in the beginning, initial skill mastery was hardly correlated at all with knowledge extraction from the programs (median $r = .29$). These low correlations remained unchanged also at posttest time for the light viewers. However, the correlations became far stronger at the end of the period for heavy viewers whose skill-mastery improved significantly (median $r = .56$), suggesting that improved skill-mastery facilitated the extraction of knowledge from the program. In other words, the evidence suggested that as amount of viewing increased, skill-mastery improved in the service of better knowledge extraction.

There were also significant age differences. Whereas the skills of second and third graders were strongly affected by the program (viewing accounting for up to 31% of classification skill mastery), those of the preschoolers were affected to a far lesser extent. Clinical observations carried out on a sample of 36 children confirmed the expected: preschoolers showed poor comprehension of even the briefest events, their attention was more easily drawn to commotion and visual change than to the critical information, and they described observed segments in quite random ways, often failing to tie them together.

Finally, there were large and systematic SES differences. It became evident that middle class children were generally more affected than lower class ones. In addition, while lower class children were affected mainly in skill areas that pertained to visual analysis (e.g., matching), middle class children were more strongly affected in skill areas that pertained to synthesis (e.g., classification, relating parts to wholes). This differential pattern was repeated in both the preschool and grade level samples. Further analyses showed that achievements in the area of analysis preceded those in the area of synthesis. Middle class children exhibited better mastery of analytic skills than lower class

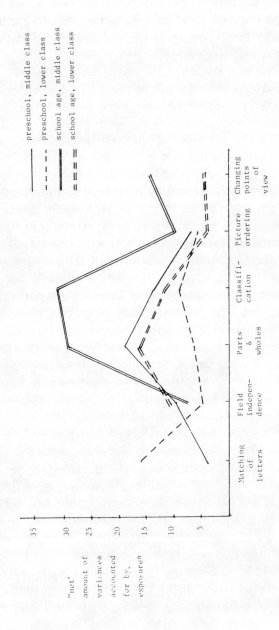

Figure 2

*After variance accounted for by pre-exposure abilities and other background variables are partialled out.

Legend:
- preschool, middle class
- preschool, lower class
- school age, middle class
- school age, lower class

Y-axis: "net" amount of variances accounted for by exposure*
(35, 30, 25, 20, 15, 10, 5)

X-axis (SKILL TESTS): Matching of letters | Field independence | Parts & wholes | Classification | Picture ordering | Changing points of view ones from the outset. Hence, there was less need for the middle class children to improve mastery in this area, while lower class children had to improve their analytic skills prior to handling synthesis. Results pertaining to a selected number of tests are graphically summarized in Figure 2.

The *Sesame Street* studies have shown that symbolic elements of television can participate in the cultivation of specific mental skills under normal conditions of exposure. Although no comparison with more television-seasoned American children was possible, it is reasonable to assume that the observed strong cognitive effects were due to the *novelty* of the program's elements. When new elements are introduced (much like when novel avant-garde films are encountered), they impose relatively new mental demands. Within limits, such demands allow the exercising of skills which can thus be cultivated; but the cultivation of skills, as the results showed, is not a simple effect. Both age and previous mastery of skills appear to play major roles in this process.

The significant and consistent age differences are perhaps of the greatest interest here. Second and third graders were more strongly affected than preschoolers, in spite of the fact that the program's *content* must have been far less novel for the former than for the latter. These age differences are consistent with the findings from a variety of areas such as style sensitivity, comprehension of metaphors, the development of pictorial interpretation, and the comprehension of television formats.

Gardner (1972) has studied the development of style sensitivity in children of varying ages (style in paintings, for instance, is part of the symbol system employed and is to be distinguished from the figural contents of the paintings). He found that in the absence of training only high school and college students can group works of arts by style and not only by figurative content. When training is introduced, even seven-year-olds succeed in grouping paintings by style, and 10- to 12-year-olds do even better. However, training is of little help to preschoolers who cannot decenter from the paintings' figurative content. They have a very strong "subject matter orientation."

In another series of studies the development of metaphoric understanding was investigated (e.g., Winner et al., 1976). When given a metaphor, six- and seven-year-olds provided totally literal interpretations of the metaphor, often also invoking imaginary "bridges" to connect the topic and its metaphoric vehicle ("The prison guard had become a hard rock" turned into a case in which a witch has made him into a rock). At age eight children begin to show some comprehension of metaphor but are still unable to connect separate domains. For example, they describe the prison guard as having muscles hard as a rock. Only by age 10 are the children able to bridge from one domain to another.

When metaphoric production was tested (Gardner et al., 1975), preschoolers turned out to be much more successful and uninhibited than older children. Their performance could be characterized as "an insensitivity to (or a willingness to disregard or cut across) conventional boundaries of experience and language." Middle childhood children, on the other hand, are more inhibited in producing metaphors, often tending to provide literal or narrational paraphrases for statements.

There are also numerous studies showing that preschoolers, by and large, do not comprehend the interaction of televised sequences, nor do they understand the interdependence of portrayed events (e.g., Noble, 1975; Collins, 1975; Leifer et al., 1971). Dorr (1977) also suggests on the basis of informal observations that smaller children interpret filmic elements such as slow motion in completely literal ways. However, all this changes with the advent of schooling, and by age 10 children interrelate sequences and quite correctly interpret most grammatical structures in stories (e.g., Mandler and Johnson, 1977), or pictorial sequences (Messaris and Gross, 1977).

The findings cited above, and those of other lines of research, strongly suggest that until about age six to seven the preschooler's mental schemata direct him or her to pick up primarily the highly *salient* and *fragmented* units of information. Overall structure and sequence of a story or television program, the constraints of good metaphor, or styles of paintings are usually not dealt with by the preschoolers. As such, structural and symbolic elements are not perceived as entailing information that the preschooler seeks to extract; they are not transformed by the child into internal representations. Hence, they cannot reinforce the mastery of transformational skills which are not invoked anyway.

It seems, then, that a child's mastery of a specific mental skill can be affected by a symbolic element to the extent that the child finds it to carry information worth extracting, and thus transforms it mentally. In other words, *the information the child is capable of extracting determines what elements are to be transformed and these, in turn, determine what skills are invoked and cultivated.*

The same is probably true within the same age group. Lower ability children address themselves to smaller chunks of information and to simpler messages, and thus transform fewer elements and are therefore less affected by them. The elements they do deal with are of the more analytic kind, cultivating more analytic skills. More skillful children, who can extract the analytic information more easily address themselves to combinational elements and thus skills of synthesis are more affected in them.

Here is where more universal achievement may be a necessary precondition (e.g., concrete operations) for the attainment of a more specific cultural achievement. However, this possibility is still open to debate. Gardner (1972) has found that ability to perform concrete operations was neither a necessary nor a sufficient precondition for style sensitivity. On the other hand, I have found children's ability to maintain a constant point of view when drawing a map to correlate (r = .57) with performance on the Piagetian tilted-bottle task.

However, it is possible also that the advent of schooling exerts its effect. Olson (1977) maintains that when the child begins to learn reading he or she moves from a preliterate stage, in which meaning is ascribed to statements on the basis of what he or she *expects,* to a literate stage in which the child regards the statements as a *reality in their own right.* Meaning, for the child, becomes *conventionalized* as he or she begins to treat statements as propositions, rather than as descriptions which map upon his or her own expectations. At that age the child *has* to learn how to negotiate the symbolic elements of a message. Indeed, at age 8-10 the symbolic structures of messages exert an observable effect on skills, a process that appears to continue until about the age of 10-12.

Still, at preschool age symbolic elements that supplant or model a skill have a better chance of affecting mastery of the skill than those that activate it. This can be seen in the *Sesame Street* results and is in agreement with the experimental findings described earlier. A child would have less difficulty learning an explicitly modeled transformation than performing the transformation on his or her own. Singer (1978) suggests that televised stories are easier to process for precisely this reason. They "supplant," so to speak, the generation of imagery that is required by story reading or even by listening to a story.

Once learned, the symbolic element can be used in an imitative way. Even if it is not yet fully comprehended, the preschooler has the ability to assign the element an "internal counterpart," perhaps no more than an internal mirror-image of it. Thus, the child can perform mental "play-backs" of zoom-ins or slow-motions but not yet reverse or transform them. As Olson (1974) observes, "the skillful use of a symbolic system involves the mastery of both its structure and its rules of transformation." Learning a supplanting element can provide only the former, not the latter.

SKILL CULTIVATION AND THE PERCEPTION OF THE PROCESSING TASK

In a cross cultural study (Salomon, 1977; Salomon and Cohen, 1978) Israeli fourth and sixth graders were compared with a similar sample of American children for amount of television viewing and mastery of related mental skills (N = 198 and 157 respectively). Television viewing was defined as "literate viewing" or the subject's ability to answer extremely simple content questions about the TV programs shown on the preceding day. This measure of TV viewing correlated only about .50 with the more common measure of self reports of TV viewing and not at all with intelligence, memory, SES, or parents' education.

To our surprise we found the Israeli children (particularly the fourth graders) to exhibit significantly more "literate viewing" than their American counterparts in spite of the fact that Israel has only one black and white channel, and only six hours of broadcasting a day. Furthermore, while 39% of the American children have three or more TV sets at home, Israeli homes have only one set. Additional data led to the conclusion that for a variety of reasons (including the coobservation of parents) Israeli children view television more "seriously." They invest more mental effort in processing its messages, and retain more of its contents, while their American counterparts spend more time at the screen but view its programs in a cognitively "shallower" way. The frequent shifting from channel to channel and the interruptions caused by commercials may facilitate the effortless pattern of TV viewing among the American children studied.

Viewing, as we have reasoned, can affect the mastery of mental skill only to the extent that mental skills have to be applied to symbolic elements in the service of knowledge extraction. The same would apply to codes that supplant skills. Thus, children who are more "serious" viewers, i.e., invest more mental effort in knowledge extraction, should have a better mastery of the relevant mental skills from the television than those who invest less mental effort. Indeed, the data corroborated this claim. Not only did the mastery of specific skills (e.g., series completion) correlate with viewing in the Israeli, but not the American sample, the Israelis showed better mastery of precisely those skills that correlated with literate viewing, but not of other skills. Thus, it appears that more "serious" viewing requires more handling of the coded messages and allows for the cultivation of the relevant mental skills.

There were also noteworthy age and SES differences. Israeli fourth graders were more strongly affected by televiewing than were sixth graders, in spite of the fact that the latter exhibited more literate viewing and had an overall better mastery of the tested skills. In addition, younger lower class children were affected more in the skill area of analysis, while older middle class ones were more strongly affected in the areas of synthesis (e.g., integrative memory). These findings are in striking agreement with the ones obtained in the *Sesame Street* study.

The cognitive effects observed in this study were far smaller than those observed in the *Sesame Street* study. It was apparently the latter's novelty which underlied its strong effects. Viewing of less novel programs, even over extended periods of time, accounts for only 6%-9% of skill-mastery variance. But note that literate viewing accounts for skill-mastery in mainly the Israeli fourth-grade sample. Two factors seem to contribute to this observation: the child's perception of what televiewing entails, or demands, and age.

Mental processes are not activated automatically upon encountering a symbolic element. For instance, not all passive sentences involve the recovery of the base structure equivalent to an active sentence (Olson and Filby, 1972). First, a symbolic or structural element is negotiated when it violates certain expectations (e.g., Kintsch, 1977). Second, there is never one and only one kind of information to be extracted, particularly when a dense symbol system is involved. One can view a television show for the characters, the actions, the settings, the outcomes, the motives, or even the hidden meanings. With the exception of instructional materials, there are seldom predetermined levels of depths or amounts of information a child is required to extract. Thus, the child is free to define the demand characteristics of the information-extraction situation to him or herself. This subjective definition, or perception of the activity, affects what and how much information is to be extracted, and thus, what elements are to be negotiated.

Scribner and Cole (1978) show how skill-cultivation by literacy is task-specific. Olson and Bruner (1974) similarly argue that "knowledge is dependent on or is limited by the purpose for which it was acquired." Bobrow and Bower (1969) have found that subjects directed to look for misspelled words or to repeat sentences processed the material at shallower levels and were subsequently less able to recall either the words or sentences than subjects whose task required processing at the level of meaning. The two groups apparently dealt with somewhat different symbolic carriers of the text.

One's social setting and prevailing norms and expectations can influence what he or she looks for in televised messages, as exemplified in our cross-cultural comparison. Thus, it is not only what information a child can extract that determines what symbolic elements will be processed, but also what the child's perception of the task is. Attempting to get at more and deeper meanings implies the processing of more and more complex elements, resulting in stronger cognitive effects. Quite obvious educational implications follow from here.

The observation that our sixth graders were less affected than the fourth graders, in spite of more literate televiewing, is equally interesting. Obviously, the skill/mastery of the sixth graders was better. Moreover, while these children could continue to acquire *new* skills, television continues to use the *same* symbolic elements. Its elements do not provide new processing demands in concert with the improving skill mastery. This, however, does not mean that no new skills can be developed by media symbol systems. First, youngsters may still encounter new symbolic elements in media such as computers, avant-garde films, and the like. Second, as the youngsters' abilities develop, so do their information expectations. At age 10 the task perception of televiewing is likely to differ from that of age eight. Thus, elements that entailed no critical information, and were not processed at one age, may become a cognitive challenge later on.

Indeed, the only skill mastery that has improved as a function of literate televiewing in the sixth-grade sample was that of chunking and synthesizing relatively large bodies of information. This finding should not surprise us. Because television messages do not increase in complexity, and because the sixth grader is capable of dealing with them effectively, he or she may in turn acquire more information from the dense messages offered by the medium—hence, the improved mastery of the chunking skill.

CONCLUDING REMARKS

The basic premise underlying the propositions presented here is perhaps best expressed by Von Bertalanffy (1965):

> If the meaning of Goethe's 'Faust,' Van Gogh's landscapes or Bach's Art of the Fugue could be transmitted in discursive terms, their authors should and would not have bothered to write poems, paint or compose, but would rather have written scientific treatises.

Media transmit not only contents. Their contents have shape and structure. Even more generic to media, each medium cultivates its own blend of symbol systems and then—through its developing technology—generates additional unique forms of expression. Does exposure to media partake in the cultivation of children's abilities?

Abilities range in generality and in the extent to which their development is contingent on specific environmental inputs. Some are universally achieved, needing little tutoring. Others are more culturally specific (still others are discipline-specific or even idiosyncratic), requiring exposure to particular inputs and specific tutorial investments. While the latter achievements, such as map reading or violin playing, may be partly dependent on more "universal" achievements, their attainment is not spontaneous. Continuous exposure to media's symbolic modes of presentation may, as the findings described above show, affect the mastery of specific mental skills.

Skill cultivation by media symbol systems appears to be a typical case of what Bruner has once called "a function creating organ." But the "organs" or rather skills thus developed appear to be extremely specific. The transfer tests used in the studies not withstanding, their applicability may be limited to the use of the same media that cultivated them. They may contribute to no more than "media literacy."

The same problem faced Scribner and Cole (1978) when they found how specific the cognitive effects of literacy are (compare these with the much more general abilities whose cultivation was followed by Luria, 1976). Yet, as they argue with respect to literacy (1978:24):

> As practice in any activity continues, we would expect the range of materials which engage it to be extended and skills to become increasingly free from the particular conditions of the original practice. Skills, then, will be more available for what has been called "far transfer," including tasks and situations that do not involve the written modality. When skill systems involved in literacy are many, varied and complex, and have wide applicability, the functional and general ability approaches will converge in their predictions of intellectual outcomes.

Seen from a developmental point of view, one would expect earlier *specific* skill improvements to gradually converge and become increasingly more general as a function of repeated application. It is not unlikely that continuous exposure to television fosters the development of increasingly more general mental skills of which we are presently unaware.

Aside from the generalizability question, there is the question pertaining to the interplay between the symbol systems children encounter and the mental activities they are *capable* of employing or *choose* to employ. As I have tried to show, only those symbolic elements that children actively address can affect skill mastery. Symbolic elements do not affect a cognitively passive child. First, certain elements cannot affect children of young ages because the children's more general cognitive development hinders them from addressing these elements. If children are relatively insensitive to sequence and structure even at age seven (Collins and Westby, 1975), how could these elements affect them?

Second, and equally important, the child's perception of the viewing (or reading) task determines what information and how much of it is to be extracted. Thus, it determines what symbolic elements will be dealt with.

Much may depend on what kinds of information a child is socially encouraged to pick up and process. The more information children attempt to, and are capable of extracting, the stronger the skill-cultivating effects of a medium's symbol systems could be. Indeed, the findings described above show that, within age groups, the more capable children show greater gains in skill mastery than the less capable ones. Even observational learning, as Olson and Bruner (1974) remind us, requires skill.

A great many questions seem to follow from here, such as: What is the utility of specific skills which are cultivated by particular symbolic elements of the media? Do they develop at the expense of other skills? How can their development be facilitated? Among the many questions there is one which may deserve the most attention. If children can acquire particular symbolic modes by observational learning (say, as the result of imitating skill-supplanting elements), can they also learn to represent the world to themselves *in terms* of these elements? Thus, can some of media's symbolic elements become internalized and be used as "tools of thought"? Some of the data presented above suggest that indeed this *may* be the case. However, much more research is needed before a more definite answer can be given.

REFERENCES

BLACK, J.B., TURNER, T.J., and BOWER, G.H. (1977). "Spatial reference points in language comprehension." Paper presented at the Annual Meeting of the American Psychological Association, San Francisco, August.

BOBROW, S.A., and BOWER, G.H. (1969). "Comprehension and recall of sentences." Journal of Experimental Psychology, 80:455-461.

BOWER, G.H. (1976). "Comprehending and recalling stories." Division 3 Presidential Address, American Psychological Association, Washington, D.C., September.

BRUNER, J.S., OLVER, R.R., and GREENFIELD, P.M. (1966). Studies in cognitive growth. New York: Wiley.

COLE, M., and SCRIBNER, S. (1974). Culture and thought. New York: Wiley.

COLLINS, W.A. (1975). "The developing child as a viewer." Journal of Communication, 25:35-44.

--- and WESTBY, S.D. (1975). "Children's processing of social information from televised dramatic programs." Paper presented at the biennial meeting of the Society for Research in Child Development, Denver, April.

DORR, A. (1977). When I was a child, I thought as a child. Manuscript prepared for book in preparation by the Social Science Research Council Committee on Television and Social Behavior.

EISNER, E. (1978). "The impoverished mind." Educational Leadership, in press.
FELDMAN, D.H. (1979). Beyond universals: Exploration of the terrain of human development. New York: Praeger.
GARDNER, H. (1972). "Style sensitivity in children." Human Development, 15:325-338.
––– (1974). The shattered mind. New York: Vintage.
––– (1977). "Senses, symbols, operations: An organization of artistry." In D. Perkins and B. Leondar (eds.), The art and cognition. Baltimore, Md.: John Hopkins University Press.
–––, KIRCHER, M., WINNER, E., and PERKINS, D. (1975). "Children's metaphoric productions and preferences." Journal of Child Language, 2:125-141.
GARDNER, H.C., SHOTWELL, J.M., and WOLF, D. (1977). "Exploring early symbolization: Styles of achievement." Paper presented at the symposium on "Fundamentals of Symbolism," Austria, July.
GOODMAN, N. (1976). The languages of art. Indianapolis, Ind.: Hackett.
GREENFIELD, P. (1972). "Oral or written language: The consequences for cognitive development in Africa, the United States and England." Language and Speech, 15:169-178.
HATANO, G., MIYAKE, Y., and BINKS, M.G. (1977). "Performance of expert abacus operators." Cognition, 5:57-71.
HUSTON-STEIN, A., and WRIGHT, J.C. (1977). "Modeling the medium: Effects of formal properties of children's television programs." Paper presented at Biennial Meeting, Society for Research in Child Development, New Orleans, March.
HUTTENLOCHER, J. (1973). "Language and thought." In G.A. Miller (ed.), Communication, language and meaning. New York: Basic Books.
KATZ, E., BLUMLER, J.G., and GUREVITCH, M. (1974). "Utilization of mass communication by the individual. In J.G. Blumler and E. Katz (eds.), The uses of mass communications, Vol. III. Beverly Hills, Cal.: Sage.
KINTSCH, W. (1977). Memory and cognition. New York: Wiley.
KJORUP, S. (1977). "Film as a meetingplace of multiple codes. In D. Perkins and B. Leondar (eds.), The art and cognition. Baltimore, Md.: Johns Hopkins University Press.
LANGER, S.K. (1942). Philosophy in a new key. Cambridge, Mass.: Harvard University Press.
LEIFER, A.D., COLLINS, W.A., GROSS, B.M., TAYLOR, P.H., ANDREWS, L., and BLACKMER, E.R. (1971). "Developmental aspects of variables relevant to observational learning." Child Development, 42:1509-1516.
LURIA, A.R. (1976). Cognitive development, its cultural and social foundations. Cambridge, Mass.: Harvard University Press.
MANDLER, J., and JOHNSON, N. (1977). "Remembrance of things passed: Story structure and recall." Cognitive Psychology, 9:111-151.
MERINGOFF, L. (1978). "The influence of the medium on children's apprehension of stories." Doctoral dissertation, Harvard University.
MESSARIS, P., and GROSS, L. (1977). "Interpretations of photographic narrative by viewers in four age groups." Studies in the Anthropology of Visual Communication, 4:99-111.
NOBLE, G. (1975). Children in front of the small screen. Beverly Hills, Cal.: Sage.
NORMAN, D.A., and RUMELHART, D.E. (1975). Explorations in cognition. San Francisco: W.H. Freeman.

OLSON, D.R. (1974). "Towards a theory of instructional means." Paper presented at the meeting of the American Educational Research Association, Chicago, April.

——— (1977). "From utterance to text: The bias of language in speech and writing." Harvard Educational Review, 47:257-281.

——— and BRUNER, J.S. (1974). "Learning through experience and learning through media." In D.R. Olson (ed.), Media and symbols: The forms of expression, communication, and education. The 73rd NSSE Yearbook. Chicago: University of Chicago Press.

OLSON, D.R., and FILBY, N. (1972). "On the comprehension of active and passive sentences." Cognitive Psychology, 3:361-381.

PERKINS, D., and LEONDAR, B. (1977). The art and cognition. Baltimore, Md.: Johns Hopkins University Press.

PRESSLEY, M. (1977). "Imagery and children's learning: Putting the picture in developmental perspective." Review of Educational Research, 47:585-622.

SALOMON, G. (1974). "Internalization of filmic schematic operations in interaction with learners' aptitudes." Journal of Educational Psychology, 66:499-511.

——— (1976). "Cognitive skill learning across cultures." Journal of Communication, 26:138-145.

——— (1977). The language of media and the cultivation of mental skills. Final report submitted to the Spencer Foundation.

——— and COHEN, A.A. (1977). "Television formats, mastery and mental skills, and the acquisition of knowledge." Journal of Educational Psychology, 69:612-619.

——— (1978). "On the meaning and validity of television viewing." Journal of Human Communication Research, in press.

SCRIBNER, S., and COLE, M. (1973). "Cognitive consequences of formal and informal education." Science, 182:553-559.

——— (1978). Literacy without schooling: Testing for intellectual effects. Vai Literacy Project, Working paper No. 2, The Rockefeller University.

SINGER, J.L. (1978). "The powers and limitations of television." In P. Tannenbaum (ed.), The entertainment function of television. Hillsdale, N.J.: Erlbaum.

———, TOWER, R., SINGER, D.G., and BIGGS, A. (1977). "Preschoolers' comprehension and play behavior following viewing of 'Mr. Rogers' and 'Sesame Street.'" Paper presented at the American Psychological Association, San Francisco, August.

VON BERTALANFFY, L. (1965). "On the definition of the symbol." In J.R. Royce (ed.), Psychology and the symbol. New York: Random House.

WINNER, E., ROSENSTIEL, A.K., and GARDNER, H. (1976). "The development of metaphoric understanding." Developmental Psychology, 12:289-297.

WORTH, S., and GROSS, L. (1974). "Symbolic strategies." Journal of Communication, 24.

Chapter 4

CHILDREN'S ATTENTION: THE CASE OF TV VIEWING

Robert Krull and William Husson

TELEVISION IS A PRINCIPAL SOURCE of information and entertainment for children. However, many researchers have wondered if television adversely affects children's ability to gather information from other sources. This chapter examines children's TV attention patterns to provide some understanding of part of this issue.

We have looked at several kinds of information and review them in the following order. First, we discuss some experimental literature on children's selective attention to complex visual stimuli. Although this literature does not deal with television directly, its findings have implications for predicting attention trends.

Second, we review literature on how viewers behave in front of the set. The number of studies in this area is small, but a coherent picture is beginning to emerge from them.

Third, we introduce new data on children's viewing. The framework for their collection grew out of the literature just mentioned and a sequence of preceding studies. The new data test alternate explanations of how attention is directed.

[83]

Finally, we develop one piece of a larger theory about what children may be thinking as they view. Its aim is to explain complicated patterns of attention without requiring abilities beyond the intellectual capacities of children.

EXPERIMENTAL STUDIES OF ATTENTION

An explanation of attention patterns in children's viewing requires consideration of at least two factors—audio/visual attributes which affect attention and the cognitive development of the children. Stimulus complexity is one attribute whose effect on attention has been examined in an effort to discern possible developmental trends.

STUDIES OF STIMULUS COMPLEXITY

Cantor et al. (1963) presented preschool children with successive sets of abstract visual images of different levels of complexity. They found that as the complexity of the image increased, in general, so did the length of timy children looked at it.

In a similar study, Faw and Nunnally (1968) examined the effect of the complexity of abstract and realistic visual stimuli on the attention of seven to thirteen year olds. They also found that subjects spent more time looking at complex images. Wohlwill (1975) found that the amount of time spent exploring slides of postage stamps and outdoor scenes increased linearly with the complexity of the stimuli. His subjects were children in grades one through eight.

These studies all show similar effects on children's attention, but the stimuli employed varied essentially along just one dimension. Extrapolating their findings to television viewers is tenuous because TV programs vary on many dimensions. Even static stimuli can be multidimensional in various ways, pre-. senting problems of interpretation. For example, Garner (1974) points out that subjects' reactions to simple dot figures cannot be explained without taking into consideration their perceptions as to the possible total number of figures and manipulations of them. There seem to be three important aspects of programs which differentiate them from static stimuli.

One major dimension which TV programs add to static stimuli is dynamism. In other words, television images change over time. Flagg (in press) for instance, cites several studies which show age and experience trends in viewer eye movements when the stimuli are static (Mackworth and Bruner, 1971; Olson, 1970; Whiteside, 1974; Zinchenko et al., 1963; Antes, 1974; Furst, 1971; Krugman, 1968; and Noton and Stark, 1971a, 1971b, 1971c). When she examined the eye movements of TV viewers, however, the age effect did not appear. Her interpretation is that television controls the rate at which information is scanned, which eliminated the developmental effect.

Two additional factors restricting extrapolation of static stimulus studies are TV program content and sound tracks. The assemblage of images into programs generally revolves around a story. Viewers' preceptions about individual TV images are probably affected by their relationship to the storyline (see Bernstein (1977) for a discussion of the importance of this variable to children's attention). The auditory portion of programs is obviously important both on its own and in interaction with program visuals. The interaction among sound, content, and sequential visual images raises the question of the relevance of individual attributes to a whole.

STUDIES OF DISTRACTION OF ATTENTION

A number of studies have sought to determine if a child's ability to ignore irrelevant stimuli in a learning task improves with age. Children were asked to recall either colors, figures, or shapes under conditions of visual or auditory distraction. Unfortunately, the findings of these studies have been ambiguous with regard to developmental trends.

Maccoby and Hagen (1965) and Hagen (1967), for example, found that auditory distraction reduced accuracy of recall for children of different ages. Other studies, on the other hand, have found improvement in resistance to distraction with age. Pick et al. (1972) asked first and sixth graders to judge the similarity of wooden animals with respect to color and shape. The experimenters varied whether subjects were told before or after exposure to the objects on what dimension they were to compare the objects. They found that older children were much quicker in judging correctly the objects if they were given the dimension of comparison in advance. The results were interpreted to indicate that the older children were better able to take advantage of the relevant attribute than were younger children. Turnure (1970) found similar developmental trends for children in the 5 1/2 to 7 1/2 age range. The older children were found to perform even better under conditions of visual distraction than under conditions without distraction.

These distraction studies indicate that older children perform better under some conditions than do younger children. However, the specification of those conditions is not clear, particularly when the findings are to be extrapolated to TV viewing. In the next section we review some of the literature on children's attention to the TV screen and try to sort out the relationship between these two sets of findings.

CHILDREN'S TELEVISION VIEWING

Although there has been concern regarding television "addicts" and "zombie" viewing styles, the bulk of TV research indicates that viewers of all ages pay varying levels of attention during programs and that concentration on the set is not nearly as intent as initially thought (Robinson, 1969; Bechtel et al., 1972; LoSciuto, 1972; Murray, 1972). Given that attention varies, the cause of the variation becomes an interesting issue.

Many attention studies have concentrated on variables specific to particular program materials. However, one generic finding is that activity on the screen or the soundtrack draws attention (Reeves, 1970; Anderson and Levin, 1976; Lasker,

1974; Flagg et al., 1976). This fits with the findings for static visual images if one considers activity on the TV screen to be a form of complexity over time. It also fits with studies showing that one of the major motivations for viewing is excitement (Greenberg, 1974; Dembo and McCron, 1976). The latter assumes that high activity is one of the factors providing the excitement viewers seek.

Data on developmental trends show that older children are more selective, more visually oriented, and more interested in complex production techniques (Ward et al., 1972; Ward and Wackman, 1973; Wartella and Ettema, 1974; Lasker, 1974). This greater discrimination on the part of older viewers also fits with some of the experimental findings described earlier. However, there is some indication that children of all ages have fairly simple views of the relationships among attributes of TV displays (Wartella and Alexander, 1978), and that they attend more intently to segments whose point is clear (Flagg, in press; Lasker, 1974).

Taking these trends and limitations into account, one would guess that children pay attention in different ways to programs of different levels of complexity and that older children are more selective, but that the discriminations are made at fairly rudimentary levels. The measures we employed seem to be at a level that should affect children.

MEASURES OF THE FORM AND
CONTENT OF TELEVISION SHOWS

We measured program variables which can be grouped into three general categories: form complexity, visual/verbal interaction, and temporal structure. All of the form complexity and most of the visual/verbal interaction measures have been used in preceding studies. The temporal structure and one visual/verbal interaction measure were added to test alternate hypotheses generated by the preceding studies. We will discuss each of these groups of variables in turn, beginning with the older variables.

PROGRAM FORM COMPLEXITY

These variables are drawn from a larger group based on the "information theory" concept of entropy. Entropy, which has been used in a good deal of theoretical and empirical work (Shannon and Weaver, 1949; Garner, 1962, 1974; Berlyne, 1971), treats complexity as a function of the uncertainty of the occurrences of stimuli. The form complexity variables measure the uncertainty of certain occurrences in TV programs.

In previous studies, form complexity has been found to affect the size of audience (Krull and Watt, 1975), the habitual tuning-in of programs (Watt and Krull, 1974), and physiological arousal (Watt and Krull, 1975). Complexity has also been found to correlate positively with viewer aggression (Watt and Krull, 1976). Finally, there is some indication of a developmental trend in preference for complexity. Young adults were found to watch and like higher levels of program complexity than either younger or older individuals (Krull et al., 1977).

The experimental studies described earlier showed that children spend more time exploring complicated stimuli and the television studies showed that children are more attracted to active and novel parts of television programs. Combining those findings with these on program complexity led us to expect that children would pay more attention to parts of programs having high form complexity.

We used four complexity measures in preliminary attention studies: set complexity, shot complexity, verbal interaction complexity, and modal complexity. More information on these variables can be found in Krull et al. (1978) and Watt and Krull (1974).[1]

VISUAL/VERBAL INTERACTION VARIABLES

In addition to the complexity variables, we used two which take into account the relationship between visual and verbal content: visual/verbal congruence and independence. These concepts were suggested by Piaget's theory of intellecutal development (Ginsburg and Opper, 1969) and the results of some of the experiments described earlier. We hypothesized that children would prefer program sequences in which they could actually see the relationships talked about (visual/verbal congruence) to those in which the meaning of speech was not supported by a visual referent (visual/verbal independence).

RESULTS OF PRELIMINARY STUDIES

GENERAL DESIGN FEATURES

We have examined attention effects in three studies of Children's Television Workshop programs. The attention data were gathered in controlled, but relatively uncontrived settings and program measures were obtained for shows very similar to those broadcast. Relationships among variables were analyzed using time series techniques and multiple regression. Readers unfamiliar with time series analysis may want to consult sources such as Box and Jenkins (1970) and Krull and Paulson (1977).

PRELIMINARY RESULTS

Our first study showed that *Sesame Street* viewers (four to five years of age) are little affected by program variables, the major factor influencing their attention being a positive correlation between adjacent attention levels. Viewers of the *Electric Company* (7 1/2 to 8 1/2 years of age) were found to react to a variety of program variables and to be less affected by attention interdependence (Krull and Husson, 1977). In a follow-up study we found indication of anticipation in the *Electric Company* attention patterns (Krull and Husson, in press).

These data imply that younger children are slow to determine whether or not they like the material presented in a program segment and so are slow to react with changes in attention. One could think of this as attention "inertia." The older children, on the other hand, appear to know program structure sufficiently well to change levels of attention in advance of changes in program material.

In the third study Krull et al. (1978) analyzed these viewing data to determine if the viewing patterns could be due to children's reacting to regularities in program variables. They found that older children are more affected by cycles in program variables and that they show some anticipation of cycles, particularly for set complexity.

Taken together, these studies provide a more complicated picture of children's behavior than we had expected. The older children do pay more attention to complex material in general, are more affected by visual variables, and are able to sort out relationships among program variables so as to anticipate patterns in some of them. These trends fit with those in the experimental literature. However, the anticipation pattern is more elaborate than one might have expected of seven to eight year olds (although Flagg, in press, pointed out that television's presenting information sequentially over time is different from most experimental settings and yields different results). Also, the young children seem much less discriminating even than we had expected.

In this chapter we have tested several alternative explanations of our data. To do so we have added several variables. Two measures of temporal structure have to do with the type of distraction used and the division of programs into segments (bits). Another visual/verbal interaction measure has been added to refine a rationale.

NEW VARIABLES

Measures for Temporal Structure

We added two measures of how parts of programs are sequenced. One of these variables, "time in show," was added to handle problems with the slide distractor. The other, "time in bit," was added to remove possible effects of the segmentation of programs.

Several researchers (Bernstein, 1977; Epstein, 1977) have reported that the slide distractor used in testing Children's Television Workshop programs produces an artificial change in children's attention from the beginning to the end of a program. The slide projector contains about 10 minutes worth of different slides. After having shown its repertory of slides once, the projector simply repeats the sequence. This repetition appears to distract children less as the viewing period progresses. The result is that segments of programs appearing earlier seem to be less interesting than segments appearing later.

To eliminate this confounding effect we measured a variable we call "time in show." It is defined as the length of time between any point in the program and the program's beginning. By using this variable as a statistical control, we expected to obtain more accurate models of viewing.

The second sequence variable we added was expected to handle two related theoretical issues. One of these involves the level of sophistication of *Sesame Street* viewers. Even though our data seem to indicate that young children are not very discriminating and show considerable attention inertia, these children may still react to large-scale changes in program material. Developing variables at this level could add significantly to our models of viewing. The second theoretical problem deals with the sophistication of *Electric Company* viewers implied by the anticipation effects.

Our data indicate that older children are able to anticipate changes in several program complexity variables by intervals of 90 seconds or more. One alternate explanation for these effects is that children are really anticipating the end of one program segment and the beginning of another. Since bit changes often involve changes in many form and content aspects of program material, it could be that the apparent anticipation of changes in program variables could merely be a statistical artifact of the change from one bit to another.

The bit change seemed both useful for clarifying the *Electric Company* models and, being a large-scale structural aspect of programs, also relevant to explanations of the *Sesame Street* models. To assess these effects we measured "*time in bit.*" It is defined as the length of time from any point in a program to the opening of the segment in which it occurs.

We expected that as the *"time in bit"* got longer, the level of children's attention would decrease. The rationale is that children would become bored with the material in a segment after a while and would stop viewing. This seems to fit with data indicating that long bits generally get lower attention (e.g., Anderson and Levin, 1976). We also expected that if older children are really anticipating the end of bits, controlling for *"time in bit"* should reduce anticipation effects for variables to statistical insignificance.

VERBAL CONCRETENESS

We decided to refine the way in which the visual/verbal interaction variables treat content. We felt that the way we conceptualized the concreteness of verbalization could have two subdimensions. One of these deals with the reference of verbalization to visually presented objects or to abstract concepts. This is the subdimension our older measures tapped.

The other subdimension deals with the visual presence or absence of the speaker as opposed to the things spoken about. We have argued that children can more easily understand the meaning of what TV characters say if a visual anchor is provided. By the same token, children may be more interested in the meaning of what is said if the source of the message is visually present on screen.

Making discriminations along both subdimensions gave the following hierarchy of concreteness levels:

(1) *Speaker "off" image "off"*—In this category, an off-screen voice, rather than a live character, is the source of the verbalization. Furthermore, there is no visual support for what the speaker is saying.

(2) *Speaker "on," image "off"*—A physically present character talks about things which are not visually represented on the screen. Statements concerning feelings, ideas, etc. predominate in this category.

(3) *Speaker "off," image "on"*—A narrator's voice speaks about objects or events which the viewer can see on the television screen.

(4) *Speaker "on," image "on"*—A character (human, muppet, or animated) appears in the same visual frame of reference as that which he is talking about. A character who is explaining how to make something, for example, would be able to point to, or refer to, whatever he or she was talking about.

We also felt that children may evaluate program segments as a whole rather than make very fine distinctions regarding language. Even if a bit were predominantly about some very concrete topic, such as naming the parts of the body, some proportion of the verbalization would probably be fairly abstract. Conversely, even very abstract bits are likely to refer to concrete aspects of the situation occasionally. We reasoned that children would not react strongly to the small amount of verbalization which did not fall into the category dominating the bit. Therefore, we coded entire bits as falling into one of the categories we just described, using the numbers given beside the categories as weights.

METHOD

SAMPLES

Television Programs

We analyzed four videotapes. Two *Sesame Street* shows were 47 (SS #1 in the tables) and 58 (SS #2) minutes in length; two *Electric Company* shows were 19 (EC #1) and 28 (EC 2) minutes in length. The EC #1 show was a truncated version of the program, but was similar to the rest of the shows in the series in other respects.

Viewing Samples

CTW provided attention data on 10 different children watching each videotape. The *Sesame Street* viewers were four to five years old; the *Electric Company* viewers were 7-1/2 to 8-1/2 years old.

PROGRAM COMPLEXITY MEASURE

Scoring the videotapes proceeded in several stages, more fully described in Krull and Husson (1977). One coder ran the videotape machine and stopped it every 30 seconds using the machine's pause control. The other coder scored the variables using a system of clocks and counters, noting the results for each interval. Videotapes were coded for one complexity variable at a time and entropy values were computed after coding was completed. Intercoder reliability for the complexity measures has been found to be high (Watt and Krull, 1974).

Visual/Verbal Interaction Measures

The verbal parts of each videotape were transcribed. Then, using the criteria described above, we determined whether each utterance fell into the congruent or independent category. Since the length of utterances varied greatly, the number of words per utterance was used as a weight. Each scale was completed by summing the number of weighted utterances in each category per 30-second interval.

Verbal Concreteness

Using the transcription obtained for the visual/verbal interaction measures and the rationale outlined in a preceding section, we assigned program segments to one of four concreteness categories. All 30-second intervals which fell within a bit were given the same score as the whole bit. Those intervals which fell within a bit were given the same score as the whole bit. Those intervals which bridged the boundary between two segments were given the score of the segment taking up more than 15 seconds of the interval. Because of the length of segments, most intervals fell completely within one segment.

Temporal Structure Measures

"Time in show" was measured by sequentially numbering the 30-second intervals into which programs had been divided. This system was chosen over absolute lengths of time because statistical analyses would yield precisely the same results with either technique and the numbering system was less cumbersome to handle.

"Time in bit" was computed by measuring the length of time between the mid-point of each 30-second interval and the beginning of the program segment in which it occurred. The mid-point of intervals was expected to be fairly representative of each whole interval.

Children's Attention Measure

The attention data were collected by CTW (see Reeves (1970) for a full description of the procedures). Children were individually shown a videotape. A colored-slide projector, changing slides every 7.5 seconds, was placed at the same height as the television set and slightly to one side. The level of attention of each child was rated every 7.5 seconds by a coder using a push-button connected to a recording device. We averaged these attention data over 30 seconds to make the measurement intervals comparable to those used for the program variables.

STATISTICAL ANALYSIS

We first computed time-domain time series statistics for the bivariate relationships among variables. Then we used those autocorrelations and crosscorrelations in ordinary least squares (OLS) multiple regressions to build our models of TV viewing.

We made a number of assumptions to guide us in building multivariate models. First, we assumed that a model with few variables would be most easily understandable. This assumption was grounded on our belief that children are not straining to bring complicated ideas about programs to a potentially relaxing activity. Second, we assumed that children are unlikely to show effects over very long time periods (this has already been discussed). In a following section we show how, although our best models seem strong empirically, there are indications these assumptions may not be warranted.

In most cases our statistical procedures worked effectively at the empirical level. However, we ran into a rare problem with one of the *Electric Company* shows—some combinations of predictor variables yielded multiple correlations greater than 1.0. The cause of this was neither multicollinearity, because the simple correlations were all below .5, nor overfitting the data, because as few as eight terms produced multiple correlations beyond the theoretical limit.

Our best explanation is that particular combinations of terms interacted in ways which violated the assumptions of ordinary least squares (see, for example, Wonnacott and Wonnacott, chap. 6). We present data regarding this point in the discussion section.

RESULTS

SESAME STREET

Table 1 shows the results for *Sesame Street*. The subscripts beside the predictor terms indicate by how many 30-second intervals the terms lead $(t + 'x')$ or lag behind $(t - 'X')$ attention.

The models for the two shows are rather similar. A fairly large amount of variance is accounted for (R^2 = .55 to .64), the bulk of this due to attention intercorrelation (Attention$_{t-1}$). However, several of the new variables also contributed. Verbal concreteness and "time in show" were both positively correlated with attention as expected; "time in bit" correlated negatively, but only for SS #1.

In general, these models indicate rather small effects on attention by the program variables. When the variance accounted for by the attention inertia and temporal structure characteristics are summed, one finds that 37% to 40% of variance in attention is due to these factors alone. This amounts to over 60% of the variance explained by all the terms in the models together. Young children, then, seem to pay attention largely as a function of attention inertia and gradually increasing boredom with the slide distractor.

There are two qualifications regarding this interpretation. One is that over 40% of the variance in attention remains unaccounted for by our models. This may be due to young children's being somewhat random in their attention (this concurs with Anderson and Levin's data on very young viewers). It may also be due to the action of program variables we did not measure (Bernstein (1977), among others, has found effects for rather different program measures).

A second qualification is that we can draw conclusions only about effects lasting 30 seconds or more. Effects of shorter duration would decay inside our measurement intervals undetected.

Table 1: REGRESSION MODELS FOR PROGRAM VARIABLES AND ATTENTION FOR SESAME STREET

Show #1

Predictor Variables	Beta	Multiple R	F	D.F.	P<
Attention$_{t-1}$	.34	.80	31.65	5/87	.001
Visual/Verbal Independence$_{t+3}$	.18				
Time in Show$_t$	.32				
Time in Bit$_{t-6}$	−.24				
Verbal/Concreteness$_t$	.32				

Show # 2

Predictor Variables	Beta	Multiple R	F	D.F.	P<
Attention$_{t-1}$	.45	.74	26.66	5/110	.001
Set Complexity$_{t-4}$	−.15				
Shot Complexity$_{t-2}$	.17				
Time in Show$_t$	.18				
Verbal Concreteness$_{t-1}$	.25				

THE ELECTRIC COMPANY

Table 2 shows the regression models for the *Electric Company*. It is clear even from a casual inspection that these results are very different from those obtained for *Sesame Street*. The total variance accounted for is larger (R^2 = .79 to .86) and much of this is due to set complexity coefficients (25% to 49% due to direct and indirect effects). These complexity coefficients show a rather odd pattern of positive and negative values, which we explain in the discussion section.

There are also significant coefficients in the other complexity variables, but their values often do not conform to our hypotheses. Shot complexity affects attention in both shows; but there are negative coefficients in each case and a positive one only for EC #1. There is a negative coefficient for verbal complexity for EC #1, and none at all for EC #2. Modal complexity is negatively related to attention in both shows, but the lags are very different, - 2 and +3. We had expected positive coefficients for all of these variables and got these rather unstable set of results instead.

Visual/verbal congruence is negatively related to attention in EC #1 and positively in EC #2. Verbal concreteness was similarly correlated in the two shows. Positive coefficients were expected for both variables.

"Time in show" is negatively related to attention in EC #1 and positively in EC #2. The reason for the difference between the values of these coefficients may be the length of the two sample shows. EC #1 is rather short and boredom with the slide distractor may not have appeared by the time the show ended.

Overall, then, these models account for a good deal of variance and the sets of predictor variables look rather similar. However, the values of the regression coefficients form odd patterns and one can reasonably ask what these and the *Sesame Street* models tell us about TV viewing in general. We will handle this issue in the following way in the next section. First, we explain the set complexity coefficients. Second, we discuss the issues of generic models of viewing. Finally, we attempt to

Table 2: REGRESSION MODELS FOR PROGRAM VARIABLES AND ATTENTION FOR ELECTRIC COMPANY

Show # 1

Predictor Variables	Beta	Multiple R	F	D.F.	P<
Set Complexity$_{t-3}$	−.23	.89	7.92	12/25	.001
Set Complexity$_{t-2}$	.32				
Set Complexity$_t$	.39				
Set Complexity$_{t+3}$	.60				
Shot Complexity$_{t-1}$	.52				
Shot Complexity$_t$	−.27				
Verbal Inter. Complexity$_{t+4}$	−.32				
Model Complexity$_{t-2}$	−.39				
Visual/Verbal Congruence$_{t-4}$	−.37				
Visual/Verbal Congruence$_{t+1}$	−.68				
Time in Show$_t$	−.25				
Verbal Concreteness$_{t-3}$	−.35				

Show # 1

Predictor Variables	Beta	Multiple R	F	D.F.	P<
Attention$_{t-1}$	−.23	.93	29.33	10/45	.001
Set Complexity$_{t-3}$	−.65				
Set Complexity$_t$	.22				
Set Complexity$_{t+4}$	−.41				
Set Complexity$_{t+5}$	−.63				
Shot Complexity$_{t-2}$	−.51				
Model Complexity$_{t+3}$	−.35				
Visual/Verbal Congruence$_t$	.48				
Time in Show$_t$	.48				
Verbal Concreteness$_{t-3}$	.62				

construct a theoretical model of viewing behavior which can realistically be expected to be within the capabilities of children.

DISCUSSION

INTERPRETING THE SET COMPLEXITY FINDINGS

The set complexity coefficients for *Sesame Street* are fairly straightforward—one significant coefficient appears for SS #1, and none appear for SS #2. This shows weak, if any, support for a relationship between this program variable and attention.

The coefficients for *Electric Company*, on the other hand, have a mixture of positive and negative values over a wide range of lags. This pattern is rather confusing if one simply wants to determine whether two variables are positively or negatively correlated. Fortunately the results of plotting the predicted attention values are quite clear.

In Figure 1 the solid line shows the actual attention scores for EC #2 and the dashed line shows the predicted attention scores. Scores for intervals four to 52 only are plotted because the complexity coefficients cannot predict attention outside that range without the application of elaborate techniques (see Box and Jenkins, 1970:chap. 7). The ordinate in the graph gives the percent of complete attention paid by viewers. The dotted line in the figure gives the level of set complexity for each interval. The values of set complexity range from 0.0 to 2.40 in the ordinate. We have deliberately not scaled the complexity values to match the attention values so that patterns in behavior of the series are more easily visible.

The fit between the predicted and actual attention curves is good, but hardly perfect (r = .50). The fit cannot be perfect since only four of the total of 10 coefficients from the regression model were used to plot predicted scores. One can also see that both sets of attention scores show a cyclical rise and fall in level. For example, there are peak high scores around intervals 4, 10, 17, 25, 31, and 43, and relatively low scores at 6, 13, 23,

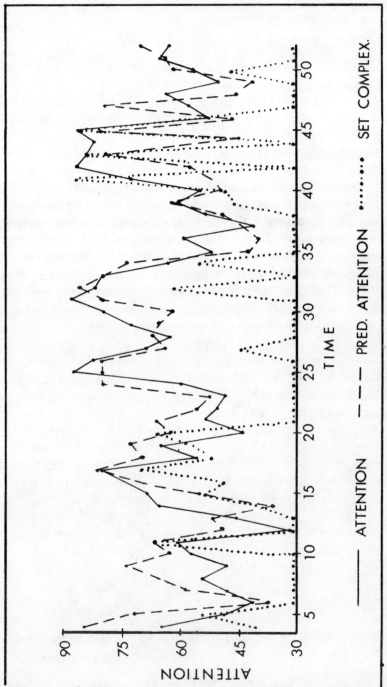

Figure 1: Realizations of Actual and Predicted Attention, and Set Complexity

28, 37, and 49. This cyclical pattern is the key to understanding the relationship of attention to set complexity.

Note that the set complexity scores also show a cyclical pattern and that in most places complexity and attention scores are high in the same general area. For example, there are high peaks in complexity around intervals 5, 11, 17, 27, 32, and 43. Note also that the attention peaks seem to come slightly ahead of the complexity peaks. For example, attention peaks are at intervals 25 and 31, and complexity peaks at 27 and 32.

So far we have seen that there are cycles in the variables, and that the fit between the paths of the variables over time is moderately good. That is, the complexity and attention scores move up and down together in value, but these movements do not match perfectly. One would expect such a pattern to give moderate positive correlations between the variables, and yet

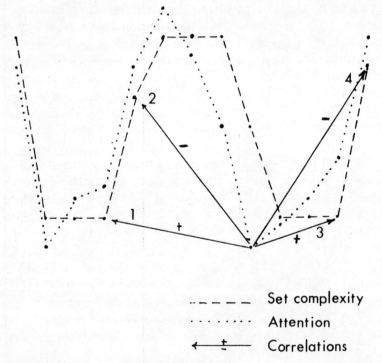

- - - - - Set complexity

· · · · · · · Attention

←——±—— Correlations

Figure 2: Correlations Between Set Complexity and Children's Attention at Various Time Leads and Lags

we obtained a mixture of positive and negative values. We will now show graphically why this occurs and then verify the result statistically.

Figure 2 shows segments of series of hypothetical complexity and attention scores. (We use hypothetical data to make our point more clearly, but the real data would yield very similar results.) We have chosen one point on the attention series and show its relationship to complexity scores at different lags by means of arrows.

Since the complexity scores behave cyclically, there are regular alternations of high and low scores. In other words, high complexity scores are surrounded by low ones and vice versa. Since the attention scores also behave cyclically, the same pattern is observed for them. The effect of these patterns on correlations can be seen by observing the change of sign of the arrows we have drawn. Arrow one points to a complexity score separated by five intervals from the attention score of interest. Because both the complexity and attention scores are low, this would imply a positive correlation as indicated by the sign on the arrow. The next complexity value, at arrow two, is much higher and a negative correlation between it and the attention score is implied. The next four complexity scores are all high and imply negative relationships to attention. (We have not drawn arrows to these points to make the figure easier to interpret.)

The first three complexity scores to the right of the attention point are all low. These imply a positive relationship between attention and complexity, as indicated by the arrow to the third point; and the relationship is an anticipatory one since attention precedes complexity. When complexity rises again, negative relationships to attention are again implied, and so on. So although the two sets of scores clearly move up and down together in time, the statistical relationship for our example points changes from positive to negative at different time lags.

When the procedure we have just described is repeated for all the points in two series one can obtain a set of correlations where we had arrows. This means that instead of having a pattern of positive and negative arrows, one would have a set of positive and negative correlations. Because the two series clearly move together, these bizarre correlations are merely a statistical artifact. This interpretation can be verified by examining the relationship in terms of cycles using spectral analysis techniques (Jenkins and Watts, 1968).

Krull et al. (1978) found that 200-300-second cycles in set complexity are fairly strongly related to cycles in children's attention and that attention shows an anticipatory lead of 30-60 seconds. These cycles are in the range suggested by the regression coefficients we have been discussing. For EC #2 the coefficients run from lag -3 intervals to lead +5 intervals, a range of 8 intervals or 240 seconds. We validated this interpretation by subtracting the predicted attention values from the actual values, as given in Figure 1, to produce a set of residuals. Then we duplicated the analysis run by Krull et al.; only this time we correlated set complexity with the residuals rather than the raw attention scores.

Krull et al. had obtained a spectral correlation of .67 for 300-second cycles; we obtained a correlation of only .22 for the residuals. This indicates that by using the coefficients from the multiple regression models we removed most of the variance in the relationship. In terms of children's behavior this means that we have verified that children are reacting to cycles in set complexity, rather than to the individual complexity values. The pattern of the regression coefficients is merely an artifact and the real correlation between the variables is positive. The children also show anticipation as found by Krull et al. Comparable results could be generated for EC #1.

THE PROBLEM OF GENERIC MODELS

In describing results of our regression analyses we pointed out differences between the findings for our sample shows. Although the overall patterns of predictor variables are similar, in several cases the predictor coefficients are neither of the same sign nor at the same lag; in a few cases, variables appearing in one equation do not appear at all in the equation for the other sample program. These differences make it difficult to draw conclusions about children's viewing in general. Sampling variability and complex interactions among variables are two possible reasons for these differences. They imply very different solutions to finding generic models.

Sampling variability could make our models of viewing look dissimilar even though they reflect the same underlying relationships among variables. Unmeasured variables in both our sample programs and viewing samples could have different values and cause our findings to look different. For example, the levels of viewing experience and of cognitive development of the children in viewing groups could be different. As a result, some children could be bored by the same material that excited other children. The outcome would then be different apparent relationships between the program and attention variables.

One way to handle sampling variability is to measure a much larger number of variables on a much larger number of programs than we did. Then one could assess the reliability of one's findings. A major problem with this approach is that models of viewing become both theoretically and statistically unmanageable when the number of variables handled becomes large. At least this approach is possible using the same theoretical and methodological frameworks we did.

Complex interactions among variables probably cannot be handled with our current techniques. For example, because our *Electric Company* models have very high multiple correlations, yet are different in several coefficients, it is likely that the relationships among program variables account for the differences. Explaining these relationships may be a little like explaining jokes—a lot of effort with ambiguous results. However, we have attempted to do this for one of our more interesting findings.

A Viewing Mini-Theory

There are several important interaction issues we could address. The particular relationship we have chosen involves variables we have already discussed in some detail. Figure 3 shows links among set complexity, attention, and three cognitive variables on which we do not have any data. We will use this model to describe how children might anticipate changes in program variables. The links and our explanation of them are exceedingly tentative, but we expect that a more elaborate model of this form will be necessary to fully explain how children view.

In the figure, direction of causality is indicated by arrows. The kind of causal relationship is indicated by a sign for linear relationships and by a schematic for nonlinear relationships. This first link, that between set complexity and attention, is linear and positive. We have already provided a rationale and data in support of this. We think that attention is also linked to a number of cognitive variables. In other words, after paying some attention, children think about what they see.

One of our links goes to expectancy of interesting program material. Considerable research has shown that receivers of repetitive stimulation develop expectations about the sequence of occurrences. The range of stimuli for which this appears to hold includes classical stimulus-response conditioning, neural firings in the brain (Callaway, 1975), and purchases made on the stock market (Christ, 1966:206). Here we are dealing with children's expectations about set changes in a program in a series to which they have had previous exposure. Our model

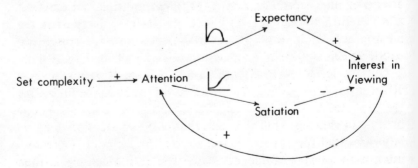

Figure 3: Theoretical Links Among Set Complexity, Attention, and Three Cognitive Variables

requires only that children are aware that there is considerable, regular change in the kind of material shown in the program. It does not require that children know the exact rhythm of the changes. In other words, our model does not require children to have cognitive stopwatches telling them precisely when set changes are going to occur.

The relationship could operate in the following way. If attention is low, expectancy is low because there is no information on which to build expectations. At moderate levels of attention, expectance would be high because children would know that the interesting material presented would continue for a short period at least. When attention is very high, expectancy would again drop because children would know the program material is soon likely to change to a different, and probably less interesting, form. The shape of the relationship would vary depending on the kind of program material and children's viewing experience. Longer cycles in programs would produce a flatter curve of the relationship. Less viewing experience would make the relationship less strong (young children would have less well-defined expectations, for example).

Another link from attention goes to a variable which could be called satiation or fatigue. When attention is low, satiation is low. In other words, when children have not watched for a while, they are not tired of watching. When attention builds, satiation could build according to logistics curve. The curve predicts little initial gain in satiation (the toe of the curve) as attention increases. The curve also predicts an upper limit on the satiation of viewers, and that attention and satiation are linearly related between the two flat sections. The reason for choosing this shape will become clear shortly.

Our model shows that expectancy and satiation could then affect interest in viewing. These relationships could be linear. As the expectation of more interesting material increases, so would interest in viewing. This presumes that children are motivated to be stimulated (Berlyne, 1971:chap. 8). As satiation increases, interest in viewing would decrease. The rationale here is that children can become so tired of viewing itself that they will not want to watch further. One link remains to complete the model.

We expect that interest in viewing affects the actual attention paid. This presumes that, if children have interests, they will act on them. However, adding this link makes our model work and produces theoretical and methodological problems at the same time. We will describe how it works first.

One thing this model can explain is how children can accurately anticipate changes in programs. If set complexity is low, attention, expectancy, and satiation will be low. Then, depending on the coefficients linking all the variables in the model, interest in viewing will be either moderately or very low. Let us explain why this is the case. Since the effects of expectancy and satiation on interest balance one another, interest would be high or low depending on the relative levels of the two variables. If satiation is very low, because viewing has just started for example, interest in viewing would be driven upward. If a program has just started, expectancy would only be moderately low even though nothing is happening yet. This level of expectancy would only lower interest slightly. The combined effects of satiation and expectancy, in this case, would be a moderately low level of interest. Completing the links, moderately low interest would lead to moderately low attention.

The upshot of this set of linkages would be that low set complexity would lead to low attention through the direct link between the variables and then to moderate attention due to the action of the loop. Children would be paying attention to the screen even though nothing had happened. They would do this because they have the energy to devote to viewing and some minimal expectations that the program will eventually provide something interesting to watch. Let us see what will happen next.

If set complexity remains low, the attention which was just built up would be driven back down. This is due to the direct link and due to the following interactions in the loop. Expectation may go down since nothing has happened. Some very small level of satiation may also have been built up due to the small amount of attention paid. The combined effect of the changes in expectancy and satiation would be to lower interest in viewing. The feedback loop to attention would push attention down.

Even though set complexity has not changed yet, attention has moved up and down. This kind of oscillation would repeat itself as long as complexity remained low. From a more prosaic point of view, these oscillations indicate that the children periodically check the screen to see if anything of interest is happening. If children have some viewing experience, these oscillations will probably take a form indicating the children are anticipating changes in program variables. (If children have little experience, they may pay attention largely as a function of satiation.)

If children expect that program material changes in quality fairly regularly, they should show moderately high expectations after nothing of interest has occurred for some period of time. Since they have not watched a great deal, satiation is low because they are still on the toe of the relationship. The result is that interest in viewing becomes fairly high. The effect of this pattern on the oscillations we have described is to produce a rise in their average level over time. When attention data are gathered from several children and the results averaged, one would see just the rising trend in attention. This would be part of the anticipatory reaction we have been describing in the chapter.

Another part of the anticipatory reaction would come once set changes actually occur. If children periodically check the screen, they can quickly react to what is shown. If set complexity rises, so will attention through the direct link. This could drive expectancy to its highest level and yet leave satiation low (again because of the nonlinear relationships we have proposed). The effect of these changes would drive interest in viewing upward directly and attention indirectly.

This explanation of anticipation is tentative, yet seems well within the mental capabilities of children. However, if this model is correct, there are broad implications both for the study of television viewing and of children's attention to stimuli in general.

The point of many television studies is to determine the effect of programs on viewers. Searching for a simple causal order may be futile. If children's viewing is a function of expectations based on previous viewing experience, then the relationship of the program materials used in a given experiment to the programs children have seen previously would be very important. If our model is correct, children's reactions may largely be a function of how well their expectations are confirmed, rather than as a result of the program attributes seen in isolation. For example, this could mean that production techniques which draw a great deal of attention in an experiment merely because they are unusual would not have the same effect if they were used repeatedly in a series of programs. If children were used to relatively calm production styles, say *Mr. Rogers' Neighborhood*, they might be overwhelmed by very fast paced programming. After some experience with the new programming, they might see the patterns in shows and find the programs rather easy to understand. This has apparently been the case in countries such as Israel, where *Sesame Street* was added to program schedules dominated by documentaries rather than action-adventure shows.

Another example would be violence experiments in which it is made clear to children that they will not be punished for exhibiting aggressive behavior. In such situations children may act aggressively after seeing a violent presentation because they do not expect negative consequences due to their actions. In real life the same children may find other ways of sublimating their aggressive drives because experience with their peers has led them to expect retribution for negative behavior.

Similar comments may be made about experimental studies on nontelevision stimuli. Most experimental designs involve control over the order of presentation of stimuli. This control could be either systematic or random, but the point in either case is the elimination of sequence "effects." If our model is correct, attributes of the sequence may be as important as the individual stimuli. For example, Berlyne (1971) argues that both over- and under-stimulation is unpleasant for subjects in aesthetics experiments. While experimenters may be able to force these conditions on subjects by controlling the choice and order of presentation of stimuli, in normal situations, the subjects have a good deal of control over what they are exposed to. This means that they can avoid over- and under-stimulation by controlling their attention levels. One tool for this control would be information about sequences of events in uncontrived, naturally occurring stimuli. The experimental subject does not have this information because it is held in confidence by the experimenter.

Children in the age range we have been discussing in this chapter probably do not have very sophisticated ideas about many stimuli; but our data indicate that they are able to understand the multidimensional organization of television programs after some practice. This calls into question the generalizability of highly controlled experiments on matters in which children can normally apply considerable experience.

NOTE

1. These variables have been called set time entropy, shot time entropy, verbal time entropy, and nonverbal dependence entropy in papers by Krull and Watt. The labels and definitions of the variables were modified slightly to make clearer what is measured. The operationalization of the variables in terms of entropies was not changed. For example, the computational formula for the operationalization of set complexity is:

$$HST = - \sum_{i-1}^{K} \frac{t_{set_i}}{t_{show}} \log_2 \frac{t_{set_i}}{t_{show}}$$

Where t_{set_i} = total time the ith set appears.

t_{show} = total time of the show

k = no. of sets

Additional information on these variables can be found in Watt and Krull (1974).

REFERENCES

ANDERSON, D.R., and LEVIN, S.R. (1976). "Young children's attention to Sesame Street." Child Development, 47(3).

ANTES, J.R. (1974). "The time course of picture viewing." Journal of Experimental Psychology, 103:62-70.

BECHTEL, R. B., and ACHELPOHL, C., and AKERS, R. (1972). "Correlates between observed behavior and questionnaire responses on television viewing." In Television and social behavior, Vol. IV. Washington, D.C.: U.S. Government Printing Office.

BERLYNE, D.E. (1971). Aesthetics and psychobiology. New York: Appleton-Century-Crofts.

BERNSTEIN, L. (1977). "Design attributes of Sesame Street and the visual attention of preschool children." Unpublished Ph.D. dissertation, Columbia University.

BLALOCK, H.M. (1969). Theory construction. Englewood Cliffs, N.J.: Prentice-Hall.

BOX, G. E. P., and JENKINS, G.M. (1970). Time series analysis: Forecasting and control. San Francisco: Holden-Day.

CALLAWAY, E. (1975). Brain electrical potentials and individual psychological differences. New York: Harcourt, Brace and Jovanovich.

CANTOR, G.N., CANTOR, J.H., and DITRICHS, R. (1963). "Observing behavior in preschool children as a function of stimulus complexity." Child Development, 34:683-689.

CHRIST, C.F. (1966). Econometric models and methods. New York: Wiley.

DEMBO, R., and MCCRON, R. (1976). "Social factors in media use." In R. Brown (ed.), Children and television. Beverly Hills, Cal.: Sage.

EPSTEIN, S.L. (1977). "A comparison of two methods for measuring children's attention to television program material." Report to the Children's Television Workshop.

FAW, T.T., and NUNNALLY, J.C. (1968). "The influence of stimulus complexity, novelty, and affective value on children's visual fixations." Journal of Experimental Child Psychology, 6:141-153.

FLAGG, B.N. (in press). "Children and television: The effects of stimulus repetition on eye activity." In J.W. Senders, D.F. Fisher, and R.A. Monty (eds.), Eye movements and the higher psychological functions. Hillsdale, N.J.: Lawrence Erlbaum.

———, ALLEN, B.D., GEER, A.H., and SCINTO, L.F. (1976). "Children's visual responses to Sesame Street: A formative research report." Report to the Children's Television Workshop.

FURST, C.J. (1971). "Automatizing of visual attention." Perception and Psychophysics, 10:65-70.

GARNER, W.R. (1962). Uncertainty and structure as psychological concepts. New York: Wiley.

——— (1974). The processing of information and structure. New York: Wiley.

GINSBURG, H., and OPPER, S. (1969). Piaget's theory of intellectual development: an introduction. Englewood Cliffs, N.J.: Prentice-Hall.

GREENBERG, B.S. (1974). "Gratifications of television viewing and their correlates for British children." In J.G. Blumler and E. Katz (eds.), The uses of mass communications. Beverly Hills, Cal.: Sage.

HAGEN, J.W. (1967). "The effect of distraction on selective attention." Child Development, 38:685-694.

JENKINS, G.M., and WATTS, D.G. (1968). Spectral analysis and its applications. San Francisco: Holden-Day.

KRUGMAN, H.E. (1968). "Processes underlying exposure to advertising." American Psychologist, 23:245-253.

KRULL, R., and HUSSON, W.G. (1977). "Children's attention to the television screen: A time series analysis." Paper presented to the Association for Education in Journalism.

——— (in press). "Children's anticipatory attention to the TV screen." Article submitted for review.

——— and PAULSON, A.S. (1978). "Cycles in children's attention to the television screen." In B.D. Ruben (ed.), Communication yearbook II. New Brunswick, N.J.: Transaction.

KRULL, R., and PAULSON, A.S. (1977). "Time series analysis in communication research." In P.M. Hirsch, P.V. Miller, and F.G. Kline (eds.), Strategies for communication research. Beverly Hills, Cal.: Sage.

KRULL, R., and WATT, J.H. (1975). "Television program complexity and ratings." Paper presented to the American Association for Public Opinion Research.

——— and LICHTY, L.W. (1977). "Structure and complexity: Two measures of complexity in television programs." Communication Research, 4(1).

LASKER, H.M. (1974). The Jamaican project. Cambridge, Mass.: Harvard University.

LOSCIUTO, L.A. (1972). "A national inventory of television viewing behavior." In Television and social behavior, Vol. IV. Washington, D.C.: U.S. Government Printing Office.

MACCOBY, E.E., and HAGEN, J.W. (1965). "Effects of distraction upon central versus incidental recall: Developmental trends." Journal of Experimental Child Psychology, 2:280-289.

MACKWORTH, N.H., and BRUNER, J.S. (1971). "How adults and children search to recognize pictures." Human Development, 13:149-177.

MURRAY, J.P. (1972). "Television in inner-city homes: Viewing behavior of young boys." In Television and social behavior, Vol. IV. Washington, D.C.: U.S. Government Printing Office.

NOTON, D., and STARK, L. (1971a). "Eye movements and visual perception." Scientific American, 224:34-43.

——— (1971b). "Scanpaths in eye movements during pattern perception." Science, 171:308-311.

——— (1971c). "Scanpaths in saccadic eye movements while viewing and recognizing patterns." Vision Research, 11:929-942.

OLSON, D.R. (1970). Cognitive development: The child's acquisition of diagonality. New York: Academic Press.

PICK, A.D., CHRISTY, M.D., and FRANKEL, G.W. (1972). "A developmental study of visual selective attention." Journal of Experimental Child Psychology, 14:165-175.

REEVES, B.F. (1970). The first year of Sesame Street: The formative research. New York: Children's Television Workshop.

ROBINSON, J. (1969). "Television and leisure time: Yesterday, today and (maybe) tomorrow." Public Opinion Quarterly, 33.

SHANNON, C.E., and WEAVER, W. (1949). The mathematical theory of communication. Urbana: University of Illinois Press.

TURNURE, J.E. (1970). "Children's reactions to distractors in a learning situation." Developmental Psychology, 2(1):115-122.

WARD, S., LEVINSON, D., and WACKMAN, D. (1972). "Children's attention to television advertising." In P. Clark (ed.), New models for communication research. Beverly Hills, Cal.: Sage.

WARTELLA, E., and ALEXANDER, A. (1978). "Children's organization of impressions of television characters." Paper presented to the International Communication Association.

WARTELLA, E., and ETTEMA, J.S. (1974). "A cognitive development study of children's attention to television commercials." Communication Research, 1(1).

WATT, J.H., and KRULL, R. (1974). "An information theory measure for television programming." Communication Research, 1(1).

––– (1975). "Arousal model components in television programming: Form activity and violent content." Paper presented to the International Communication Association.

––– (1976). "An examination of three models of television viewing and aggression." Human Communication Research, 3(2).

WHITESIDE, J.A. (1974). "Eye movements of children, adults, and elderly persons during inspection of dot patterns." Journal of Experimental Child Psychology, 18:313-332.

WOHLWILL, J.F. (1975). "Children's responses to meaningful pictures varying in diversity: Exploration time vs. preference." Journal of Experimental Child Psychology, 20:341-351.

WONNACOTT, R.J., and WONNACOTT, T.H. (1970). Econometrics. New York: Wiley.

ZINCHENKO, V.P., CHZHI-TSIN, B., and TARAKANOV, V.V. (1963). "The formation and development of perceptual activity." Soviet Psychology and Psychiatry, 2:3-12.

Chapter 5

CHILDREN'S UNDERSTANDING OF TELEVISION PEOPLE

Byron Reeves

A DOMINANT CONCERN IN RESEARCH on children and television is the extent to which children will assimilate the specific behaviors and attitudes shown on television into their own lives. Researchers typically seek to measure aggressive responses to violence, demand for sugared cereal and candy for those heavily exposed to Saturday morning advertising, or the development of political cognitions for those who begin watching public affairs programs. Though there certainly are exceptions, the attitudes, behaviors, ideas, and themes of television have been more important in media research than the characters who express them.

When researchers have focused on the portrayals of television people, they have tended to study single groups of people, usually a minority group. Recent studies have concentrated on

AUTHOR'S NOTE: This chapter was completed as part of a project grant from the Graduate School, University of Wisconsin-Madison. Parts of the literature review in this chapter appeared in an earlier paper, "Children's perception of television characters," coauthored by Ronald Faber, University of Wisconsin-Madison, and presented at the Sixth Annual Telecommunication Policy Research Conference, Airlie, Virginia, 1978.

the portrayal of black people on television (Dominick and Greenberg, 1970; Fife, 1974), portrayals of women (Tuchman, 1978; Miller and Reeves, 1976), and most recently the elderly (Aronoff, 1974; Petersen, 1973). Although these studies deal with people on television, two aspects of the ways in which the portrayals are studied should be noticed. First, most of the studies on television people rely on content analyses. Research questions have typically asked about the frequency of portrayals, changes in the portrayals over time, or the types of programming the people appear in most often. While these studies provide necessary information about what content may have an impact on children, they do not link television messages with actual attitudes and behaviors.

Second, people on TV are usually studied in isolation from the other people on television. For example, the frequency of blacks in prime-time television has been traced for the past several years. While this strategy is valuable in determining changes in media content and the potential of the portrayals to have an impact, it also assumes that the single attribute of people which has been focused on, race in this example, is an important attribute relative to other attributes that might be apparent if additional characters were included. It is possible in these cases that researchers may isolate attributes which are important in the adult world, but which are not primary attributes used by children to understand television portrayals.

Very seldom has research concentrated on more general perceptions of television people, especially the impressions that children hold of *how people or groups of people are different.* Television provides children with possibly the most complete presentation of different types of people they are likely to see during childhood. Focusing on the attributes that children use to *differentiate* television portrayals may tell us more about media impact on how children categorize and relate to people than the study of any one group of people or type of person. The ways in which children learn to differentiate people may be very important in determining which attributes of people are dominant in children's real-life perceptions and dealings with other people.

This chapter will examine the impressions that children form of television characters, concentrating especially on age and sex differences in those perceptions. The general concern in this discussion will be the possible impact of television on children's perceptions of people in real life. Although neither the psychological literature nor the literature in mass communication has consistently dealt with specific criterion variables in the study of impression formation, three concerns in the area of children and television will be discussed as they relate to children's impressions of television characters: (1) the impressions of television characters which predict children's attraction to television portrayals and identification with specific television characters; (2) the possible interaction effects on children's own behavior of perceptions of characters and perceptions of the attitudes and behaviors expressed by the characters; and (3) the extent to which impressions of television characters are generalized to perceptions of real people. Before the television research is reviewed, studies examining children's perception of people in general will be discussed. It is the more general process of impression formation and person perception which could both affect and be affected by children's perceptions of people on television. A final section of the chapter will discuss a research plan for further study in this area, concentrating on the application of developmental theories to the study of children's learning from television and specifically to the study of children's perception of television people.

THE PERSON PERCEPTION LITERATURE

A first difficult question in the review of this literature is establishing boundaries for a search; this is a problem noted by most who have attempted reviews in this area (Flavell, 1968; Tagiuri, 1969; Shantz, 1975). Research in this general area has been variously labeled role taking, person perception, impression formation, empathy, role enactment, role perception, and social cognition. There appear to be both subtle and important differences in these areas depending on the specific interests of those conducting the research. In a review attempting to integrate all of these areas, Shantz (1975) organized the research around five questions; what is the other seeing, feeling, thinking and intending, and what is the other like? It is the latter question which will be the focus here, not because the other questions are irrelevant to the study of children's reactions to television, but because the others have not generated much, if any, media research. Furthermore, it is the question of what other people are like that relates most to the reasons mentioned above for studying children's perceptions of television characters.[1]

A second question deals with the organization of a review in the area of person perception. The optimal organization would probably center on propositions of a single unifying theory, though few research areas in the social sciences, including person perception, can claim such assistance. The literature reviewed here is organized around two central issues in the area which have guided most of the research; the content and organization of children's descriptions of other people. Content refers to the number of traits and the type of traits a child uses to describe others. Questions about organization are concerned with the complexity and abstractness of impressions and with the ability to handle discrepant information. Within these areas, it is also necessary to review differences in research method. Unfortunately, there appear to be more differences between the studies based on methods than on important differences in theoretical perspective.

This is not to say, however, that research in person perception has not been influenced by theory. As Shantz noted, most of the research on the development of social cognitions has been based on cognitive-developmental theories, especially the theories of mental development proposed by Piaget (1970) and Werner (1948). According to Kohlberg (1969), these theories generally assume that: (1) development involves transformations of cognitive structures, defined as organizational wholes or systems of internal relations; (2) children's learning and maturation interact in the process of development; (3) cognitive structures involve actions upon objects, and (4) the direction of development is toward an equilibrium of the organism-environment interaction. Working from the same assumptions of cognitive-developmental theories, more specific theories of role taking have been proposed by Flavell (1968) and Selman (1971). Flavell defines role taking as the "ability to predict the visual experience of another person." He proposes five sequential psychological recognitions that are required for children to develop mature abilities to deal interpersonally with other people: (1) knowledge of the existence of an alternative perspective; (2) perception of a need to understand that perspective; (3) prediction of the other perspective with accuracy; (4) maintenance of the other perspective; and (5) application of these conditions and an ability to translate them into an effective communication message.

Selman, who actually sees role-taking abilities as a theoretical link between the logical stages of Piaget and the moral reasoning stages of Kohlberg, suggests that children progress through stages of role-taking abilities. These stages progress from an egocentric view that *all* perspectives are similar to an understanding of the possibility of mutual role taking (both people simultaneously taking their own and another's perspective). Between these two stages children become able to infer accurately other people's intentions, feelings, and thoughts, and also realize that their own thoughts and feelings can be the object of another person's thinking. These theories, however, have been applied almost exclusively to other areas of research in social cognition, especially to questions about what others are thinking and feeling. There are currently no studies which have attempted to relate levels of role taking with changes in person perception.

When a single theory has been used in person perception research it has most often been Werner's organismic theory (Gollin, 1958; Scarlett et al., 1971). Researchers have assumed that the development of impressions of others will follow Werner's orthogenetic principle, which states that "development proceeds from a state of relative globality and lack of differentiation, articulation, and heirachic integration" (Werner, 1957).

A shift from concrete to abstract methods of conceptualization is fundamental to this developmental change. Two other aspects of this development, which are especially relevant to studying perceptions of other people, are: (1) the ability to differentiate between self and others, which allows children to perceive other people as different and independent from themselves, and (2) the ability to differentiate between external and internal dimensions of personality, which enables children to combine different aspects of personality into an integrated impression.

CONTENT OF IMPRESSIONS

Most studies in person perception have been concerned with changes in children's impressions at different ages. These studies typically ask children to write impressions of people they know or see in experimental films, or to check off words from a list that they feel describe various people. Not surprisingly, these studies have consistently found an increase in the number of traits children use at older ages (Maddock and Kenny, 1973; Peevers and Secord, 1973; Livesley and Bromley, 1973; Scarlett et al., 1971). This increase, however, has not been linearly related to maturation. Livesley and Bromley found that a major shift in the number of traits used occurs between the ages of seven and eight. The increase in traits mentioned between these two age groups was larger than the difference between eight and 15 year olds. This period of greatest change coincides with the approximate age when children are entering the subjective and self-reflective stages in Selman's theory. In these stages children learn to make inferences about others and to understand sequentially the uniqueness of their own and others' viewpoints.

While age differences in the number of traits employed is the most consistent finding, several researchers have also reported sex differences. These studies primarily find that girls use more traits than boys (Livesley and Bromley, 1973; Beach and Wertheimer, 1961; Wegner, 1974); however, this sex difference may simply reflect girl's greater verbal skills at these ages.

Differences in the number of traits used also varies in relation to characteristics of the person being described. Scarlett et al. (1971), for example, found that first, third, and sixth grade boys use significantly more constructs to describe other boys than girls. Livesley and Bromley, using children of both sexes, also found more terms being used to describe males. A greater number of constructs are also used when describing people the child likes than for disliked others (Supnick, 1964; Peevers and Secord, 1973; Livesley and Bromley, 1973). Third and fifth grade boys in the Scarlett et al. study used significantly more terms to describe boys they liked than boys they disliked. Among third graders, there was no difference between liked and disliked females; however, for the fifth graders, disliked girls elicited more traits than liked girls. Supnick (1964), on the other hand, found that by high school boys used more traits for liked girls than disliked ones.

Two additional characteristics have been found to influence the number of traits employed in descriptions. Children use more traits to describe people their own age than for adults (Livesley and Bromley, 1967, 1973). Finally, more traits are used when describing well known people than for those less well known (Yarrow and Campbell, 1963).

The type of traits children employ has also been found to change with age. Younger children tend to focus primarily on physical appearance (Watts, 1944; Livesley and Bromley, 1967, 1973; Brierley, 1966; Pratt, 1975). Most of these studies found a noticeable decrease in physical appearance descriptions around seven years old; this decrease again corresponds to the time most children have moved into the higher stages of role taking.

Sex differences in the type of traits children use have also been found. Girls seem to emphasize personality terms such as bossy or friendly (Livesley and Bromley, 1967; Brierley, 1966) and interpersonal and social skill traits like nurturance (Yarrow and Campbell, 1963; Campbell and Radke-Yarrow, 1956; Supnick, 1964; Beach and Wertheimer, 1961). Boys, on the other hand, focus more on nonconforming and aggressive behaviors (Yarrow and Campbell, 1963; Dornbusch et al., 1965). Dornbusch et al. found that, of the 12 top categories of traits used by males and females, 11 were on both lists. However, the frequency of using any specific categories differed by sex.

ORGANIZATION OF IMPRESSIONS

Organization of impressions typically refers to the complexity, abstractness, or hierarchical integration of impressions. Unfortunately, researchers have used different categories to conceptualize organizational traits. These categories make it almost impossible to directly compare results across studies; however, there appears to be a definite developmental trend running through most findings which is consistent with Werner's orthogenetic principle. Studies have found that as children grow older their impressions become more qualified (Leahy, 1976; Livesley and Bromley, 1973); more situationally specific (Peevers and Secord, 1973); more complex (Yarrow and Campbell, 1963; Livesley and Bromley, 1973); and there is a greater use of abstract traits (Scarlett et al., 1971; Livesley and Bromley, 1973) and internal and dispositional traits (Pratt, 1975).

The final attribute of impression formation to be discussed is the way children integrate conflicting information about people. As we have just pointed out, children are increasingly able to use qualifiers and recognize that behaviors are situationally determined. Thus, it should not be surprising that older children more frequently mention both positive and negative characteristics of people (Peevers and Secord, 1973; Gollin, 1958; Livesley and Bromley, 1973). Gollin (1958) looked at the ability to handle conflicting information about people by showing children age 10 to 17 a five-scene film in which the main character was portrayed in both positive and negative ways. Children were then asked to write their impressions of the main character. Responses were coded for the presence of inferences and concepts. Inferences were scored if the subject tried to explain or ascribe a motive for any action in the film and concepts were coded when the respondent attempted to account for the diversity of the actor's behavior. The use of inferences increased most dramatically between 10 and 13 years old and continued to increase between 13 and 16. Concepts were relatively rare among the younger children, but were used by about half of the 16 year olds. In the two oldest age groups (13 and 16), females used significantly more inferences and concepts than males.

In summary, researchers have found that impressions become more detailed as children grow older. With increasing age, children also become more aware of the temporal and situational factors affecting the behaviors of others. Older children are more frequently able to deal with conflicting behaviors, and their impressions of others change from being univalent to divalent. Sex differences are less clear. It appears that girls use more traits in describing people than boys and also emphasize personality and psychological traits more than boys. Girls also appear to comment on and account for conflicting behaviors more. Several researchers have hypothesized that females are both quicker and more likely to stereotype people than males (Sarbin, 1954; Kohn and Fiedler, 1961; Shapiro and Tagiuri, 1959); however, all of these studies have been conducted with adult subjects. Whether girls are also more likely to stereotype people than boys is still an open question.

STUDIES ON PERCEPTIONS OF TV CHARACTERS

Compared to the literature on children's perceptions of people in real life, the number of studies which focus on children's perceptions of television characters as a special group of people is very small. Further, few of the studies just reviewed can be compared to similar media studies where TV characters have been the object of perception because most of the media research has centered on only one or two questions. The purpose of most of the television research has been to identify character attributes that are important in children's attraction to various characters. In this sense, researchers have begun with characters which children identify with and then asked questions about the attributes of those characters which predict the attraction. Only a couple of recent studies have been concerned with the attributes that children use to differentiate and describe characters independent of other criterion variables such as identification.

Reeves and Greenberg (1977) found four primary dimensions that third, fifth, and seventh grade children used to differentiate a sample of 14 prime-time and Saturday morning entertainment characters. A multidimensional scaling system was used to determine the dimensions.[2] These scaling models assume that a

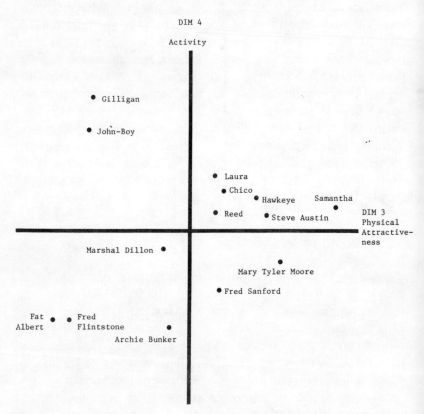

Figure 1a

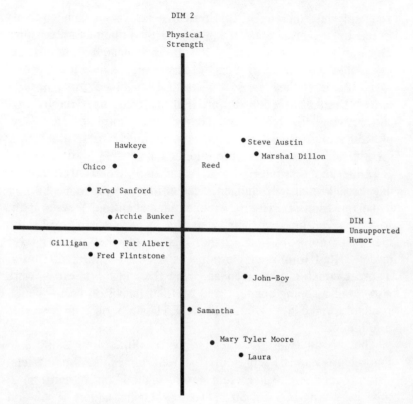

Figure 1b

set of some number of independent dimensions underly the perception of a larger set of stimuli. In this study the stimuli were television characters and the dimensions were expected to represent the attributes children used to differentiate the characters. The output of multidimensional scaling is a space locating each television character (stimulus), on each of the dimensions. The geometic distances between the characters can be interpreted as the perceived similarity between the characters.

In relation to most studies about children's perceptions of other people, this method has the advantage of not suggesting the attributes that children should use to describe others. The geometric representation of the television characters in this case was not determined by attributes of television characters selected by the researcher or by responses to open-end questions. Children judged the perceived similarity between all possible pairs of characters, using as the basis for the judgments whatever attributes they chose to think about. In order of importance, the attributes found were humor, strength, attractiveness, and activity. Figures 1a and 1b show the sample of characters plotted along four spatial dimensions which represent the four attributes used to differentiate the characters.[3]

Dimension 1, humor, shows that children perceive characters like Fred Flintstone, Gilligan, Fred Sanford, and Archie Bunker to be the funnier characters while Marshal Dillon, Steve Austin, John-boy Walton, and Laura were the characters perceived to be the least humorous.[4] Further analysis of this attribute also revealed that humor was not necessarily a desirable attribute. Those characters perceived as being the most humorous were also rated as being unsupported by their television peers—which probably makes them more like the classic boob than desirable role models.

The second two attributes (shown as dimensions 2 and 3 in Figures 1a and 1b) represented stereotypic evaluations of television characters. Characters rated highest on dimension 2, physical strength, were Steve Austin, Marshal Dillon, Reed, and Hawkeye. Characters highest on dimension 3, physical attractiveness, were Samantha, Mary Tyler Moore, Steve Austin, and Hawkeye. The final dimension, activity, differentiated the characters on the basis of the number of different things they did in their television roles. Characters highest on that attribute were Gilligan, John-boy Walton, Laura, and Chico.

A replication of this study was recently completed which attempted to find the same four attributes using a different sample of children (grades 6 and 8) and a different sample of television characters (Reeves and Lometti, 1978). Among other new characters in the sample were three additional women to balance more evenly the ratio of TV men and women. Essentially the same four dimensions emerged. The one important difference was that dimension 2 from the original study, physical strength, more clearly differentiated TV characters in the replication in terms of sex. In fact, dimension 2 in the second study was the only attribute which clearly separated the male· and female television characters in the sample. Another difference in the replication was that the attribute smart was also negatively related to humor.

The most striking finding in the two studies, however, was that there were no age or sex differences in the number or content of the four attributes used to differentiate the characters. This finding was unexpected and was especially divergent from the expectations about boys and girls' use of the second two dimensions, strength and attractiveness. It was expected that children would stereotypically orient to just one of these physical descriptors; males depending on the attribute strength and females on physical attractiveness. In this study, however, the boys were just as likely to differentiate the characters using the attribute attractiveness as were the girls, and the girls were just as likely to use the attribute strength as the boys.

When compared with the psychological literature on person perception, the absence of sex and age differences is very conspicuous. As mentioned in the previous review, older children develop more complex perceptions of others which are dependent on increasingly inferential qualities rather than merely physical descriptions. Sex differences included the use of more attributes by girls and the emphasis on personality and psychological traits. In terms of children's perceptions of television characters, however, none of these findings were confirmed. The location of the various characters along the four dimensions discussed was almost identical for children from grades three to eight, and for children of both sexes.

Unfortunately, there appear to be at least two possible explanations for these differences—one theoretical and one methodological. At first, it seemed appropriate to make predictions about children's perceptions of television characters from theory and research concerned with their perceptions of actual people. The expectation was that television characters represent people who should be evaluated and categorized similar to people in real life. The lack of correspondence between the two literatures, however, suggests a counter hypothesis.

While the perceptual skills of children are developing to the extent where cognition is abstract, inferential, and generalized, children may also be learning that television, unlike real life, requires only the most simple evaluations. Consequently, while older children are making complex personality inferences about peers, for example, they may have learned early that television characters need only be evaluated on the basis of whether they are funny or serious. A similar rationale could be applied to the lack of sex differences in the perception of TV characters. The sex-typed use of certain attributes to describe others may apply only to real people and not to the special case of television people.

An unreported analysis of the data used in Reeves and Greenberg (1977) offers some support for this suggestion. Most multidimensional scaling models assume that all subjects use the same dimensions in differentiating the concepts used to generate the geometric spaces. The particular scaling method used in the original study (INDSCAL, Carroll and Wish, 1974), however, allows for individual variations from a total group solution. While the model still assumes that all individuals use the same dimensions to differentiate the concepts, the salience of each dimension for each individual is given which roughly corresponds to a correlation between a dimension calculated separately for each individual, and the same dimension for the total group.[5] These salience scores can be interpreted as the importance of each dimension for each individual (or subcategory of people, e.g., an age group or sex).

Table 1 shows the average salience scores for third, fifth, and seventh grades on the four dimensions of humor, strength, attractiveness, and activity. For the first dimension, humor, there is a clear trend toward greater salience with increasing age (from 436 to 724). For the remaining three dimensions the opposite occurs; the dimensions become less salient with increasing age. These data suggest that by seventh grade, children have formed a relatively unidimensional view of the importance of the dimensions compared to the third graders who view the dimensions with almost equal importance. It should be noted that this suggestion applies only to the perceived *importance* of the dimensions and that this analysis does not contradict the previous finding that children in all three grades used each of the four dimensions to differentiate the portrayals.

There is also some indication that the actual attributes that emerge from descriptions of real people are different from those used to describe television characters. The major attributes which Livesley and Bromley report in their studies include attributes such as nice, kind, good, temper, helpful, bossy, generous, and smart. The primary attribute in the television studies, humor, does not even rank in the top 10 attributes. Additional implications of the idea that perceptions of television people become more simple as children develop will be discussed in the final section.

In comparing these literatures it is important to note differences in the methods typically employed to study person perception among children. There has been little uniformity in the ways in which the actual attributes and the organization of the attributes have been studied, and it is relatively easy to speculate on differences in study results which could be attributed solely to research procedures. The methods used most often in the psychological literature have been either children's free descriptions of people, semantic differential scales, or the use of adjective check lists where children indicate which attributes

Table 1: **AVERAGE SALIENCE SCORES FOR THREE AGE GROUPS FROM AN INDSCAL ANALYSIS OF DATA ON SIMILARITIES AMONG 14 TELEVISION CHARACTERS**

	Humor *DIM 1*	Strength *DIM 2*	Attractiveness *DIM 3*	Activity *DIM 4*
Total Group (n = 202)	.596	.372	.340	.326
Third Grade (n = 67)	.463	.456	.400	.387
Fifth Grade (n = 66)	.692	.372	.325	.320
Seventh Grade (n = 69)	.724	.289	.295	.272

they feel apply to various people.[6] Critics of these methods have argued that research results could be due as much to different abilities to use language as to developmental shifts in person perception. This criticism seems especially applicable to the finding that children use increasingly more attributes to describe others as they develop.

The two studies on children's perception of television characters relied on a multidimensional scaling procedure which does not require that children describe characters or rate them on various attributes supplied by the researcher. Children only rate the *similarity* of all possible pairs of characters in each study, using as the basis for their judgments whatever attributes *they* choose to think about. The dimensions which emerge in the spaces are then assumed to represent fundamental psychological processes by which the children differentiate the people in the space. Other data are then used to determine how each of the dimensions should be conceptualized. Researchers have criticized this method because it is a mathematical procedure which attempts to obtain maximum parsimony (i.e., the fewest number of dimensions) from the data. In this sense, the fewer number of dimensions that emerge using this method could possibly be attributed to the scaling procedure used rather than simple perceptions. Problems have also been pointed out concerning children's ability to make relative comparisons using the words "alike" and "different" (Palermo, 1973).

There is only one study in the psychological literature which attempted to use multidimensional scaling to study children's perceptions of peers (Olshan, 1971). Similar to the television studies, the author found that three dimensions adequately represented the data, as well as that no age differences existed in the number of dimensions used to differentiate peers. Although this study did not find age differences in the complexity of perception, there were differences in the actual attributes that emerged. The primary attributes that third, sixth, and ninth grade children used to describe peers were good/bad and many friends/few friends. A smart/dumb dimension was found for third and sixth graders, adult/child for third graders, and male/female for sixth graders. In addition to the similarity with the television studies in terms of perceptual complexity, this study also suggests that TV people and real people may be evaluated using different attributes even when the method for determining the perceptions (multidimensional scaling) is held constant.

One study is currently underway which is attempting to separate differences in the attributes ascribed to people and television characters which can be attributed to methods versus actual differences in the perception of the people (Alexander and Wartella, in progress). Until the methodological issue is resolved, it will be difficult to argue with certainty that television people are evaluated differently than real people; however, the lack of any differences in the studies using multidimensional scaling at least suggests at this time the possibility that more uniformity exists in the perception of television people than researchers have typically expected.

ORGANIZATION OF IMPRESSIONS
ABOUT TELEVISION CHARACTERS

Similar to the psychological literature on person perception and children, the focus of media researchers has been on the content of children's perceptions of television characters. Most researchers, however, point out that perceptions of other people have both content and organizational aspects (Livesley and Bromley, 1973). Questions that could be asked about the organization of children's impressions of television characters deal with how children relate the various content statements into meaningful unified impressions.

Only one recent study has attempted to study the organization of children's perceptions of television characters (Wartella and Alexander, 1978). Children in grades 2, 5, and 8 were asked to describe TV characters "so that someone would know what he was like and why he was like that." The study found two age-related differences in the organization of children's perceptions of television people: (1) greater use of internal descriptors (e.g., motivational and personality characteristics); and (2) increased use of causal descriptions (e.g., describing reasons and/or motivations for characters' behaviors). No sex differences in these trends were reported.

Unlike the studies on the content of perceptions of TV characters, these results support the expectations of age-related differences in children's organization of impressions as suggested by past research in the general area of person perception. It should also be noted that while the television studies on content of perception used methods different from those typically employed in psychological studies, the single study on organization of television impressions used a method much more consistent with the previous literature. Despite methodological problems, however, *the limited number of attempts to study the perception of television characters suggests that there are differences in the actual attributes children use to describe real people and television people, although the perceptions seem to be organized in a similar manner.*

WHY STUDY CHILDREN'S
PERCEPTION OF TELEVISION CHARACTERS

Few of the psychological studies on children's perceptions of other people suggest other variables that may be dependent on the content or organization of children's impressions of others. The actual perceptions of others and the process of organization and development seem to be themselves the criterion concerns. It has been suggested that the absence of data linking research in social cognitions to social behavior merely reflects a traditional gap between the study of conceptual, motivational, and behavioral processes (Kagan and Kogan, 1970). Shantz (1975) observed that "the relation between social cognition and interpersonal behavior may be one of the largest unexplored areas of developmental psychology today."

This is not the case with research on the effects of television. The primary rationale for studying perceptions of television characters has been to study the attributes of characters which are related to children's desires to model their behavior. Consequently, most of the research in this area has actually taken as a starting point children's desires to identify with characters and then asked which attributes of the characters are related to that attraction.

Generally, age and sex differences in the attributes which predict children's attraction to TV characters have been much greater than differences in the attributes they use to describe the characters. This was very apparent in the studies which identified humor, strength, attractiveness, and activity as the primary attributes that differentiated TV characters (Reeves and Greenberg, 1977; Reeves and Lometti, 1978). The strength and activity dimensions were excellent predictors of whether boys at all ages wanted to "be like" or "do things like" the characters in the sample. The attractiveness dimension was an equally good predictor of the same measures for girls. Furthermore, the primary attribute which differentiated the characters, humor, was not a predictor of identification for either sex at any age.

Sex differences in the importance of the attributes in choosing role models are especially interesting in relation to the lack of sex differences in the *use* of the attributes to discriminate among the same characters in the same study. Boys were just as likely as girls to differentiate characters on the basis of physical attractiveness, yet the attractiveness of characters was only useful to the girls in choosing television role models. Similarly, girls were just as likely to differentiate characters on the basis of strength, although strength was only important to the boys in identifying with characters.

The key suggestion from this finding is that cognitive structures for boys and girls are the same while the use of the structures is completely different. This is different from saying that only males use the attribute of strength and, therefore, strength is only a predictor of television effects for males. Males use both strength and attractiveness, but only one attribute is applicable to their modeling decisions. The counterpart process existed for girls' use of attractiveness. While others have suggested that little data exist to support stereotypic differences in the ways males and females describe and orient to other people (Maccoby and Jacklin, 1975), these results constitute a conspicuous exception.

The television studies that have focused only on the attributes which predict attraction to TV characters have essentially confirmed the same stereotypic evaluations using several different methods. Miller and Reeves (1976) reported similar stereotypic rationales for model choices. After third through sixth grade children had indicated their favorite television characters in open-ended personal interviews, boys said they chose the characters primarily because they were strong or tough, and girls reported choosing models because they were good looking or well dressed. Using a multidimensional measure of identification in a survey of third through sixth graders, the same pattern of prediction was found for the attributes strength and attractiveness (Reeves and Miller, 1977). Similar findings for these stereotypic attributes were also found in two other studies (Greenberg et al., 1976; Miller, 1976).

Although the attributes strength and attractiveness have been consistent predictors of modeling, the most powerful predictor, and one for which large sex differences have been found, has been the sex of television characters. Several studies have demonstrated that children are most favorable toward same-sex characters (Miller and Reeves, 1976; Reeves and Miller, 1977; Miller, 1976). There are, however, important differences in the willingness of boys and girls to nominate opposite-sex models. Two different studies report that no boys chose opposite-sex television characters as people they would like to "be like," while approximately one-third of both samples of girls chose male characters as primary role models (Miller and Reeves, 1976; Miller, 1976). Further, boys were more likely to name any television model than girls (Miller and Reeves, 1976).

It is important to remember that in most of the studies on character attributes which are related to identification, television models have been determined before children are asked to describe their primary attributes. Further, when children do describe the characters, they are usually asked to name the features of the character that made them choose the character as a model. This strategy could be criticized in that it would by definition ignore other attributes of TV characters which may not predict identification, but which could be important for other reasons. For example, the primary attribute which differentiated TV characters in two past studies, humor, was not found to be related to any identification measures, yet it should probably not be assumed that there are no consequences of that particular perception. While researchers have concentrated almost exclusively on impressions of characters which predict identification, there are other criterion variables which may further explain how television people impact on children.

A first question deals primarily with the content of the attributes children associate with television characters and involves the generalization of TV perceptions to person perception in general. Television represents a primary source for meeting new people, especially for younger children, and typically the variance in the types of people is nowhere greater than on television. As noted in several studies in the area, the attributes which children use in describing television characters are obviously dependent on the number and types of people there are to observe. Humor would not be an important attribute of television characters, for example, if there were only serious characters on TV. The variance in television portrayals could then influence the attributes which children use not only to differentiate television people, but also people in real life. People in real life may be evaluated primarily on the basis of humor even though children might not have naturally settled on that attribute solely on the basis of the people they meet in real life.

This question becomes more important if, in fact, the attributes which relate to television and real people are found to be different. Comparing the results of the television studies with those in the general area of person perception at least suggests that these attributes may be different. Not all of the four primary attributes found to differentiate television characters appear in similar lists involving children's perceptions of real people. A study in progress is attempting to find out (1) if there are unique sets of television attributes and real person attributes, and (2) whether high television viewers are using primarily television attributes to evaluate real people (Reeves and Faber, in progress).

A second important contribution of this research area may be a better understanding of the effects of attitudes and behaviors expressed on television. It is probably an error to assume that effects of television on children can be totally attributed to either TV people or their actions. Typically, we study the effects of people and actions as if they were independent and additive. It is assumed that what we know about the behaviors on television (e.g., number of violent acts, altruistic behavior, information about occupations) can be added to what we know about the characters who express them (e.g., that they are funny, attractive, or strong) to gain a full understanding of the impact of the medium. It is highly probable, however, that the two *interact* to produce effects. The same act of violence, for example, may have an impact if expressed by a strong, active male but have no impact or negative impact if attempted by an attractive female. Studying these interactions could be very important in understanding how children relate television content to their own lives.

DEVELOPING IDEAS ABOUT TELEVISION AND TELEVISION PEOPLE: GUIDELINES FOR FUTURE RESEARCH

Several questions still remain concerning children's perceptions of television characters. The validity of studying impressions of TV portrayals at least assumes that children can recognize the consistency of a role both within and between the same program. When, for example, do children realize that a character remains constant throughout a program or that the same individual appears at the same time every week? Are there differences in the impressions held of one-time characters versus characters who are developed, although with little variance, across different episodes? When do children begin combining and organizing scattered character attributes into unified impressions? How do children combine attributes and what happens when they receive information about characters that runs counter to past impressions or forces them to combine both positive and negative information? Is there some minimum level of development that these impressions must reach before they begin to determine how and if children assimilate television behavior into their own lives? Are there developmental changes in children's orientation to television characters versus TV actions and events? Finally, what effect does children's understanding of the nature and purposes of television in general have on their impressions of television people? Will children form and apply impressions differently if they believe TV is a "magic window" versus a source of fantasy dreams? The list could easily be extended; however, it is apparent even from these questions that an understanding of how perceptions of television people *develop* should be an important goal of any further research in this area.

This is hardly a novel suggestion. Certainly one of the more obvious trends in research on children and television is the attention to developmental changes in children's ability to understand their environment and especially to process information. Most researchers have pointed out that it is not sufficient merely to describe age-related differences in children's interpretation of or reaction to television messages, but it is also important to understand the developmental explanations of why the differences occur. Consequently, research has been dependent on theories of development taken mostly from child psychology. Media researchers now advocate the use of theories describing the development of logical abilities, moral reasoning, and role taking, and indeed the names of Piaget, Kohlberg, Bruner, and Selman are appearing more frequently in communication journals.

Attention to cognitive development theories has increased our understanding of children as active information processors and has focused more attention on process-oriented learning rather than stimulus-response learning models. The application of these theories to the unique case of children's perceptions of television characters, however, has met with mixed success.

Children's organization of impressions, for example, were found to change according to developmental theory; although, the content and number of impressions ran counter to developmental expectations. There seems to be growing evidence in this research area as well as other areas of media research that despite general developmental changes in the direction of increasing complexity of reasoning and perception, some aspects of children's understanding of television becomes more simple as children gain more experience with the medium.

Several explanations of this inconsistency are possible. First, the theories could be wrong. Children may become less complex as they age; a suggestion which obviously runs counter to common sense, data from numerous other research areas, and even findings from this specific area which indicate that organization of impressions of TV characters becomes more complex as children develop. A second possibility is that television is an experience to which the theories do not apply. Perhaps there are unique aspects of the medium and the process by which messages are disseminated that make learning from television a special case. This interpretation would, of course, also contradict several demonstrations of children's learning from television which for the most part conform to the expectations of the theories and help to demonstrate that learning from television is in some ways similar to learning from other information sources (e.g., parents and peers). A third possible explanation, and one which will be more seriously developed, is that when developmental theories are used to understand how children learn from television and how television comes to have an influence in development, the theories are often applied to the wrong variables or at an inappropriate level of abstraction.

One major difficulty in accurately describing the impact of television on children is determining exactly what is responsible for different effects (McLeod and Reeves, forthcoming). A review of media effects research shows that several aspects of the medium and even the medium itself have been held responsible for changes in children's attitudes and behaviors. These different attributes of television range from very specific isolated pieces of content to abstract properties of the television experience including specific behaviors (e.g., sexual behavior, consumption of alcohol, helping peers); categories of behavior (e.g., physical and verbal aggression and altruistic behavior); categories of people on television (e.g., women, black people, the elderly); specific television programs; categories of programs (e.g., situation comedies, action adventure, news); and aspects of the medium itself (e.g., physical properties of messages and understanding of the television industry). Furthermore, it is likely that these various aspects of television interact in their influence on children.

Given this large number of possible variables that may influence children's learning from television, a difficult question becomes whether various developmental theories can be similarly applied to children's understanding of each of these aspects of television. The theories themselves describe the most general aspects of development (e.g., logical abilities) and may be misleading when applied to specific television situations (e.g., perception and understanding of television messages) if more abstract levels of understanding are not accounted for first. If in fact each of the various aspects of television just described are related and hierarchically influential—that is, understanding of television at higher levels of abstraction influence the understanding of specific aspects of TV messages and people—then the application of these theories solely to the more detailed aspects of television may be inappropriate.

This lack of attention to various levels of understanding television may explain differences between traditional notions of development and findings in the area of children's perceptions of television characters. As was suggested in the literature review, it may take a more complex cognitive structure to realize that television and television people require only the most simple evaluations. Applying developmental theories which predict increasing complexity of person perception to the perception of television characters *independent* of the development of children's conception of the medium in general may account for present study results. Increasingly complex cognitive abilities may cause increasingly simple perceptions of television content.

Consider this example. Increasing logical abilities may enable children to learn from adults and by experience that watching entertainment television is basically a fantasy dramatic experience. Children may then realize, on the basis of this more general orientation to television, that a primary evaluation of television people should reflect their entertainment potential; hence, television characters are differentiated on the basis of humor, not because of their similarity to people in real life, but because of a more abstract understanding of the context in which they appear. In this example, the application of a general developmental principle to children's perception of a specific part of television would be inaccurate, although application of the theory to understanding the medium would be totally appropriate and useful. The major point is that developmental characteristics of children's understanding of the more abstract characteristics of television may need to be considered as a mediator between general theories of development and children's learning from specific elements of television content.

If television is a unique experience for children, that is, if television information is evaluated and used differently than information from nontelevision sources, then it would seem appropriate for media studies to focus on a developmental scheme which relates as closely as possible to the exact stimulus (i.e., television) which is expected to interact with the structures of children's reasoning. This does not necessarily imply that a totally independent set of developmental stages be designed which will describe the development of a child's conception of television. Current evidence suggests that children's learning from television is not independent, for example, of the development of logical abilities (e.g., Ward and Wackman, 1973). What does seem appropriate, however, is further testing of the generalizability of developmental theories to children's television experiences, and more importantly, the reduction or translation of the more abstract theories into logically consistent statements about children's conception of television.

The specific questions now become more difficult: (1) What are the various dimensions or attributes of television as a medium that will influence children's perceptions of more specific aspects of television content, including impressions of television people; (2) How should children's understanding of these aspects of television be organized into hierarchical stages which represent an increasingly complex conception of television; and (3) How do the various theories of cognitive development relate to a progressive conception of television.

Some progress has been made in mass communication research in terms of defining attributes of children's perception and interpretation of television that may contribute to an understanding of how children learn from television messages. Less attention has been given to the relationship of mediating variables which help explain the conditions under which media will have an impact on children. There appears to be a growing recognition that different children will respond to the same message in different ways depending on several third variables (McLeod and Reeves, forthcoming). Examples of these mediating or conditional variables include children's perceived reality of television messages (Hawkins, 1977; Reeves, 1978), parent attempts to control and interpret television messages (Atkin and Greenberg, 1977), children's identification with primary television characters (Noble, 1975; Reeves and Miller, 1978), and the various gratifications children derive from exposure to television (Greenberg, 1974; Brown et al., 1974).

While several of these conditional variables most likely represent attributes of television for which children progressively develop more complex conceptions, a recognition of the necessity of accounting for these variables in addition to information about children's exposure to media is relatively new. The majority of research in this area has not looked at how these perceptions of the medium and its messages change developmentally, but rather the major interest has been whether they add to the understanding of media effects at single age levels. Another reason that little attention has been paid to developmental changes in these mediating variables is that typically they have been used to explain perceptions of specific television messages rather than perceptions of the entire medium. In the area of perceived reality, for example, questions have more often dealt with whether Kojak is like detectives in real life rather than whether the medium represents life as it really exists (Reeves, 1978).

In defining the dimensions along which children's perception of television changes, an attempt has been made to account for the research that has suggested third variables which either augment or diminish the impact of television on children. Other dimensions have been suggested by recent attempts to conceptualize the development of children's understanding of television along specific dimensions such as visual literacy (Salomon, 1974), and by recent attempts to define a more comprehensive list of similar dimensions (Dorr, forthcoming).

Dorr's work was based on a similar contention that the conceptions children have of television as a medium will have implications for the role that television plays in their lives. She says that "If we unravel some of the mysteries of the constructions children make of television, perhaps we shall come closer to understanding what television can provide for them." Dorr specifies several dimensions of a conception of television in terms of questions that children must deal with in order to develop an "adult" viewpoint. A first question is "What, really, are those things in the box?" Development along this dimension begins with a child's equation of television images with actual people, places, and events. In this context, the linkage between television and the real world takes place without regard for any unique properties of television and television information becomes yet another source of facts about the real world to be assimilated equitably with information from all other sources. In other words, the mediational characteristics of television are completely ignored.

Somewhere between this conception of television and a more complete recognition of television as a medium, children maintain a belief that social interaction with television characters is possible, despite a growing recognition that two-dimensional representations are somehow different from their three-dimensional real-life counterparts. Noble (1975), for example, argues that an important reason television appeals to children is because it provides them with an opportunity for parasocial interaction, and anecdotal evidence abounds concerning children's disappointment on learning that television people do not recognize and know them when they meet in real life. The most likely end point of children's development of a mediational conception of television is a full understanding that the medium is not literally a "magic window" on the world despite its potential to portray realistically the real world.

There are several implications of children's development along this continuum for perceptions of television characters. First, if television people are evaluated with no concern for the context in which they appear, as they apparently would be by children who believe television presents things exactly as they appear in real life, then TV people would have as much chance of impacting a child's general conception of what people are like as real-life people. This may be particularly important to the extent that the television people a child meets are markedly different from those they have contact with in real life or are not even present in real life. At an early stage on this dimension, television may maximally influence children's ideas and expectations about what a wide variety of other people are actually like.

Moving beyond this stage, but still holding on to the possibility of interaction with television characters, children may develop a conception of people in terms of how they should interact with others. Any real-life person not willing to live up to the often fantastic nature of television people may be evaluated as boring and not worth the child's attention. This may also lead to a relatively passive orientation to interaction where the child assumes other people should assume primary responsibility for conducting conversation. More than one elementary school teacher has noted that television people are a hard act to follow in the classroom. Children often demand that teacher presentations be colorful and fast-paced, and that the presenter exhibit the same style as television entertainers.

Finally, a full realization of the *mediational characteristic of television* may substantially influence children's perceptions of television people at least by making possible the perception that television people are neither exact duplications of reality nor capable of personally knowing individual members of their audience. At least the possibility exists that children would recognize that television people are to be evaluated differently than real-life counterparts. More detailed perceptions of television people at this level may be dependent on children's conception of television along other dimensions (e.g., ideas about the nature of drama and the social functions of media); however, the major recognition of the *possibility* of differences may be an essential and prerequisite notion.

A second dimension deals with the *nature of television drama* in terms of conceptions of story lines and plots and conceptions about people as actors and about appropriate orientations to the dramatic experience. Dorr described one aspect of this dimension in terms of "What can be understood in a story?" As adults, we are prone to think about the impact of television in terms of entire programs or even multiple episodes and program types. The evidence from developmental psychologists seems clear, however, that children must develop a conception of action which requires more than processing individual program vignettes. Recent work cited by Dorr indicates that children only gradually acquire the concept of an ideal plot, or one in which the most elementary characteristics of a story are present including an initiating event, attempt at resolution, and the consequences of the resolution (Mandler, 1977; Stein, 1977). Before this fundamental conception of a story develops, children apparently attend only to isolated pieces of television stories, never grasping the relationships between program segments. For example, the random sequencing of events in crime drama programs seems to have little detrimental effect on second graders' ability to recall story information whereas fifth graders retain far less of the material, likely because it is inconsistent with their expectations of how the story should ideally be organized (Collins and Westby, 1975).

The implications of this conception of television for the perception of television people may be dramatic. First, it may be impossible for younger children to develop a conception of television people using any information which is not obtainable from isolated program segments. Perceptions which require the collation of information from two seemingly unrelated parts of a story would simply never be possible. For example, the moralizing at the end of a "Shazam" or "Isis" segment, which attempts to set straight all of the good and bad behaviors committed by the various characters, would not be part of a younger child's perception of the characters. Similarly, any information in the plot or storyline which could color a perception, such as information about characters' motives and the consequences of actions, would also be ignored (Collins et al., 1974). For very young children, this aspect of a conception of television may even have implications for whether a child can recognize that the same character is appearing throughout a single story or in the same role every week. All but the most simple time and situation specific perceptions would not be possible.

Two other aspects of a conception of television drama may affect perceptions of television people; an understanding of what it is to be an actor and an understanding of the nature of drama itself. For young children a willing suspension of belief in trade for benefits of the dramatic experience is hardly a common orientation to television entertainment. The evaluation of dramatic characters may be heavily influenced by the recognition that television drama, like stage drama, is performed by individuals in temporary roles, who are instructed by directors to elicit certain responses and behave in certain ways, and who are all performing a creation of an author who is not present and only indirectly identified, if at all. How might impressions of characters change, for example, as children learn about the artificiality of actual television production settings, or learn about the cleverness of TV stuntmen?

The recognition of television characters as actors may even determine whether the actor or the role is the object of the perceptions. When elementary school children were asked to name TV characters they would most like to "be like," fifth and sixth graders, unlike younger children, often named actors independent of their television roles (e.g., Lee Majors instead of Steve Austin or the Six Million Dollar Man [Miller and Reeves, 1976]). The attribution of causality to characters' thoughts and behaviors may produce entirely different character impressions if authors, producers, and directors are held accountable for actions rather than the characters themselves.

A third possible dimension of a conception of television, which may be closely related to the first two, is an understanding of *the nature of the television industry and the economics of commercial television.* This dimension might range from a totally naive or even nonexistent conception of why programs are presented on television to an understanding that television is primarily available because it makes money for those who produce it by allowing them to sell the attention of millions of people to advertisers. Dorr (1978) reported that no children in any of the elementary school grades had an accurate understanding of the economic system of audience size, advertising, and income. This suggests that development along this dimension might require either higher levels of logical abilities or more experiences with similar ventures or even both. Among the sixth graders in Dorr's sample, one quarter did have some idea that television programs were broadcast to make money although they knew nothing of how that process worked.

It is more difficult to speculate exactly what development along this dimension may mean for the perception of television people. It is even possible that this conception of television may not be operative until children are relatively advanced in their overall conception of the medium. A recognition of the economic incentives that motivate the production of television, however, may have implications for children's evaluation of the credibility of both television people and their attitudes and behaviors. If children realize that producers are trying to make characters appealing (or not appealing depending on their role in the programs) so they will watch them, then children may be more apt to disregard attributes of the characters that only contribute to their appeal or to focus their attention on more subtle characteristics that are less artificial and not present only to promote attention. Also possible would be a total disregard of television characters due to an incredulous attitude toward television. As Dorr's data indicate, however, this conception may be more appropriate for adolescents and even adults because few children come close to a well developed economic understanding of the medium.

Why do children watch these TV programs? The answers to this question may describe a fifth dimension of a conception of television related to children's understanding of the social functions of the medium. Although seldom discussed developmentally, several researchers have recently suggested that knowledge of *the uses and gratifications of television for audiences* will increase the ability to predict how messages will be used and with what impact (Katz et al., 1974; McLeod and Becker, 1974; Lometti et al., 1977). Most of the research conducted to determine the actual reasons why people use television has been with adults, although the functions found in studies with children and adolescents have not been extremely different. Greenberg (1974), for example, factor analyzed open-ended responses to questions about why English children watched television and found seven reasons: learning, habit, arousal, companionship, forgetting, relaxation, and passing time.

Very little is known, however, about how these functions of television develop and even less is known about the relationship of the conceptions to the impact of television messages and characters. Preliminary evidence suggests knowledge of these functions may be an excellent predictor of learning from the media. In a recent study of learning from television news, elementary school children who reported watching news to learn were much more likely to remember facts from an experimental news program than those children who said they watch news for entertainment reasons, e.g., "I watch news because it's fun," or "I watch news just to see the pretty pictures" (Drew and Reeves, 1978a). In addition to the actual uses children have for different messages, their perceptions of the intentions of the sources of television messages may also be important. In a second study on children and television news, children's ideas about why news was on TV was a good predictor of the child's use of the message (Drew and Reeves, 1978b). Furthermore, causal analyses indicated these were independent perceptions which differentially predicted both exposure to news and learning from news stories.

Several questions remain in this area, however. When, for example, do children understand that television may be a formal source of information and learning as well as entertainment? When do they know that different types of programs, such as news versus situation comedies, may be used to satisfy different needs? When, in fact, can television begin to satisfy *any* needs or be used for any reason?

Despite these remaining research questions, it is relatively easy to speculate on how this conception of television may affect children's perceptions of television people. In fact, as suggested earlier, it is this conception of television which may relate directly to the finding that as children develop, their perception of TV characters becomes more unidimensional and simple (Reeves and Greenberg, 1977; Reeves and Lometti, 1978). The perception that television serves primarily an entertainment function may determine that television characters be evaluated solely in terms of their potential to provide entertainment (e.g., whether they are funny or serious). Similar perceptions of television people may result from other perceived functions of television as well as mixes of functions. When children realize, for example, that news and entertainment are not similar types of content and that they serve different functions, they may begin to evaluate the people that appear in those programs using entirely different sets of attributes.

A final conception of television relates to children's *ability to understand the language of visual presentations* and especially the use of complex visual techniques such as slow motion, flashbacks, camera angles, zooms, and fades. Although little research has been published on the development of a capacity to process correctly visual information, these abilities clearly have implications for understanding current television drama. Visual techniques often carry the essence of meaning in television messages and to the extent they are ignored or misinterpreted, children may form incomplete or idiosyncratic impressions of television people. Perhaps the best current evidence is an example cited by Dorr (1978) of children trying to make sense of slow motion as an indicator of bionic strength in the "Six Million Dollar Man." The five- to seven-year-old children she spoke with wondered how Steve Austin could catch the bad guys when he is running so slowly.

In summary, five dimensions of a conception of television have been proposed: (1) understanding the mediational characteristics of television; (2) understanding the nature of drama (including knowledge of actors, plots, and storylines); (3) economic understanding of television and the television industry; (4) knowledge of the uses and gratifications of various types of television formats (e.g., entertainment and news); and (5) understanding the visual grammar of television. It should be remembered that the major rationale for discussing these dimensions was to better understand how children form impressions of TV characters and how they are likely to use impressions of television people in forming conceptions of the real world. Further, these dimensions should provide a link between abstract theories of development and specific television behaviors and characterizations.

The most difficult questions, however, still remain. What are the specific relationships between the development of abilities in the areas of logic, role-taking, and moral reasoning and the development of a conception of television along the dimensions described? Some of these relations have been suggested here, although a systematic review of all those possible remains to be written. In any future consideration at least two criteria for establishing these relationships seem important. First, the independence, comprehensiveness, and sequencing of the proposed dimensions should be determined. On reviewing the five dimensions proposed here, it is apparent, for example, that an understanding of the mediational characteristic of television may be a prerequisite for understanding the nature of drama or the social functions of the medium. It is even possible that dimensions such as this should be combined to form a more abstract continuum of understanding.

Second, it is important that we know the *functional* relationships between cognitive development and a conception of television. As other authors have pointed out (Shantz, 1975), it will be important to differentiate between coincidental development in two areas (e.g., role-taking abilities and person perception or logical abilities and a conception of television) and determinant relationships (e.g., nonegocentric understanding of other people's perceptions as a predictor of children's identification of television character's motives for behavior). This determination will likely be very difficult because development in all of these areas is at least to some extent related to age. In determining the various functional relationships between different areas of cognitive development, it will also be necessary to determine where the critical changes in a conception of television occur. Even more importantly, however, will be an identification of the television experiences that facilitate the development of a conception of television by promoting confusion which can be resolved only by higher order thinking. For example, does seeing an actor perish in one episode only to reappear the next week contribute to a child's understanding of the nature of drama?

While the proposed dimensions of a conception of television were discussed mostly in terms of their implications for the study of children's perceptions of television characters, they likely could be applied to other research areas in children and television as well as to other media and other audiences. Again, the major benefit of this conception should be that more abstract theories in other areas of the social sciences can be applied to the specific elements of television—people, behaviors, social interactions, etc.—mediated by a consideration of the child's conception of the medium. The key question to which this conceptualization should relate asks when is television different from everything else. When indeed is the medium at least part of the message.

NOTES

1. Research dealing with children's descriptions of other people is usually classified under the title person perception. Although others have used this title to describe different categories of research, this title here refers only to those studies about how children formulate and organize impressions of what other people are like.

2. These spaces are the result of a multidimensional scaling analysis of the perceived similarities among all possible pairs of the 14 television characters. Children were first asked to rate the similarities of the character pairs on a five-point scale. The

resulting matrix of character by character similarity ratings was then input into the INDSCAL multidimensional scaling program which yielded the four-dimensional solution shown in Figure 1. Children were then asked to rate each of the 14 characters on nine unidimensional univariate measures (funny, strength, attractiveness, reality, age, support received from television peers, activity, and goodness). Sex was the ninth unmeasured attribute. The unidimensional measures were then related to the multidimensional spaces using multiple regression procedures to conceptualize each of the dimensions in the spaces. See Reeves and Greenberg (1977) for further details of the analysis procedure.

3. The unidimensional ratings did not include polar adjectives (e.g., funny versus serious), but rather asked if the attribute was applicable or not (e.g., funny versus not funny). Polar adjectives should probably not be assumed for children in the absence of evidence that the adjectives do in fact represent different ends of the same continuum.

4. The INDSCAL model (for INdividual Differences SCALing) uses as input an m x n x n (subjects x concepts x concepts) matrix of similarity scores. This means that for such subject or subgroup, a separate concept by concept similarity matrix is input. The output for INDSCAL consists of two matrices as opposed to one for the n x n input. All of the subgroup similarity matrices are first combined into a group space and a coordinate value is computed for all concepts on each dimension. A second matrix defines subgroup weights for each dimension based on the similarity ratings for each subgroup. Mathematically, the use of salience scores adds a weighting factor to the computation of ordinary Euclidean distances. The formula for distance in INDSCAL is:

$$d_{jk} = \sqrt{\sum_{t=1}^{n} W_{it} (Y_{jt} - Y_{kt})^2}$$

where W_{it} is the weighted metric for subgroup i; d_{jk} is the distance between stimulus j and k, and Y_{jt} and Y_{kt} are the coordinates of stimulus j and k on dimension t.

5. For a detailed review of the methods researchers have used to measure both the content and organization of children's impressions of others, see Livesley and Bromley, 1973:39-45.

REFERENCES

ALEXANDER, A., and WARTELLA, E. (forthcoming). Children's impressions of television characters and real people.
ARONOFF, C. (1974). "Old age in prime time." Journal of Communication, 24:86-87.
ATKIN, C.K., and GREENBERG, B.S. (1977). "Parental mediation of children's social behavior learning from television." Paper presented to the Theory and Methodology Division of the Association for Education in Journalism, Madison, Wisc.
BEACH, L., and WERTHEIMER, M. (1961). "A free response approach to the study of personal cognition." Journal of Abnormal and Social Psychology, 62:367-374.

BRIERLEY, D. (1966). "Children's use of personality constructs." Bulletin of the British Psychological Society, 19:72.

BROWN, J.R., CRAMOND, J.K., and WILDE, R.J. (1974). "Displacement effects of television and the child's functional orientation to media." Pp. 93-112 in J.G. Blumler and E. Katz (eds.), Annual review of communication research, Vol. 3. Beverly Hills, Cal.: Sage.

CAMPBELL, J., and RADKE-YARROW, M. (1956). "Interpersonal perception and behavior in children." American Psychologist, 11:416.

CARROLL, J.D., and WISH, M. (1974). "Models and methods for three-way multi-dimensional scaling." Pp. 57-105 in D.H. Krantz (ed.), Contemporary developments in mathematical psychology. San Francisco: W.H. Freeman.

COLLINS, W.A., BERNDT, T.J., and HESS, V.L. (1974). "Observational learning of motives and consequences for television aggression; a developmental study." Child Development, 45:799-802.

COLLINS, W.A., and WESTBY, S.D. (1975). "Children's processing of social information from televised dramatic programs." Paper presented at the biennial meeting of the Society for Research in Child Development, Denver, April.

DOMINICK, J., and GREENBERG, B. (1970). "Three seasons of blacks on television." Journal of Advertising Research, 10:21-27.

DORNBUSCH, S., HASTORF, A., RICHARDSON, S., MUZZY, R., and VREELAND, R. (1965). "The perceiver and the perceived: Their relative influence on the categories of interpersonal cognition." Journal of Personality and Social Psychology, 1:434-440.

DORR, A. (forthcoming). "When I was a child, I thought as a child." In an edited volume by the Committee on Television and Social Behavior of the Social Science Research Council. Washington, D.C.: Lawrence Ehrlbaum.

DREW, D., and REEVES, B. (1978a). "Learning from a television news story." Paper presented to the Radio-Television News Division of the Association for Education in Journalism, Seattle, Wash.

——— (1978b). "Children's exposure to television news: Antecedents and effects." Manuscript in progress.

FIFE, M. (1974). "Black image in American TV: The first two decades." Black Scholar, 6:7-15.

FLAVELL, J.H. (1963). The developmental psychology of Jean Piaget. Princeton, N.J.: Van Nostrand.

——— (1968). The development of role-taking and communication skills in children. New York: Wiley.

GOLLIN, E. (1958). "Organizational characteristics of social judgment: A developmental investigation." Journal of Personality, 26:139-154.

GREENBERG, B.S. (1974). "Gratifications of television viewing and their correlates for British children." Pp. 71-92 in J.G. Blumler and E. Katz (eds.), Annual review of communication research, Vol. 3. Beverly Hills, Cal.: Sage.

———, HEALD, G., WAKSHLAG, J., and REEVES, B. (1976). "TV character attributes, identification and children's modeling tendencies." Paper presented to the International Communication Association, Portland, Oregon, April.

HAWKINS, R.P. (1977). "The dimensional structure of children's perceptions of television reality." Communication Research, 3:299-320.

HOLLOS, M., and COWAN, P.A. (1973). "Social isolation and cognitive develop-

ment: Logical operations and role-taking abilities in three Norwegian social settings." Child Development, 44:630-641.
KAGAN, J., and KOGAN, N. (1970). "Individual variation in cognitive processes." In P.H. Mussen (ed.), Carmichael's Manual of child psychology, Vol. 1. New York: Wiley.
KATZ, E., BLUMLER, J.G., and GUREVITCH, M. (1974). "Utilization of mass communication by the individual." Pp. 19-34 in J.G. Blumler and E. Katz (eds.), Annual review of communication research, Vol. 3. Beverly Hills, Cal.: Sage.
KOHLBERG, L. (1966). "A cognitive-developmental analysis of children's sex-role concepts and attitudes." In E.E. Maccoby (ed.), The development of sex differences. Stanford, Cal.: Stanford University Press.
––– (1969). "Stage and sequence: The cognitive-developmental approach to socialization." In D.A. Goslin (ed.), Handbook of socialization theory and research. New York: Rand-McNally.
KOHN, A., and FIEDLER, F. (1961). "Age and sex differences in the perception of persons." Sociometry, 24:157-164.
LEAHY, R. (1976). "Developmental trends in qualified inferences and descriptions of self and other." Developmental Psychology, 12:546-547.
LIVESLEY, W., and BROMLEY, D. (1967). "Studies in the developmental psychology of person perception." Bulletin of the British Psychological Society, 20:67.
––– (1973). Person perception in childhood and adolescence. New York: Wiley.
LOMETTI, G.E., REEVES, B., and BYBEE, C.R. (1977). "Investigating the assumptions in uses and gratifications research." Communication Research, 4:321-338.
LUNZER, E.A. (1960). Recent studies in Britain based on the work of Jean Piaget. London: National Foundation for Educational Research.
MACCOBY, E., and JACKLIN, C. (1975). The psychology of sex differences. Stanford, Cal.: Stanford University Press.
MADDOCK, R., and KENNY, C. (1973). "Impression formation as a function of age, sex and race." Journal of Social Psychology, 89:233-243.
MANDLER, J.M. (1977). "A code in the node: Developmental differences in the use of story schema." Paper presented at the biennial meeting of the Society for Research in Child Development, New Orleans, March.
McLEOD, J.M., and BECKER, L.B. (1974). "Testing the validity of gratification measures through political effects analysis." Pp. 137-164 in J.G. Blumler and E. Katz (eds.), Annual review of communication research, Vol. 3. Beverly Hills, Cal.: Sage.
McLEOD, J.M., and REEVES, B. (forthcoming). "On the nature of mass media effects." In an edited volume by the Committee on Television and Social Behavior of the Social Science Research Council. Washington, D.C.: Lawrence Ehrlbaum.
MILLER, M.M. (1976). "Factors affecting children's choices of televised sex role models." Unpublished paper, Department of Communication, Michigan State University.
––– and REEVES, B. (1976). "Dramatic TV content and children's sex-role stereotypes." Journal of Broadcasting, 20:35-50.
NOBLE, G. (1975). Children in front of the small screen. Beverly Hills, Cal.: Sage.
OLSHAN, K.M. (1971). "The multidimensional structure of person perception in children." Unpublished Ph.D. dissertation, Rutgers University.
PALERMO, D. (1973). "More about less: A study of language comprehension." Journal of Learning and Verbal Behavior, 12:211-221.

PEEVERS, B., and SECORD, P. (1973). "Developmental changes in attribution of descriptive concepts to persons." Journal of Personality and Social Psychology, 27:120-128.

PETERSEN, M. (1973). "The visibility and image of old people on television." Journalism Quarterly, 50:569-573.

PIAGET, J. (1962). Play, dreams and imitation in childhood. New York: Norton.

––– (1970). "Piaget's theory." In P.H. Mussen (ed.), Carmichael's Manual of child psychology, Vol. 1. New York: Wiley.

PINARD, A., and LAURENDEAU, M. (1964). Causal thinking in children. New York: International Universities Press.

PRATT, M. (1975). "A developmental study of person perception and attributions of social causality: Learning the what and why of others." Unpublished Ph.D. dissertation, Harvard University.

REEVES, B. (1978). "Children's perceived reality of television and the effects of pro- and anti-social TV content on social behavior." Journalism Quarterly, in press.

––– and FABER, R. (forthcoming). "The distinguishing attributes children use in their impressions of real people and television characters."

REEVES, B., and GREENBERG, B. (1977). "Children's perceptions of television characters." Human Communication Research, 3:113-127.

REEVES, B., and LOMETTI, G. (1978). "The dimensional structure of children's perception of television characters: A replication." Human Communication Research, in press.

REEVES, B., and MILLER, M. (1978). "A multidimensional measure of children's identification with television characters." Journal of Broadcasting, 22:71-86.

ROBERTS, D. (1973). "Children and communication." In I.D. Pool, F.W. Frey, W. Schramm, N. Maccoby, and E. Parker (eds.), Handbook of communication. Chicago: Rand-McNally.

RUBIN, K.H. (1973). "Egocentrism in childhood: A unitary construct?" Child Development, 44:102-110.

SALOMON, G. (1974). "Annual report of the first year of research on cognitive effects of the media." Submitted to the Spencer Foundation, Hebrew University, Jerusalem, Israel, September 30.

SARBIN, T. (1954). "Role Theory." In G. Lindzey (ed.), Handbook of social psychology. Cambridge, Mass.: Addison-Wesley.

SCARLETT, H., PRESS, A., and CROCKETT, W. (1971). "Children's descriptions of peers: A Wernerian developmental analysis." Child Development, 42:439-453.

SELMAN, R. (1971). "Taking another's perspective: Role-taking development in early childhood." Child Development, 42:1721-1734.

SHANTZ, C.V. (1975). "The development of social cognition." In E.M. Hetherington (ed.), Review of child development research, Vol. V. Chicago: University of Chicago Press.

SHAPIRO, D., and TAGIURI, R. (1959). "Sex differences in inferring personality traits." Journal of Psychology, 47:127-136.

SHRAUGER, S., and ALTROCCHI, J. (1964). "The personality of the perceiver as a factor in person perception." Psychological Bulletin, 62:289-308.

SINGER, J.L. (1973). The child's world of make-believe: Experimental studies of imaginative play. New York: Academic Press.

STEIN, N.L. (1977). "The role of structural variation in children's recall of simple stories." Paper presented at the biennial meeting of the Society for Research in Child Development, New Orleans, March.

SUPNICK, J. (1964). Unpublished Senior Honors Thesis. Clark University, Worcester, Mass.

TAGIURI, R. (1969). "Person perception." Pp. 395-449 in G. Lindzey and E. Aronson (eds.), The handbook of social psychology, Vol. III. Reading, Mass.: Addison-Wesley.

TUCHMAN, G., DANIELS, A.K., and BENET, J. (eds.) (1978). Hearth and home: Images of women in the mass media. New York: Oxford University Press.

WACKMAN, D.B., and WARTELLA, E. (1977). "A review of cognitive developmental theory and research and the implication for research on children's responses to television." Communication Research, 4:203-224.

WARD, S., and WACKMAN, D.B. (1973). "Children's information processing of television advertising." Pp. 119-146 in P. Clarke (ed.), Annual review of communication research, Vol. 2. Beverly Hills, Cal.: Sage.

WARTELLA, E., and ALEXANDER, A. (1978). "Children's organization of impressions of television characters." Paper presented to the International Communication Association, Chicago.

WATTS, A. (1944). The language and mental development of children. London: Harrap.

WEGNER, D. (1974). "The development and articulation of attributes in person perception." Unpublished Ph.D. dissertation, Michigan State University.

WERNER, H. (1948). Comparative psychology of mental development. New York: International Universities Press.

――― (1957). "The concept of development from a comparative and organismic point of view." Pp. 125-148 in D.B. Harris (ed.), The concept of development. Minneapolis: University of Minnesota Press.

YARROW, M., and CAMPBELL, J. (1963). "Person perception in children." Merrill-Palmer Quarterly, 9:57-72.

Chapter 6

CONSTRUCTIVISM: THE DEVELOPMENT OF COMMUNICATION IN CHILDREN

Jesse G. Delia and Barbara J. O'Keefe

IN RECENT YEARS FACE-TO-FACE INTERACTION has come to be seen as the paradigm case of communication. In the process, conceptions of communication taking the speaker-audience situation as their focus have largely given way to positions defining communication not in terms of influence, but in terms of the creation of meaning in interaction. In this view, communication is seen as an ongoing, reciprocal process in which the actions of each party to an interaction are constantly being interpreted and given meaning by the others involved. Because any action an individual performs or any aspect of his or her appearance is subject to interpretation, the aphorism "one cannot not communicate" has become an accepted dictum of communication theory (Watzlawick et al., 1967).

The peculiarity in this conception of communication is that, as Weiner et al. (1972) observe, communication is made coterminous with processes of perception. However, because perception is a constructive, interpretive process, meaning is a ubiquitous feature of human life. People do, after all, exist in meaningful, symbolic worlds, not in an "environment." They understand and construct their realities by constantly making inferences about all the various situations in which they find themselves, not simply in interaction situations. Considered in this way, it seems unreasonable to identify the creation of meaning as the central characteristic of human interaction qua communication. Rather, it is the central characteristic of human existence.

Above all, what does seem distinctive about face-to-face interaction is the necessity for interactants to adjust and adapt to each other. When an individual interprets an utterance or action, he or she gives that utterance or action meaning in terms of his or her assessment of the other's intentions and view of the situation. When an individual constructs an utterance or action, communicative choices are based on an assessment of what the other will infer from that utterance or act. The knowledge upon which the individual relies in acting appropriately is his or her ongoing interpretation of what is socially shared and understood in the situation. It is in just this sense that face-to-face interaction is characterized by interpersonal adjustment and adaptation. Thus, while the creation of meaning is a central process in face-to-face interaction, the crucial function that such communication serves is not to provide bases for individual interpretations of experience, but rather to generate and reaffirm social or shared interpretations.

In this essay we explore developmental aspects of interpersonal perception processes underlying the ability to manage the production of meaning in interaction. We will argue that understanding how language is used in creating shared meaning requires understanding the processes by which interactants make cognitive assessments of one another's characteristics, emotional states, beliefs, intentions, and situational understandings. This is, of course, not a new or startling thesis. Many theorists from Piaget (1955) and Mead (1934) forward have argued that a primary determinant of the child's developing ability to manage communication is an increasing capacity for understanding the listener's frame of reference (role-taking or social perspective-taking).

The obtained empirical relationships between particular perspective-taking measures and particular assessments of communicative skill, however, have been strikingly low, particularly in early and middle childhood (see the summaries of Glucksberg et al., 1975; and Shantz, 1975). This appears largely attributable to conceptual and methodological limitations within this research tradition. Most of the analyses have involved the use of perspective-taking tasks either tapping the child's ability to predict what is seen by someone in a different physical location or dependent on cognitive and linguistic skills having little to do with interpersonal perception. For example, in Feffer's (1959) broadly used perspective-taking task the child is required to construct, remember, and maintain a story line across several perspectival transformations. The communication tasks typically employed in this research also are open to severe criticism. Simply referential communication tasks such as that developed by Krauss and his coworkers typically have been used (see Krauss and Glucksberg, 1970). In Krauss' task two children who alternate as speaker and listener are separated by a screen so that they cannot see one another. The speaker's job is to describe a novel or "low codable" figure (usually an odd-shaped geometric design) so that the listener can pick the specific figure described from an array of such figures. The usual dependent measure is an accuracy score reflecting successful communications across a number of trials. In addition to being a narrow and highly specific criterion by which to assess general effectiveness in communication, successful encoding and decoding of such descriptions appear dependent on a variety of perceptual, memory, and vocabulary skills unrelated to sensitivity to interpersonal perspectives and communicative adaptation (see Higgins, 1976).

Equally important to these methodological problems has been the general reliance on very global notions of perspective-taking or role-taking as bases for conceptualizing the relationship of interpersonal perception to communicative development. In our estimation there is much more to interpersonal perception than just role-taking. Speakers certainly make inferences about listeners' perspectives and in so doing they have to differentiate between their own and the listener's knowledge and beliefs. However, interactants also make inferences about attitudes, traits of character, intentions, and the like. To reduce all these specific qualities of interactants' perceptions to the level of perspective-taking underlying the perceptions seems unjustifiably narrow. This is especially so because there is considerable research showing that with age and social experience interpersonal perceptions change not only in the direction of more fully representing others' viewpoints, but in a variety of other ways as well (see Chandler, 1977; Shantz, 1975). For example, as we note below, with development such perceptions become more differentiated, more abstract, more organized, and more stable. Any effort to investigate the interrelations of development in interpersonal perception and communication processes must involve analysis of the kinds of cognitive/perceptual developments that relate to particular skills in communication.

The remainder of this chapter presents a constructivist approach to the developmental study of the relationship of interpersonal perception and communicative ability. We will first elaborate our general constructivist theoretical framework and then summarize some of our developmental communication research carried out within it.

INTERPERSONAL CONSTRUCTS, SOCIAL PERCEPTION, AND THE ANALYSIS OF COMMUNICATIVE DEVELOPMENT

Constructivism as an approach to communication study gives primary attention to analysis of stable individual differences in person's communicative abilities (Delia, 1977). This focus is achieved through the integration of George Kelly's (1955) theory of personal constructs with aspects of Heinz Werner's (1957) comparative-organismic theory as the basis for analysis of interpersonal perception processes underlying communicative development.

THE CONSTRUCTIVIST APPROACH TO SOCIAL PERCEPTION

Personal Construct Theory and Social Perception.

As both Crockett (1965) and Delia (1977) have noted, Kelly's theory of personal constructs provides a framework within which the cognitive processes involved in interpersonal perception can be conceptualized. Kelly takes as his model human beings in their scientist-like aspects. He contends that, like the scientist, all people seek to understand and order the world so that the occurrence of events can be anticipated and control exerted over them. The goal of prediction is accomplished through the use of a system of cognitive structures (constructs) which functions as an interpretive perceptual frame. Constructs, then, are organized schemas or patterns of expectation within which events are construed or interpreted. Any event can make sense only in so far as it is ordered within the construct system.

Applied to the perception of human action and social situations, this view implies that each individual develops a system of constructs or cognitive schemas through which an understanding is erected of the characteristics, qualities, knowledge, intentions, and emotional states of other persons. The perceiver construes and attributes qualities to others through the application of interpretive schemas. Understandings of other people are always in terms of images or impressions. The other is never simply a reflected reality. We can never directly apprehend another's intentions, inner qualities, or attitudes. Rather, in interpersonal perception an impression of the actions or attitudes of the other is inferred through interpreting aspects of the other's appearance and behavior within particular schemas brought by the perceiver to the social situation.

Perceivers, of course, differ widely in the number, pattern of organization, and content of the constructs or schemas they develop for construing the social world. Moreover, a perceiver spontaneously uses only a small portion of the available schemas in construing any particular situation or person. Consequently, the nature of a person's impression of another or of a social situation to a significant degree will be a function of the complexity, content, and implicit rules of use characterizing his or her interpersonal construct system.

Wernerian Organismic-Developmental Theory and the Developmental Analysis of Interpersonal Constructs.

As was noted earlier, the role of interpersonal perception in communicative development is typically approached through invoking the concept of role-taking and arguing that developments in cognitive perspective-taking or role-taking ability underlie the ability to formulate listener-adapted messages (e.g., Flavell et al., 1968). However, after reviewing an extensive body of research on communicative development, Glucksberg et al. (1975) concluded that available conceptions of role-taking are simply too general to be of much utility for analysis of the cognitive foundations of communicative adaptation and its development. Other reviewers have also noted the limited utility of the role-taking concept in providing a useful and comprehensive understanding of the development of interpersonal perception abilities (see Chandler, 1977; Shantz, 1975).

In fact, the conflation of all developmental changes in interpersonal perceptions into some global role-taking concept appears to underlie many of the disputes concerning the nature and rate of development of children's interpersonal perceptions. For example, Borke (1971, 1972) has argued that children cannot be considered to be without role-taking ability because children as young as three are capable of discerning affective moods in others (e.g., can make judgments as to which person is "happy" in a particular situation by observing physical expressions such as smiling directly corresponding to the mood). Chandler and Greenspan (1972) have argued against Borke's view by noting that in a social interaction a child of this age is incapable of realizing when another "knows" something different from the child himself or herself. This theoretical argument clearly reflects the confusion of related processes at different developmental levels (and implying different cognitive operations). On the one hand, the child is called on to coordinate behavioral expressions and inner states; on the other, the child is required to infer how another person understands or interprets some event or situation. Recent experimental work (e.g., Kurdek and Rodgon, 1975), in fact, has contributed to clarifying such disputes through differentiating the various cognitive capacities likely to be possessed by children of differing ages.

Thus, if progress is to be made in understanding the development of interpersonal perception processes and the relationship of such processes to the development of communicative abilities, general conceptions of role-taking must be replaced by more refined concepts. One perspective within which such concepts can be fashioned is provided by the integration of Kelly's theory of personal constructs with Werner's developmental ideas. The heart of Werner's (1957:126) orientation is stated succinctly in his Orthogenetic Principle: "Whenever development occurs, it proceeds from a state of relative globality and lack of differentiation to a state of increasing differentiation, articulation, and hierarchic integration." Specific assessments of the effect of underlying cognitive structure on psychological and behavioral processes is approached through comparative analysis within a series of developmental axes derived from this principle.

Of these, the axis of egocentrism-perspectivism is of particular interest because of its close parallel to the idea of role-taking. In Wernerian theory, as in Piaget's similar framework (see Langer, 1969; Mehrabian, 1968), egocentrism in no way refers to selfishness or an inordinate concern with personal well being (Elkind, 1970). Rather, as Looft (1972:74) has noted, the developmental axis refers to a process in which the child gradually comes "to differentiate cognitively among several aspects of an event and between his own and others' points of view."

Moreover, as was noted earlier, egocentrism is only one of a number of axes along which developmental changes in cognitive processes can be conceptualized. In addition to changing from egocentric to perspectivistic, children's interpersonal perceptions have been shown to change with age in their complexity, stability across situations, abstractness and sensitivity to motivations and psychological states, integration and organization, and in a host of other ways (see Chandler, 1977; Shantz, 1975). Within constructivism, such changes are seen to reflect changes along interrelated developmental axes—globality-differentiation, diffuseness-integration, concreteness-abstractness, egocentrism-perspectivism, and lability-stability, to name the most important. As discussed below, the point is this: Taken alone, such concepts as role-taking and egocentrism are too general to be of great utility in understanding either the development of interpersonal perception or the relationship of interpersonal perception to communication.

Following the Orthogenetic Principle and its derivative developmental axes, the development of personal constructs can be conceived as proceeding in the direction of increasing differentiation and hierarchic integration. This means both that the normal individual can be expected to develop, with social experience, an increasingly large number of interpersonal constructs and that the patterns of relationship among constructs can be expected to become increasingly complex and organized. The number of constructs individuals use to describe peers does, indeed, increase systematically with age (see Delia, Burleson, and Kline, 1978; Livesley and Bromley, 1973; Scarlett et al., 1971). More importantly, research has shown systematic changes with development in the quality of constructs. For example, following Wernerian developmental theory, Scarlett et al. (1971) observed (1) that the dominant type of construct shifted with age from egocentric (e.g., "*we* play kickball together" or "he hits *me*") to nonegocentric (e.g., "she plays kickball" or "he's always hitting people"), and (2) that the preceding shift was accompanied by a slightly later shift from a predominance of concrete constructs to a predominance of abstract, dispositional qualities (e.g., "she's athletic" or "he's a bully"). Systematic developments in the integration and organization of children's impressions also have been observed (Delia, Burleson, and Kline, 1978; Press et al., 1973).

There is, then, a shift in the understanding of others from attention to surface features of behavior construed in diffuse and primarily egocentric fashion to construal of their inner qualities within integrated networks of discrete abstract constructs. As Werner (1957) and Heider (1958) have both emphasized, such shifts represent perception of the invariant dispositional properties of the social world; with development, others come to be perceived as agents who operate independently of the perceiver, behaving with some degree of consistency over a broad range of situations.

The same kinds of differences in quality and organization distinguish impressions formed by young adults with noncomplex as compared to those with complex sets of interpersonal constructs. As a result of differential ranges of social experience, of the variety of individual reactions to interpersonal conflicts, and of a host of other factors that are, at best, poorly understood, any group of adults will contain some individuals with highly differentiated, abstract, hierarchically integrated, developmentally advanced sets of interpersonal constructs and others with sparse, globally organized, developmentally primitive sets of constructs (see Crockett, 1965). A number of studies have supported the general hypothesis that those with more differentiated and abstract sets of interpersonal constructs are less reliant on simplifying social schemes in understanding networks of interpersonal relations (Delia and Crockett, 1973; Press et al., 1969), develop conceptions of others less dominated by overall evaluation and affect (Delia, Crockett, Press, and O'Keefe, 1975; O'Keefe and Brady, 1978; Rosenbach et al., 1973), form more integrated—and hence, more temporally stable—impressions of others (Delia, Clark, and Switzer, 1974; Klyver et al., 1972; Mayo and Crockett, 1964; Nidorf and Crockett, 1965), and more effectively shift from their own points of view in understanding and organizing others' perspectives in social situations (Crockett et al., 1975; Hale and Delia, 1976; Press et al., 1975).

In sum, by fusing Kelly's theory with Wernerian developmental theory, a perspective is gained from which to assess a wide range of relatively stable aspects of cognitive structure. Rather than reducing the analysis of psychological development to a single construct, the constructivist perspective invites analysis of psychological structure within an interrelated system of developmental axes: differentiation, integration, abstractness, and so on. These dimensions, of course, are not independent. Thus, in much of our research the degree of differentiation of interpersonal impressions (cognitive complexity), or the level of abstractness of elicited interpersonal constructs (construct abstractness) is taken to be a good overall index of the developmental status of interpersonal construct systems. Indeed, considerable research has shown that development along the various developmental axes is positively correlated (e.g., see Applegate, 1978; Delia, Clark, and Switzer, 1974; O'Keefe and Delia, 1978b). However, even though development along these various axes is moderately and positively correlated, they are both analytically and empirically distinguishable. This fact provides the point of departure for analyses relating particular aspects of interpersonal construct system development to particular developments in communicative ability.

INTERPERSONAL PERCEPTION AND THE DEVELOPMENT OF BEHAVIORAL STRATEGIES FOR LISTENER ADAPTATION

Even given a more refined analysis of the development of social construal processes, however, conceptualizing the relationship of interpersonal perception to communicative behavior remains a problem. A fundamental difficulty in attempts to relate developments in social perspective-taking to communication, for example, is the presumption that interpersonal perception is related directly to behavior. Researchers apparently expect that if children can conceptualize differences between their own knowledge and that of others (i.e., if they can nonegocentricly take others' perspectives), their perceptions will result directly in adaptations in messages directed to others. However, understanding is developmentally prior to the achievement of behavioral control over the communicative code. Within general analyses of language acquisition, for example, it has long been recognized that comprehension of linguistic forms precedes their use. Similarly, for social understandings to affect communicative performance requires both the recognition that these understandings have implications for one's communicative tasks and their integration within some set of behavioral mechanisms (syntactic forms, strategies for message formulation, etc.) through which functional control over the communicative code is exercised. If these developments separate the achievement of a particular level of social understanding from the use of that level of understanding in communication, then the low correlations between assessments of social perspective-taking and communicative behavior are not surprising, particularly among younger children who should be just beginning to recognize the communicative implications of their construals of others' psychological states and to acquire control of strategic communication.

Thus, within the constructivist framework the connection between cognition and behavior is not seen to be straightforward and simple, but to involve a developmental process in which control is acquired over behavior at progressively more abstract levels. The child is seen as having to develop the necessary cognitive capacities and the appropriate level of control over communication to accomplish his or her functional aims. For fully functional communication, this will require that the child develop requisite conceptual and social-cognitive abilities and that these abilities be integrated with control over communication at the nonverbal behavioral, linguistic, sociolinguistic or socio-cultural, and tactical/strategic levels.

In sum, within the constructivist perspective emphasis is placed on the connection between event-specific perceptions and communicative behavior. An individual's communicative choices are seen as premised on his or her particular beliefs about the listener toward whom a message is directed. At the same time, within the constructivist viewpoint corresponding attention is given to the influence of stable psychological processes that influence the character of context-specific perceptions. While the formulation of a particular strategic message will be taken to reflect the communicator's tacit inferences and predictions concerning the listener's likely responses to alternative strategies, analysis is carried out through consideration of the stable qualitative characteristics of the communicator's interpersonal construct system. The inference of trans-situationally stable features of the interpersonal construct system is thus the theoretical backbone of the constructivist approach.

Thus, while preserving the tie between context specific perceptions and behavior, the constructivist approaches social behavior through analysis of the stabilities in individuals' interpersonal construct systems. Therefore, the constructivist seeks to show how important stable aspects of communicative behavior can be understood by focusing on the developmental status of communicative processes. Such an approach surely loses much in understanding the totality of contextually embedded interactions. However, such an approach serves to bring into bold relief the qualitatively different processes which situated interactants employ. Moreover, by not treating every interactant as equally adept at participating in the process of managing social meanings, we are led to insights that can be applied by researchers studying communication as a contextually emergent process.

INTERPERSONAL PERCEPTION PROCESSES AND COMMUNICATIVE DEVELOPMENT: RESEARCH APPLICATIONS

THE DEVELOPMENTAL ANALYSIS OF INTERPERSONAL PERCEPTION IN STRATEGIC COMMUNICATION

The foregoing analysis of the role of interpersonal perception processes in the development of strategic communication was clearly supported in a recent study conducted by Delia and Clark (1977). The investigation was designed to ascertain whether children differing in age and cognitive complexity varied in their abilities spontaneously to attribute characteristics to listeners and to utilize those attributions in formulating listener-adapted messages.

The study was conducted as an extension of an investigation undertaken by Alvy (1973). In his study the child was presented in an interview six pairs of pictures which depicted potential audiences. The two forms of each picture differed in representing the central figure, the listener, as varying along an important, typically emotional or psychological, dimension. For example, one pair of pictures showed a boy playing with several toys; the boy in one picture was smiling and obviously friendly, and, in the other, the boy was frowning and clutching the toys in a possessive posture. The child was asked to direct messages to each of the two figures in each situation in order to accomplish some interpersonal goal. For instance, the child was asked to indicate how he or she would ask first the smiling boy and then the frowning boy if he or she could play with one of the toys. Alvy's study clearly demonstrated that with advances in age children increase in ability to adapt communications to listeners. However, his design did not permit assessment of the developmental relationship between person perception processes and communicative adaptation, because he explicitly called attention to the central distinction between the listeners prior to the child's encoding of the message. The child's perception of the listeners' characteristics, hence, was accomplished not through cognitive interpretive processes, but through explicit direction.

By contrast, Delia and Clark's study systematically investigated the relationship between processes of interpersonal perception and communicative adaptation. Subjects were 40 males equally divided among four age groups (six, eight, ten, and twelve year olds) and with an equal number of complex and noncomplex subjects within each age level (cognitive complexity was assessed by counting the total number of constructs used in describing a liked or disliked peer; see Crockett, 1965). Subjects completed Alvy's multisituation communication task by (1) spontaneously describing each of the 12 figures in the six situation pairs, (2) directing to each figure a message aimed at accomplishing the assigned interpersonal task, and (3) (after the two figures within the same situation were paired) indicating differences in the members of each pair of listeners and the effects, if any, those differences would have on the construction of messages.

Delia and Clark found that in every case involving the construction of messages spontaneously adapted to the listener, the child first spontaneously represented the communication-relevant characteristic in the listener. In other words, making communication-relevant attributions of the listener characteristics was a *necessary condition* for communicative adaptation. However, attributing potentially relevant characteristics to the listeners alone was *not a sufficient condition* for the production of the listener-adapted communications. In fact, in the cases where the communication-relevant characteristics of the listeners were represented, listener-adapted communications were constructed in only 35.56% of the cases among six year olds, 50% among eight and ten year olds, and 69.49% among 12 year olds.

Analyses of children's spontaneously constructed messages and of their explanations of the effects of listener characteristics on message choices led to the characterization of the development of interpersonal perception and listener-adapted communication in terms of a series of interrelated progressions in which: (a) The ability to identify in (attribute to) listeners characteristics potentially relevant to particular communicative tasks precedes the recognition of the relevance of those characteristics to communicative adaptation. (b) Subsequently, the relevance of particular listener characteristics to the outcome of the child's communicative efforts is understood, but the communicative code is not controlled by the child; as a consequence, although the outcomes of communicative efforts can be predicted, there is no message adaptation between listeners. (c) Finally, behavioral control over strategic communication is achieved, first with the use of global, undifferentiated adaptational strategies, and subsequently with differentiated and refined strategies integrated with the capacity to erect more dispositional and more refined understandings of listeners.

All along the developmental course, children of a given age who possessed relatively complex systems of interpersonal constructs for perceiving persons (cognitive complexity) excelled the performance of those with noncomplex construct systems.

In general, the level of response manifested by cognitively noncomplex children of one age had been evidenced by complex children two years younger. That is, this study showed marked individual differences in social-cognitive and communicative performance as a function of the complexity of children's interpersonal cognitive systems.

An alternative approach to the analysis of the role of interpersonal perception in the development of behavioral control over communication is reflected in studies carried out by Clark and Delia and others. In these studies, messages were analyzed for strategic control over communication via coding schemes reflecting a hierarchic ordering of the underlying mode of representing the listener's perspective implied in the strategies themselves. For instance, in some of the studies a system for coding children's and adolescents' persuasive strategies produced in response to simple persuasive situations was developed which reflected the level of perspective-taking implied in the form of the request and each appeal (Clark and Delia, 1976, 1977; Delia, Kline, and Burleson, 1978; Ritter, forthcoming). At the lowest level the children evidenced no recognition of the perspectives of the other; for instance, they assumed the other was already aware of their needs and wants. At the second level the children indicated a low level of recognition that the other held different views by making explicit their needs or desires, but elaborating them only in terms of advantage to themselves. At the third level, a still higher level of awareness of the other's perspective was represented, as evidenced by the children's specific inclusion of counter-arguments and refutation within their messages. Such considerations obviously indicate awareness that the persuadee may not evaluate the situation or desirability of the proposed outcome the same as does the child. At the final level, the child constructed messages making advantage to the persuadee primary. While the view of the other was responded to at the third level through the inclusion of counter-arguments, at the fourth level another's view was manipulated through making it the dominant focus of persuasion. O'Keefe and Delia (1978b) applied a similar hierarchic principle in coding young adults' rationales for their strategic behavioral choices. Ritter (forthcoming) developed a conceptually parallel system for coding adolescents' responses to situations calling on the communicator to deal with his or her having hurt another's feelings (also see Applegate and Delia, forthcoming, who use a similar system for analysis of children's interpersonal communication).

Applegate and Delia (also see Applegate, 1978) constructed other hierarchically ordered coding systems. Their schemes were based on an integration of constructivist developmental principles with Bernstein's (1974) analysis of role- and person-centered communication. Bernstein argues that different modes of social organization create, and are themselves sustained through, different modes of speech. Within some social groups, social organization is rooted in the conceptualization of social relations as based on an intermeshing of role and status positions. In other social groups, persons are individuated and speech is elaborated in accommodation to the individuality (rather than position-centeredness) of perspectives. Applegate and Delia argue that such a difference in modes of conceptualization and communication can be seen to reflect not simply different speech styles, but different underlying developments in the system of interpersonal constructs through which persons are conceptualized and communications formulated. Applegate and Delia developed hierarchic systems to score the position-/person-centeredness overtly elaborated in messages constructed in response to both regulative situations (controlling others' behavior) and interpersonal situations (dealing with others' feelings and affective states).

The hierarchies for coding the subjects' messages in each kind of context contained three major levels with three hierarchically ordered sublevels within each major level. Thus, the systems included nine ordered levels. The ascending levels of the hierarchies reflected an increasing degree of adaptation and person-centeredness in the speech of the participants.

Appeals falling within the lowest major level of the regulative appeal hierarchy subsumed the individual perspectivity of addresses within general rules, commands, and forms of punishment designed to govern the thought and behavior of the listener on the basis of his or her assigned role within the family, peer group, classroom, and so forth. At the lowest major level of the interpersonal appeal hierarchy the feelings, motives, intentions, etc., of speaker and others were either explicitly denied or ignored as a legitimate basis for defining the situation. The three ascending sublevels within this major level (levels 1, 2, and 3) represented the speaker's increasing elaboration of the rules operating within the regulative or interpersonal situation, but in no way acknowledged the autonomy and uniqueness of the individual perspectives involved.

Appeals falling within the second major level of each hierarchy did not explicitly elaborate the subjective features of the speaker's and/or other's perspectives. However, appeals at this major level did implicitly recognize the autonomy of the other's perspective by encouraging the message recipient to reason through the situation for him or herself as a means of regulating or (in the interpersonal contexts) understanding the feelings and behaviors involved. Typically, this was accomplished through the elaboration of consequences and general principles which were relevant to the context. The appeals scored within the ascending sublevels of this major level (levels 4, 5, and 6) increasingly elaborated and encouraged the other to come to his or her own understanding of the need for modifying behavior (regulative context) or encouraged the other to explore non-psychological reasons for the existing interpersonal problems (interpersonal context). Subjective motives, intentions, or feelings were not explicitly elaborated.

Appeals at the highest major level in each hierarchy were those in which the participant evidenced sensitivity to the unique features of the context and of the perspectives of interactants and explicitly elaborated such features in speech. The three sublevels within this major level (levels 7, 8, and 9) reflected increasing elaboration of psychological factors as well as more explicit efforts to encourage the other to see his or her feelings and behaviors in relation to those of others (i.e., to engage in perspective-taking) as a basis for regulating behavior or resolving interpersonal problems.

Given a concern with indexing the underlying adaptive quality of communicative appeals, Applegate and Delia also coded the rationales provided for the communications. The two hierarchies used to score regulative and interpersonal rationales were grounded in the same developmental progression from concrete and normative rationales for communication to rationales representing adaptation to the specific psychological character of the listener.

Each of these hierarchic coding systems mentioned above is ordered by a particular developmental axis (e.g., egocentrism to perspectivism in the case of Clark and Delia's, Ritter's, and O'Keefe and Delia's; and concreteness to abstractness/role-centeredness to psychological-centeredness in the case of Applegate and Delia's). Consequently, by applying such systems in research with children of differing ages, developmental hypotheses relevant to the maturation of communicative skills can be directly tested. Indeed, recent research has revealed systematic age-related developments within these hierarchies across childhood and adolescence (e.g., Applegate and Delia, forthcoming; Clark and Delia, 1976; Delia, Burleson, and Kline, 1978; Ritter, forthcoming).

Hierarchic schemes in which the underlying conceptual principle ordering categories reflects interpersonal cognitive processes permit the researcher to transcend the particulars of specific situations by coding for the structural effect of underlying psychological processes on situationally located perceptions and communicative strategies. Furthermore, independent assessments of aspects of construct system content and organization permit identification of the kinds of construct system developments underlying such strategic developments. For instance, research has shown that the development of control over communication is significantly related to the communicator's interpersonal cognitive complexity (Clark and Delia, 1977; Delia and Clark, 1977; Delia, Kline, and Burleson, 1978; O'Keefe and Delia, 1978b).

The more refined analyses of Applegate and Delia (forth-coming) and Delia, Kline, and Burleson (1978), however, suggest that it is the development of abstract constructs useful in representing others' psychological states that most strongly underpin control over higher-order strategies reflected in most of the coding systems employed to date. Delia, Kline, and Burleson report that cognitive complexity, but not construct abstractness relates significantly to the level of perspective-taking implied in persuasive strategies among kindergarteners and first-graders. However, construct abstractness also emerges as a significant predictor of strategy level during middle to late childhood and is a superior predictor in adolescence. They report an overall correlation among kindergarteners to twelfth-graders (N = 211) of construct abstractness and the level of persuasive strategies of .60 (.33 with age partialled out). Similar results are reported by Applegate and Delia among first-grade and third-grade children for the relationship of cognitive complexity and construct abstractness to both persuasive and inter-personal communication strategies. Applegate and Delia also report correlations between their hierarchic codings of communicative appeals in both regulative and interpersonal contexts and the abstractness of elicited constructs ranging from .37 to .75 and averaging .55 across four studies involving diverse adult populations. Quite similar correlations were obtained for the relationship of construct abstractness to hierarchic codings of the rationales for message choices. Moreover, in one study involving three months of naturalistic observation, Applegate and Delia found expected differences in the role-centeredness/person-centeredness of spontaneous communication among day care teachers with relatively concrete versus abstract interpersonal construct systems.

Even more precise interconnections between particular features of the social-cognitive system and particular aspects of communicative behavior have been identified by O'Keefe and Delia (1978b). Undergraduate students were asked to form an impression of a person unknown to them on the basis of a wide array of supplied information. Subsequently, they assumed a role requiring them to direct a persuasive message toward this unknown other. After writing their persuasive messages, they decomposed them into discrete adaptations, appeals, and arguments and provided justifications for each message choice. In support of the view that specific social-cognitive factors should be related to specific ranges of communicative behavior, the level of appeal justification (defined in terms of the level of social perspective-taking reflected in the justification) was shown to be principally related to the use of flexible, abstract modes of social perception, while the number of adaptations, appeals, and arguments was principally related to the differentiation of the interpersonal construct system.

In pilot research, Burleson (1978) has taken a somewhat different approach by seeking to define the content of interpersonal constructs requisite to control over communication addressing a particular kind of problem or context. His initial work has sought to identify individuals whose construct systems are dominated in content by constructs discriminating among others by reference to interpersonal relations and relation-relevant characteristics; he has found that when dealing with another's hurt feelings, such individuals employ strategies overtly displaying greater sensitivity to psychological states and feelings than do those who discriminate among others in nonrelationally centered ways.

SOCIAL CONSTRUING, SOCIOLINGUISTIC KNOWLEDGE, AND SITUATIONAL CONSTRAINTS ON COMMUNICATION

An integral part of communicative development is gaining the ability to control language in accordance with the sociocultural organization of the event of communication. Many sociolinguists have made this argument (e.g., Hymes, 1974), stressing that in learning a language, we learn not only the linguistic code, but also the sociocultural rules for its use. Within our own dominant culture these rules take the form of shared understandings as to who is to be called what under what circumstances, who has the floor in a conversation and how speaker-switching is to be accomplished, how one makes a comment relevant to the previous utterance, and how topic switching is to be conducted, and so on.

Unfortunately, no research has yet been undertaken directly relating the social-cognitive abilities of the child to his or her ability to make appropriate sociolinguistic choices. However, the ability to maintain and control conversation and to participate effectively within the community understandings governing social interaction can be seen to depend heavily on the ability to construe the other's knowledge and to anticipate his or her view of the situation.

To learn to organize communication within the rules governing speech usage within his speech community, the child must learn not only how to speak formally, colloquially, or with baby-talk, but also how to recognize the conditions for the use of these code varieties; he must learn not only how to construct a sentence, but also how to fit that sentence to the preceding one and into the context of interaction; he must learn not only the rules governing the assignment of titles and honorifies, but also how to use and interpret violations of these rules. To be a fully competent member of a speech community, the child must ,learn to do all these things, yet he must be able to recognize and sustain the other's perspective on the situation in order to understand the other's characteristics and/or to see how the other defines the situation (and thus what code is appropriate), to see how the other expects the conversation to progress (and thus, what utterances and topics are appropriate), to represent the other's knowledge as it is similar and different from his own (and thus, what conversational transitions are necessary to maintain the connectedness of discourse), to recognize the social role of the other, and to see how the other sees himself (and thus, what title or name is appropriate).

Although some investigators have interpreted their studies of sociolinguistic development through reference to social-cognitive developments (e.g., Bates, 1976), research explicitly testing specific connections between social-cognitive and sociolinguistic developments remains to be done. However, given the conceptual ties we have just noted, it seems worthwhile to investigate the general hypothesis that appropriate use of sociolinguistic rules directing the forms and functions of speech in various situations is contingent on particular developments in interpersonal perception abilities.

Importantly, by studying the development of interaction processes from this point of view, the possibility is achieved for fusing sociolinguistic and strategic analyses of sequential aspects of actual interaction. As we have pointed out, it is evident that children must master an enormously complex system of tacit rules governing the conduct of situated interaction. However, they must also learn to strategically manage interaction to accomplish their aims. To maintain the orderliness of talk in speech situations requiring the accomplishment of socially defined joint tasks, the child must learn to coordinate all of his communicative choices and adapt them together toward the defined goals of the speech event. Indeed, the very process of coordination so fundamental to the conduct of situated interaction is not straightforwardly accomplished through shared social knowledge, but, as Feffer (1970) has so cogently argued, represents a problem requiring the cognitive coordination of perspectives. Hence, to manage joint tasks, the child must be able not simply to erect a cognitive assessment of the other and his perspectives, but also to give the assessment of the other and his perspective detailed and sustained consideration as the basis for continually and flexibly integrating his behavior with that of the other (see O'Keefe et al., 1978).

One implication of the foregoing is that aspects of the sociocultural understandings governing interaction may become strategic resources to be self-consciously managed in the accomplishment of individual communicative aims. For example, children and adults doubtlessly differ in their abilities to manage topic shifts so as to smoothly, though strategically, move conversation onto a desired subject. It is a straightforward extension of our previous research to suggest that such management of the resources of sequential talk is probably dependent on individual differences in underlying social-cognitive abilities.

In addition, it is evident that the sociocultural frame within which interaction is conducted places constraints on communication that require the adaptation of behavior for the successful accomplishment of interpersonal tasks. For example, Delia (1976) has commented at length on the probability that there is a culturally defined class of contexts which are framed or understood as rhetorical situations in which the primary function of talk is persuasive or manipulative; such a definition of the situation obviously will impose considerable constraints on the range of strategies the speaker either can appropriately or will need to employ. For instance, in all likelihood the speaker would have to find ways of reassuring his listeners that he or she is without self-gain motives.

In the same way, situationally emergent constraints also should limit the range and character of strategies open to the communicator. The shared organizing schemes structuring interaction serve only as general guidelines within which situationally emergent understandings are continually elaborated as further constraints on interaction. Following the lead of sociological symbolic interactionists (e.g., Blumer, 1969), analysis of such emergent constraints can be approached through consideration of the issues faced in the interactional negotiation of a social definition of reality (see Ball, 1972).

Every interaction is characterized by implicit negotiation of the definition of the situation, an answer to the question, "What's going on here?" Participants in an interaction must generate some shared conception of the interaction situation and the norms governing conduct in that situation. These understandings take the form of beliefs about what the situation is and beliefs which form general constraints on action conducted within that situation. All aspects of the situation facing the participants in interaction are subject to negotiation; hence, in the course of an interaction, a number of more specific issues may arise. Acceptable solutions to these issues must be generated in order for joint action to proceed smoothly.

The first of these more specific issues is the question of the identities of the individuals involved in the situation. Each actor generates strategies for self-presentation and altercasting, representing respectively his solutions to the problems of his own and the other's situational identity. Given their identities, participants also must construct an acceptable definition of their relationship. Their understanding of their relationship takes the form of beliefs about how their identities are related and beliefs about how action is to be conducted within their relationship ("relational rules"—additional constraints within which actions are formulated). In addition, issues may arise over the focus of interaction, those aspects of reality toward which attention is jointly and explicitly directed. Of course, at times the overt focus of interaction may be on some aspect of the definition of the situation or the identities and relationship of the interlocutors. However, most often these aspects of the reality will simply be assumed and taken for granted. In such cases, the focus of interaction will involve whatever is the overt subject of talk. Importantly, even the most mundane and pedestrian subjects are open to negotiation, as can be seen in the existence of routine strategies for introducing and switching topics in conversation. It is only the focus of interaction which serves as the subject for the explicit negotiation of social reality.

These, then, are the fundamental and implicit issues in every interaction, since in the process of constituting social reality, interactants must constitute the interaction situation itself. Only the focus of interaction is directly and explicitly defined by participants; the other issues (situations, identities, and relationships) typically are negotiated implicitly, because it is the interactants' beliefs about these aspects of the interaction that constrain their choice of strategies.

Hence, we find that the interaction proceeds not only within a set of socio-historically inherited constraints (e.g., sociolinguistic rules, definitions of prototypical situations and contexts), but also within a set of situationally emergent constraints. The individual must create strategies which actualize his intentions, but which do so within the constraints imposed by the contextually constituted definitions given to situation, self, other, relationship, and the focus of interaction. He must introduce his projects into the interactional agenda, securing for his concerns focused attention. The strategies generated thus must not only actualize his intentions, but must also be appropriate within the constantly emerging definition given to reality in interaction.

Clark (1978) has recently investigated the role of situational constraints on strategy selection within our framework. She manipulated the persuader's desire for maintaining certain definitions of the relationship between himself and his persuadee. When it was essential in a compliance-gaining encounter that a positive relationship be maintained with the persuadee, altercasting strategies were employed in which a positive self for the persuadee vis-a-vis the persuader was created. Such strategies were seldom employed, however, when it was not essential that a positive relationship be maintained. Similarly, when the speaker's own self-interest was placed at risk by having to persuade another, self-presentational strategies were employed fashioning the necessary situational identity for the persuader; when self-interest was not at issue, little attention was given to self-presentational concerns.

While only suggestive, this line of work points to the importance of embedding analyses of strategic communicative development within some understanding of the situationally emergent constraints on communication. While the work remains to be completed, we expect both that there are identifiable developmental patterns in effective strategic adaptation to such constraints and that such adaptation will be shown to be dependent on developments in the interpersonal construct system.

A CONCLUDING NOTE

It should be apparent that we have presented not simply a conception of communicative development, but the outline of a general approach to social communication. This approach emphasizes the reciprocal creation of meaning in communication as the joint product of a socially shared code for the public expression of thought and the individual interpretive processes involved in the interpretation and control of language and social contexts within socio-cultural and situationally emergent constraints. Accordingly, a generalized version of the position presented in this chapter would stress the interpretive processes by which individuals define situations and understand the perspectives of others within them in interpreting and using language and in following social rules in making the adaptations necessary to joint conduct. What we have provided, we hope, is the first approximation to a framework in which social-cognitive factors can be related to language in understanding how communication works. It is social perception as a constructive-interpretive process that underlies the interactive and reciprocally adjustive processes we find in communication and exchange. Communication is a process of jointly managing meaning not simply through behavior exchange, but through a process of ongoing reciprocal interpretation.

REFERENCES

ALVY, K.T. (1973). "The development of listener adapted communication in grade-school children." Genetic Psychology Monographs, 87:33-104.

APPLEGATE, J.L. (1978). "Four investigations of the relationship between social cognitive development and person-centered regulative and interpersonal communication." Unpublished Ph.D. dissertation, University of Illinois at Urbana-Champaign.

––– and DELIA, J.G. (forthcoming). "Person-centered speech, psychological development, and the contexts of language usage." In R. St. Clair and H. Giles (eds.), The social and psychological contexts of language. Hillsdale, N.J.: Erlbaum.

BALL, D.W. (1972). " 'The definition of situation': Some theoretical and methodological consequences of taking W.I. Thomas seriously." Journal for the Theory of Social Behavior, 2:61-82.

BATES, E. (1976). Language and context. New York: Academic Press.

BERNSTEIN, B. (1974). Class, codes and control: Theoretical studies towards a sociology of language. New York: Schocken.

BLUMER, H. (1969). Symbolic interactionism: Perspective and method. Englewood Cliffs, N.J.: Prentice-Hall.

BORKE, H. (1971). "Interpersonal perception of young children: Egocentrism or empathy?" Developmental Psychology, 5:263-269.

––– (1972). "Chandler and Greenspan's 'Ersatz Egocentrism': A rejoinder." Developmental Psychology, 7:107-109.

BURLESON, B.R. (1978). "Relationally oriented construct system content and messages directed to an affectively distressed listener: An exploratory study." Paper presented at the annual meeting of the Speech Communication Association.

CHANDLER, M.J. (1977). "Social cognition: A selective review of current research." In W.F. Overton and J. McCarthy (eds.), Knowledge and development, Vol. 1: Advances in theory and research. New York: Plenum.

——— and GREENSPAN, S. (1972). "Ersatz egocentrism: A reply to H. Borke." Developmental Psychology, 7:104-106.

CLARK, R.A. (1978). "The impact on selection of persuasive strategies of self interest and desired liking." Unpublished manuscript, Department of Speech Communication, University of Illinois at Urbana-Champaign.

——— and DELIA, J.G. (1976). "The development of functional persuasive skills in childhood and early adolescence." Child Development, 47:1008-1014.

——— (1977). "Cognitive complexity, social perspective-taking, and functional persuasive skills in second- to ninth-grade children." Human Communication Research, 3:128-134.

CROCKETT, W.H. (1965). "Cognitive complexity and impression formation." In B.A. Maher (ed.), Progress in experimental personality research, Vol. 2. New York: Academic Press.

———, MAHOOD, S.M., and PRESS, A.N. (1975). "Impressions of a speaker as a function of variations in the cognitive characteristics of the perceiver and the nature of the speaker and the message." Journal of Personality, 43:168-178.

DASEN, R.P. (ed.) (1977). Piagetian psychology: Cross-cultural contributions. New York: Wiley.

DELIA, J.G. (1976). "A constructivist analysis of the concept of credibility." Quarterly Journal of Speech, 62:361-375.

——— (1977). "Constructivism and the study of human communication." Quarterly Journal of Speech, 63:66-83.

———, BURLESON, B.R., and KLINE, S.L. (1978). "A structural analysis of the organization of impressions in kindergarteners to twelfth-graders." Unpublished manuscript, Department of Speech Communication, University of Illinois at Urbana-Champaign.

DELIA, J.G., and CLARK, R.A. (1977). "Cognitive complexity, social perception, and the development of listener-adapted communication in six-, eight-, ten-, and twelve-year-old boys." Communication Monographs, 44:326-345.

———, and SWITZER, D.E. (1974). "Cognitive complexity and impression formation in informal social interaction." Speech Monographs, 41:299-308.

DELIA, J.G., and CROCKETT, W.H. (1973). "Social schemas, cognitive complexity, and the learning of social structures." Journal of Personality, 41:413-429.

———, PRESS, A.N., and O'KEEFE, D.J. (1975). "The dependence of interpersonal evaluations on context relevant beliefs about the other." Speech Monographs, 42:10-19.

DELIA, J.G., KLINE, S.L., and BURLESON, B.R. (1978). "A constructivist analysis of communicative development in childhood and adolescence." Paper presented at the anual meeting of the Speech Communication Association.

ELKIND, D. (1970). Childhood and adolescence. New York: Oxford University Press.

FEFFER, M.H. (1959). "The cognitive implications of role-taking behavior." Journal of Personality, 27:152-168.

——— (1970). "A developmental analysis of interpersonal behavior." Psychological Review, 77:197-214.

FLAVELL, J.H., in collaboration with BOTKIN, P.T., FRY, C.L., WRIGHT, J.W., and JARVIS, P.E. (1968). Role-taking and communication skills in children. New York: Wiley.

GLUCKSBERG, S., KRAUSS, R., and HIGGINS, E.T. (1975). "The development of referential communication skills." In F.R. Horowitz (ed.), Review of child development research, Vol. 4. Chicago: University of Chicago Press.

HALE, C.L., and DELIA, J.G. (1976). "Cognitive complexity and social perspective-taking." Communication Monographs, 43:195-203.

HEIDER, F. (1958). The psychology of interpersonal relations. New York: Wiley.

HIGGINS, E.T. (1976). "Social class differences in verbal communicative accuracy: A question of 'which question?' " Psychological Bulletin, 83:695-714.

HYMES, D. (1974). Foundations in sociolinguistics: An ethnographic approach. Philadelphia: University of Pennsylvania Press.

KELLY, G.A. (1955). The psychology of personal constructs (2 vols.). New York: W.W. Norton.

KLYVER, N., PRESS, A.N., and CROCKETT, W.H. (1972). "Cognitive complexity and the sequential integration of inconsistent information." Paper presented at the Eastern Psychological Association Convention.

KRAUSS, R.M., and GLUCKSBERG, S. (1970). "Socialization of communication skills." In R.A. Hoppe, G.A. Milton, and E.C. Simmel (eds.), Early experience and the processes of socialization. New York: Academic Press.

KURDEK, L.A., and RODGON, M.M. (1975). "Perceptual, cognitive, and affective perspective-taking in kindergarten through sixth-grade children." Developmental Psychology, 11:643-650.

LANGER, J. (1969). Theories of development. New York: Holt, Rinehart, and Winston.

LIVESLEY, W.J., and BROMLEY, D.B. (1973). Person perception in childhood and adolescence. New York: Wiley.

LOOFT, W.R. (1972). "Egocentrism and social interaction across the lifespan." Psychological Bulletin, 78:75-92.

MAYO, C.W., and CROCKETT, W.H. (1964). "Cognitive complexity and primacy-recency effects in impression formation." Journal of Abnormal and Social Psychology, 68:335-338.

MEAD, G.H. (1934). Mind, self, and society. Chicago: University of Chicago Press.

MEHRABIAN, A. (1968). An analysis of personality theories. Englewood Cliffs, N.J.: Prentice-Hall.

NIDORF, L.J., and CROCKETT, W.H. (1965). "Cognitive complexity and the organization of impressions of others." Journal of Social Psychology, 66:165-169.

O'KEEFE, D.J., and BRADY, R.M. (1978). "Cognitive complexity and attitude change." Unpublished manuscript, Department of Speech Communication and Theatre, University of Michigan.

O'KEEFE, B.J., and DELIA, J.G. (1978a). "Construct comprehensiveness and cognitive complexity as predictors of the number and strategic adaptation of arguments and appeals in a persuasive message." Unpublished manuscript, Department of Speech Communication, Theatre, and Journalism, Wayne State University.

——— (1978b). "Construct comprehensiveness and cognitive complexity." Perceptual and Motor Skills, 46:548-550.

———, and O'KEEFE, D.J. (1978). "Interaction analysis and the analysis of interaction." Unpublished paper, University of Illinois.

PIAGET, J. (1955). The language and thought of the child (M. Gabain, trans.). New York: World.

PRESS, A.N., CROCKETT, W.H., and DELIA, J.G. (1975). "Effects of cognitive complexity and of perceiver's set upon the organization of impressions." Journal of Personality and Social Psychology, 32:865-872.

PRESS, A.N., CROCKETT, W.H., and ROSENKRANTZ, P.S. (1969). "Cognitive complexity and the learning of balanced and unbalanced social structures." Journal of Personality, 37:541-553.

PRESS, A.N., SCARLETT, H.H., and CROCKETT, W.H. (1973). "The organization of children's descriptions: A Wernerian developmental analysis." Paper presented at the biennial meeting of the Society for Research in Child Development.

RITTER, E.M. (forthcoming). "Social perspective-taking ability, cognitive complexity, and listener-adapted communication in early and late adolescence." Communication Monographs.

ROSENBACH, D., CROCKETT, W.H., and WAPNER, S. (1973). "Developmental level, emotional involvement, and the resolution of inconsistency in impression formation." Developmental Psychology, 8:120-130.

SCARLETT, H.H., PRESS, A.N., and CROCKETT, W.H. (1971). "Children's descriptions of peers: A Wernerian developmental analysis." Child Development, 42:439-453.

SHANTZ, C.U. (1975). "The development of social cognition." In E.M. Hetherington (ed.), Review of child development research, Vol. 5. Chicago: University of Chicago Press.

WATZLAWICK, P., BEAVIN, J.M., and JACKSON, D.D. (1967). Pragmatics of human communication: A study of interactional patterns, pathologies, and and paradoxes. New York: W.W. Norton.

WERNER, H. (1957). "The concept of development from a comparative and organismic point of view." In D.B. Harris (ed.), The concept of development. Minneapolis: University of Minnesota Press.

WIENER, M., DEVOE, S., RUBINOW, S., and GELLER, J. (1972). "Nonverbal behavior and nonverbal communication." Psychological Review, 79:185-214.

Chapter 7

LANGUAGE AND COGNITION
IN THE DEVELOPING CHILD

Norman Elliott

WATCHING A CHILD GROW through the years involves two particularly intriguing aspects of development: the child coming to understand his environment and his or her learning to talk with others. Whether as parents, relatives, or other observers, we intuitively deal with cognitive growth and linguistic development as distinct phenomena. We commonly attribute to the child prelinguistic comprehension and intention and treat the infant's babbling as prerational speech. But we also intuitively assume an obvious relationship between the two distinct phenomena. Noting the child distinguishing between orange juice and lemonade by calling the latter "lemon juice" or commenting that "she's really smart" after the utterance of a particularly adult-like sentence, reflects our belief in the interconnection between the development of language and thought in children.

At the general level, can we say that a relationship between development of thought and language exists? A survey of the developmental literature leaves little doubt that scholars believe there is a general and necessary relationship between linguistic and cognitive growth.[1] It is considerably less clear, however, just what that relationship is. As Schaff (1973:84) notes:

[187]

> Theoretically, developmental psychology ought to provide the most
> important data for . . . the problem of the relationship between
> thinking and language. Unfortunately, it does not. . . . [A]nalysis of
> the relevant available literature reveals that such is the case.

Schaff's frustration seems well motivated as scholarly work
dealing with the relationship between cognitive growth and
language development yields no consensus on the matter. Indeed, this work is characterized by a number of explicit positions in opposition to each other on the one hand, and writers
who are less explicit in their assessments, thereby permitting the
possibility of a number of different descriptions of the relationship on the other. For example, Slobin (1972:180), operating
from the perspective of "Cognitive Prerequisites for the Development of Grammar," holds that "a child cannot begin to use a
given linguistic form meaningfully until he is able to understand
what it means." By contrast, Luria (1961:28) approaches the
relationship in terms of "The Role of Speech in the Formation
of Mental Processes" and investigates "the readjusting of mental
processes under the influence of speech."

The search for a general relationship is frustrated by the
instance of various descriptions that apparently conflict. Jerome
Bruner (1966:37, 47) indicates that "the very use of language
presupposes certain underlying cognitive processes required for
its use" followed by the observation that:

> One is thus led to believe that, in order for the child to use language
> as an instrument of thought, he must first bring the world of
> experience under the control of principles of organization that are in
> some degree isomorphic with the structural principles of syntax.

To add to the confusion, the same data and theories are often
used to support differing descriptions of the relationship. Particularly, Piaget's extensive work is often cited as evidence for a
full range of possible relationships:

> This confirms Piaget's theory that knowledge has its roots in activ-
> ity, and that its logical organization is not derived from language. . . .
> [T]he prudent conclusion can be drawn that language acquisition is
> closely linked to cognition in two fundamental ways: first because
> meaning implies knowing, and second because the linguistic rule
> system is an example of human organizational abilities that permit

not only construction of a grammar but also that of physics and logic. [Sinclair, 1975:224, 237.]

The developing child masters syntax of speech before syntax of thought. Piaget's studies proved that grammar develops before logic and that the child learns relatively late the mental operations corresponding to the verbal forms he has been using for a long time. [Vygotsky, 1962:46-47.]

In agreement with Piaget's theory, no specific symbol system or medium is a prerequisite for the development of preoperatory to formal thinking. [Furth and Youniss, 1975:167.]

Considerable thought and investigation have left the nature of the general relationship between cognitive and linguistic development unresolved. Edward Sapir (1921:15-17), whose notions on the role of language in concept formation are well-known as the Sapir-Whorf hypothesis, voices this lack of resolve. In one place, he says:

It is, indeed, in the highest degree likely that language is an instrument originally put to uses lower than the conceptual plane and that thought arises as a refined interpretation of its content. The product grows, in other words, with the instrument, and thought may be no more conceivable, in its genesis and daily practice, without speech than is mathematical reasoning practicable without the lever of an appropriate mathematical symbolism.

While on the next page he concedes that:

The point of view we have developed does not by any means preclude the possibility of the growth of speech being in a high degree dependent on the development of thought. . . . We see this complex process of the interaction of language and thought actually taking place under our eyes. The instrument makes possible the product, the product refines the instrument.

My effort to obtain an understanding of the general relationship between the development of thought and language is initially motivated by the lack of consensus itself. As with Averroes (1954:318), "[T]hose things whose causes are not perceived are still unknown and must be investigated, precisely because their causes are not perceived." Both in and out of the academic community, we strive for and value understanding of phenomena at a broad, generalized level. That we commonly use highly general conceptualizations to interpret our observations seems apparent enough. In short, it would be nice to have a general description of the relationship between language and thought in the developing child.

A different perspective, however, might be brought to bear on the matter. It could be argued that the failure of any general relationship to emerge is a function of the highly complex and interactive nature of the relationship itself. The complexity of the relationship is such that any general account of it would be so imprecise as to be inappropriate.

While I think the major premise of this argument is reasonable in some cases, I am not persuaded to its conclusion. Failure to describe the mediation of air pressure, for example, in the relationship of heat to the physical state of water is imprecise, but does not invalidate a useful understanding. More directly, the complex and interactive nature of the relationship between stimulus properties and certain neurophysiological events involved in visual perception does not preclude generalized descriptions of, say, figure-ground preferences. In fact, the articulation of a highly generalized relationship can facilitate the evolution of a more precise understanding as seems to be the case of work into psychological drive and behavior (Bradac and Elliott, 1975). Furthermore, the suggestion that the relationship between linguistic and cognitive development is not amenable to general description is, itself, speculative. Not enough is known about the details of this relationship to necessitate the rejection of a general description as inappropriate. In sum, it would still be nice to be able to make a general developmental description of the language-thought relationship, or at least have a clearer basis for the determination that no general relationship holds.

There is yet another perspective, however, from which to view the need for clarification of this relationship. Regardless of the appropriateness of a general conceptualization, researchers continue to hold such conceptualizations. Work has been influenced by assumptions, to varying degrees of explicitness, about the relationship between cognitive growth and linguistic development. In some instances one relationship is assumed to operate, while another is held in other instances. The resultant research is influenced both in terms of the problems posed and in the design of the investigations. Mosher and Hornsby (1966), for example, treat cognitive development as an independent variable with language behavior being dependent. This contrasts with a series of studies by Khomskaya, Martsinovskaya, and others that Luria (1969) describes where verbal behavior is controlled or treated as independent to account for differential performances on various perceptual and functional tasks.

If conduct of research will be underlain and guided by broad assumptions, then a clarification of our assumption about the developmental relationship between thought and language seems a worthy enterprise. At the least, such a clarification would provide a common framing for the assessment of data and collation of disparate lines of research.

This inquiry will attempt to determine what general relationship exists, if any, between the development of thought and language. The relevant theory and research is first examined with an eye to selecting those possible positions that seem likely. I suggest three: the cognitive, the linguistic, and the reciprocal positions. The *theoretical* relationship between cognitive and linguistic development described by each of these three positions is then used to generate a more testable model of association. Results of a study are presented to permit specification of these general theoretical relationships in terms of the *empirical* relationships observed in a sample of children.

THE POSSIBILITIES

THE COGNITIVE POSITION

The cognitive position describes a relationship where cognitive development precedes and influences the development of language. The work of Piaget, which focuses on the developing structure of thought as it underlies various human abilities and behaviors, is an obvious source of the position that linguistic growth is dependent on an antecedently developing cognitive framework. The excellent interpreter-critic of Piaget, John

Flavell (1963:270), capsulizes the Piagetian view of the thought-language relationship, especially as it was expressed in Piaget's earlier works:

> The major theme of *The Language and Thought of the Child* (and, in a sense, all of the early books) is that the child's cognitive structure, the kind of logic his thinking possesses, gets expressed in his use of language. Thus, language behavior is here treated as the dependent variable with cognition as the independent variable; language is viewed essentially as a symptom of underlying intellectual orientation.

In a test of this conceptualization, Parisi and Antinucci (1970) focus on the comprehension and expression of spatial relationships. Piaget and Inhelder's (1948) work indicates that children first acquire notions of *simple* topological space, then only later develop the concepts of *dimensional* or Euclidian space. To these, a third level of conception can be added for *complex* spatial relations such as "along" and "through." Using a drawing task, Parisi and Antinucci observed Italian children applying a variety of spatial locatives including "in" and "on" (simple), "in front of," "below," and "beside" (dimensional), and "along" and "through" (complex). They found that the children had little trouble in correctly using the simple locatives, somewhat more difficulty with the dimensional words, and encountered the most problems with the complex spatial words. This synchronous evidence is consistent with Roger Brown's (1973) longitudinal data in which the three children he observed were using "in" and "on" while not expressing the more complex spatial notions.

These same general findings have been obtained in studies looking at the conception and expression of negation conducted by the McNeills (1968) and Bloom's (1970) investigation of possession. Of crucial importance here is the implication that children develop a concept (such as spatial location, general negation, object possession) *prior to* their ability to express that concept linguistically. Such observations and inferences underlie the general cognitive position that cognitive growth precedes and influences linguistic growth.

Slobin (1974:114) expresses the cognitive position when he concludes that "the work of Piaget's school strongly suggests that language more often *reflects* rather than *determines* cognitive development." The cognitive position is summarized below.

LINGUISTIC POSITION

The linguistic position posits the opposite relationship where cognitive growth is seen as a consequence of language use and development. Central to the linguistic position is the notion that speech is a necessary and compelling mediator of increased cognitive growth. A child progresses through a series of increasingly different and complex uses of language, which consequently result in changes in cognitive functioning. Muller (1969:166) takes this perspective when he cites Boutan's studies in the early 20th century as having "shown that, until the development of language, the baby acts more or less like an animal; as soon as he begins to speak, he acts differently and solves problems which an animal would not be able to deal with."

But the linguistic position stems most identifiably from the distinct philosophical perspective of human mentality in Soviet psychology. In an interesting view of the historical background for current developmental research, Alexander Luria (1969: 128) describes the "idealistic" psychology of the West where "the higher psychological functions ... are seen as primitive

Figure 1: COGNITIVE MODEL

1. Cognitive development precedes and influences linguistic development.
2. Linguistic development, like other human capabilities, is a product of an underlying, more fundamental growth of intelligence.

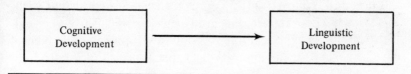

forms of existence of the mind." Even Piaget, whom he lauds
for recognizing the close interrelation of the child's speaking
and thinking, must be similarly criticized for treating the child
initially as a creature of deep instincts whose behavior is only
later influenced by social interaction.

This basic stance is contrasted with the "materialistic"
psychology of the Soviet Union which posits that the child is
crucially a social being from birth. Luria (1969:128) outlines
the linguistic approach:

> The task is to trace how the forms of association connecting the
> child with surrounding adults are changed; how the elementary,
> direct forms of association which initially have an emotional-active
> character gradually become conditioned by speech; how this verbal
> behavior becomes separated from overall behavior into a special
> activity depending on a system of language; and how on the basis of
> these complex forms of verbal associations new forms of mental
> activity, which are social in their origin and speech-conditioned in
> their structure, begin.

While the cognitive position looks first to developing cognitive states, then to language use as reflectons of these states, the
linguistic approach starts with language behavior then moves to
resultant changes in cognition as consequences of this behavior.

Just as Piaget is thought of as the leading theorist of the
cognitive approach, the linguistic view is most often associated
with Lev Vygotsky. The causal role of language in thought
development is described by Vygotsky (1962:56) in his classic
work, *Thought and Language:*

> All the higher psychic functions are mediated processes, and signs
> are the basic means used to master and direct them. The mediating
> sign is incorporated in their structure as an indispensable, indeed the
> central, part of the total process. In concept formation, that sign is
> the *word,* which first plays the role of means in forming a concept
> and later becomes its symbol.

Luria and Yudovich (1956) provide evidence consistent with
this view. They report the study of a pair of five-year-old
identical twins who exhibited poor development of language
and, importantly, the absence of "typical forms" of intellectual

behavior such as role playing, common object play, and organized drawing. The twins were then separated and housed in different nursery school groups. After three months the experimenters observed obvious improvements in these indicants of cognitive development. They reasoned that the separation drastically increased the need to communicate (other than with each other), which was responded to by developing the "speech forms of normal intercourse," which in turn permitted changes in their cognitive functioning.

A long series of Soviet studies attempts to specify the evolution of verbal associations (the development of word meanings by children from *using* words) and their generalization into higher-order associations. For example, Samsonova found that verbalization "led to the elaboration of finer and firmer discriminations" by children of subtle stimulus differences, Shipilova and Surina report that such discriminations are made from 1.5 to 3 times faster than silent judgments, and Lyublinskaya demonstrated the role of verbal labels in identifying the critical attributes of objects for making such discriminations.[2]

These studies and others, along with several investigations of his own, have led Luria to describe the mediating role of language in thought development in terms of the succession of first "orienting" responses, then "releasing" them, and finally serving a "selective" and even "preselective" function in guiding behavior in a given environment. For Luria (1969:135), the evidence is clear as to "the unity of thinking and speech and the description of the stages in the formation of thinking together with *their dependence* on the formation of word meanings [emphasis mine]."

RECIPROCAL POSITION

While Piaget's cognitive position focuses on the child and the primacy of intellectual growth attendant to the child's contact with and action on his or her environment, the linguistic perspective of Vygotsky, reversing this focus, concenters on the social context into which the child is born. The former describes language development as underlain by the internally inspired growth of thinking, while the latter views thought as the product of an externally motivated expansion of language use and capacity. In apparent appreciation of both views, Jerome Bruner (1964:1) presents the general underpinnings of the reciprocal position:

> I shall take the view . . . that the development of human intellectual functioning from infancy to such perfection as it may reach is shaped by a series of technological advances in the use of mind. Growth depends upon the mastery of techniques and cannot be understood without reference to such mastery. These techniques are not, in the main, inventions of the individuals who are "growing up;" they are, rather, skills transmitted with varying efficiency and success by the culture—language being a prime example. Cognitive growth, then, is in a major way from the outside in as well as from the inside out.

For Bruner, understanding the relationship between thought and language requires this initial insight. Specifically, he views development as a function of the media used by individuals to represent their experience with the environment. Development, from this perspective, can be described as the successive employment of three ordered modes of representation: enactive, iconic, and symbolic. The enactive mode is representation through appropriate action. Like bicycle riding or tying knots, aspects of experience are represented as motor responses. Iconic medium, by contrast, represents events through images available and derived from the perceptual field. Representation by

Figure 2: LINGUISTIC MODEL

1. Linguistic development precedes and influences cognitive development.

2. Cognitive development is mediated by language and can be viewed as the product of linguistic development.

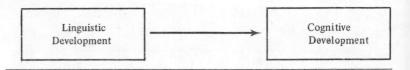

symbolic media adds additional capabilities including arbitrariness and remote reference.

The reciprocal position on the relationship of cognitive and linguistic development can now be specified. From infancy, young children interact with their environment by increasing employment of representational devices of experience. Intellectual development proceeds as individuals are increasingly more able to represent past experience for present and future use. The very young child accomplishes such "learning" primarily through enactive means. As the level of cognitive functioning rises, the child's representation of experience also changes, moving from the domain of action, to that of images, and finally to the use of symbols. In this way language, being the most obvious instrument of symbolic representation, is crucially influenced by antecedent cognitive development. *Its* employment by the child, however, becomes the primary source of subsequent intellectual growth. Bruner (1964:13-14) observes that:

> Translation of experience into symbolic form, with its attendant means of achieving remote reference, transformation, and combination, opens up realms of intellectual possibility that are orders of magnitude beyond the most powerful image forming system.

A variety of experiments demonstrate these effects of linguistic representation on increased cognitive growth. For example, Bruner and Olver's (1970) findings in a study of object grouping and equivalence imply a link between linguistically less-developed children and perceptually bound problem-solving strategies (iconic representation) which contrasted with the perceptually freed strategies (symbolic representation) of older children with a more progressed development of language. This general implication is supported by Bruner and Kenney's (Bruner, 1964) experiment on two-dimensional classification, Mosher and Hornsby's (1966) "twenty questions" studies, Olson's (1966) studies of conceptual strategies, and others.

These findings point to the crux of the reciprocal position that cognitive development progresses prior to the advent of language, compelling increasingly more powerful means of representing experience, and climaxing with the "most power-ful" mode, language. The availability of linguistic representation of experience results in a qualitative shift in the child's under-standing, problem solving, and so forth. As Olver and Hornsby (1966:85) conclude:

> With the development of symbolic representation, the child is freed from dependence upon moment-to-moment variation in perceptual vividness and is able to keep the basis of [judgment] invariant.

In sum, work from the Brunerian point of view supports a reciprocal relationship between cognitive and linguistic develop-ment[3] where the cognitive position is taken to be correct for younger, *presymbolic* children. But,

> Once the child has succeeded in internalizing language as a cognitive instrument, it becomes possible for him to represent and systemati-cally transform the regularities of experience with far greater flex-ibility and power than before. [Bruner, 1964:4]

For this reason, the relationship changes such that the linguistic position is thought to be the appropriate one for older, *sym-bolic* children.

SUMMARY

In attempting to describe the general relationship between language and cognition in the developing child, three possibil-

Figure 3: RECIPROCAL MODEL

1. From the beginning of life, cognitive development precedes and influences linguis-tic development.

2. When language becomes a general means for representing experience, language can be said to precede and influence cognitive development.

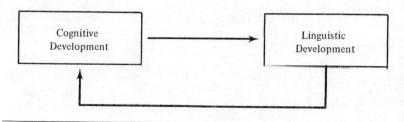

ities have been identified: (1) the *cognitive position,* consistent with Piaget, which holds that linguistic development is a product of the underlying, antecedent growth of cognition; (2) the *linguistic position,* following Vygotsky, which views cognitive development as a mediated result of increased development and use of language; and (3) the *reciprocal position,* suggested by Bruner, where cognitive development precedes and influences language development in younger children to a period when symbolic media become the general means for representing experience. After this period, the relationship becomes reversed and increased language development produces growth to higher cognitive levels.

Clearly, the temptation to assume that a given position represents the "core" of a particular scholar's developmental theory should be avoided. In most cases, the works reviewed constitute attempts at understanding early human development in terms of the processes and behaviors believed by the investigators to be most demonstrative of that development. My purpose has been to describe how the relationship between language and cognitive growth, treated globally, is expressed or implied in these works. Given this aim, the reader should be clear that while these positions are consistent with the theories referenced, they are in some ways selective, and more obviously nondetailed, when compared to the comprehensive developmental perspectives of the scholars reviewed.

These three positions provide theoretical guidance for describing a general language-cognition relationship in development. It will now be useful to specify these alternative relationships empirically. To do this the cognitive and linguistic functioning of a group of children was observed.

THE EMPIRICAL RELATIONSHIP

Data were collected from 37 children living in Iowa City and Coralville, Iowa, and Columbus, Ohio. These children were selected for study because of their accessibility to the investigator, the belief that they are, as a group, fairly representative of

American middle-class children, and the group's diversity of age. The children's ages ranged from 3 years, 10 months to 8 years, 10 months. Such a range of ages, I believe, permits investigation of cognitive and linguistic functioning through a variety of levels of development. The investigator was either known by the parents of these children, or was recommended by a friend of the parents, which permitted observation and testing of the children in their own homes without the presence of others.

Two measures, one of cognitive development and another of linguistic development, were needed.[4] Because the purpose of this investigation was to examine the relationship of thought and language development at the general level, I believed it to be important to approach the measurement of these constructs from a broad conception. Thus, for measuring the construct "general cognitive development" (and likewise "general language development"), a strategy which sought to assess growth of the common underlying process in terms of a wide range of different manifestations of it was favored.

COGNITIVE DEVELOPMENT

Cognitive development of the children is assessed from performance on a number of primarily Piagetian-type tasks in five areas of intellectual functioning: (1) time, distance, and velocity concepts, (2) classification and inclusion relations, (3) spatial relations and proportion, (4) transformational imagery, and (5) visual perception of illusion. Within each of these areas, the child's performance on the various tasks was used to generate a component score for that area of functioning. The five component scores were then cross-correlated for submission to a factor analysis. Factor analyzing the intercorrelations of these five tests provided evidence for treating the five scales jointly as a measure of a single dimension (general cognitive development). Confirmation of the unifactorial interpretation of these five scores then permitted construction of a single measure of overall cognitive development.

LINGUISTIC DEVELOPMENT

Stemming from the assumption that the level of development of children's linguistic capacities may not be accurately reflected in their language use, studies have usefully employed "recognition tasks" to measure language competence. As with cognitive development, measurement of the children's levels of linguistic functioning was approached broadly using such recognition tasks to assess their understanding of sentences in different grammatical forms. One set of tests contained passive sentences (the cowboy hit the Indian versus the Indian was hit by the cowboy) while another set measured recognition of sentences having undergone extraposition (when he got tired, John went to bed versus John went to bed when he got tired). While these two measures were designed for sensitivity among the more linguistically immature members of the sample, a third procedure was used to discriminate more sophisticated language competence. Borrowing heavily from Carol Chomsky's (1969) experiments, a third component measure was generated for understanding of more complex syntactic structures. These three scores, along with a measure of vocabulary development, were used to assess the overall language development of the children.

Specifically, language development was measured on (a) recognition of passivized transformational variants, (b) recognition of extraposed transformational variants, (c) understanding of complex reduced structures, and (d) vocabulary development. As before, these four component measures were intercorrelated and a factor analysis gave evidence that they are underlain by a common dimension (general language development). The four scores were then used to construct a single measure of linguistic development.

ASSESSING THE EMPIRICAL RELATIONSHIP

The relationship between language and thought in the developing child is assessed by means of correlation and regression analyses of the data. In particular, these techniques are used to scrutinize the empirical relationships between linguistic (LD) and cognitive development (CD) across time. An understanding of the dimension of time in analysis of developmental phenomena provides a useful rationale for specifying this study's analytic procedure.

"Development" is just change associated with time. Cognitive and linguistic development, as processes, are essentially observable as changes in state over time (standardly interpreted as "progressive" or "regressive" change over time). The pervasive scale of development is time; in terms of any particular developing individual, that pervasive scale is age. So to speak of the development of language, for example, of a particular child, we must treat the child's language observed at age four (time 1) as less developed in a consideration of language development that includes knowledge (from observation) of that child's language at age seven (time 2).

In statistical terms, development implies that the average observation of a state in four year olds represents "less development" when a similar average of observations of this state for seven year olds is known. If our purpose is understanding and explaining various developmental processes taken one at a time, this pervasive age scale is often useful as an informal marker of subsequent stages in development, especially as particular developmental processes roughly relate to one another or to "overall" development. If, on the other hand, our purpose is to understand and explain the co-occurence of two developmental processes *in terms of one another,* changes in both processes associated with this pervasive age scale are confounded with the unique interdependence of the two processes. The nature and extent of dependence of one developmental process on another is clouded by the change in that dependent process that necessarily (i.e., it is "developmental") occurs over time.

Taking the cognitive model for example, what is of interest here is the change in language than can be systematically understood *only* with knowledge of change in cognition. In any developmental study, time (or age) is a crucial and pervasive dimension. In a developmental study of the relationship between two processes though, time is a crucial but theoretically uninteresting dimension. In the present example, the analyst might naively specify the relationship CD → LD by accounting for change in LD from change in CD. This makes the double error of ignoring the crucial effect of time on values of LD while confounding the uninteresting effects of time with CD. The relevant question for analysis is how much (or to what extent) change in LD is understandable from knowledge of change in CD alone. So stated, the analysis logically must proceed by first removing, or otherwise controlling for, that part of the change in LD that is given by knowledge of change in time (or age) alone. The analyst then is in a position to relate additional change in LD directly to CD. As AGE is confounded (i.e., correlates highly) with innumerable physiological, social, and experiential dimensions of growth, direct assessment of the unique variation in LD explainable from CD can only be made after these confounding and theoretically uninteresting influences are removed.

COGNITIVE MODEL

Starting with the cognitive position, the association between growth of thought and language can be presented in a more empirically specifiable form if certain assumptions about the relationship are made explicit. This theoretical position describes cognitive development as temporally antecedent to language development and responsible for its growth. In other words, this position posits a particular causal relationship, such that CD is temporally prior to LD and changes in CD will produce systematic changes in LD. Interpretation of the empirical relationship is further simplified by assuming that the causal relationship is linear and that LD generally increases with age.

Thus described, the cognitive position is represented by a theoretical model which treats language development as a linear function of age and cognitive development (AGE, CD → LD). Empirical assessment of the model is made by regressing LD scores, in two steps, on Age (AGE → LD) and cognitive development (AGE, CD → LD).[5]

The analytic intent here is initially to determine if the overall model is viable; that is, does the model (AGE, CD) account for a substantial and significant portion of variation in language development across the sample with a tolerable amount of error.[6] But more importantly, is the hypothesized *causal* role of cognitive development on variation in language development supported by the data? This assessment can be made from the joint perspective of causal variable (CD) influence and effect variable (LD) determination. More specifically, empirical support for the causal claim of the cognitive model requires *both* evidence that (a) CD accounts for a significant portion of LD variation beyond what is accounted for by AGE, and (b) variation in LD is sufficiently determined by change in CD (i.e., AGE does not significantly improve the determination of LD variation beyond what is attributable to CD).

Throughout the three models, the strong positive correlations of age with the various causal variables raises the potential for interpretive confusion in assessing relative independent variable effects on dependent variable change. To avoid this potential for confusion due to high collinearity, evidence of (a) and (b) was sought in terms of the semipartial correlation of LD and CD, controlling CD alone for age (or the value and significance of R^2 change resulting from the addition of CD on the second step to the AGE → LD regression) and the unbiased reestimation of beta values (and appropriate F-tests of significance) produced by applying Huang's (1970) method of imposing linear restrictions on the coefficients.

LINGUISTIC MODEL

Analytic assessment of the linguistic position proceeds like the analysis of the cognitive position. In this case, however, the aim is to account for changes in cognitive development, and crucially, the CD dependence on language development. Appropriately, CD is treated as a linear function of age and LD (AGE, LD → CD) and comparable regression analyses are made.

RECIPROCAL MODEL

Recall that the reciprocal position describes a relationship like the cognitive model for younger presymbolic children (CD → LD) which changes to parallel the linguistic model (LD → CD) in older symbolic children. Performance on a transformational imagery test[7] was used to divide the children into presymbolic (N = 16) and symbolic (N = 21) samples. The analytic procedure described earlier was then applied separately to each of the two samples employing the appropriate models from the reciprocal view. Information was also generated on the "alternative" to the reciprocal model (i.e., the opposite of the

Table 1: INDEPENDENT CONTRIBUTIONS OF CAUSAL VARIABLE AND AGE TO FUNCTIONAL DETERMINATION OF EFFECT VARIABLE CHANGE AND REESTIMATED REGRESSION COEFFICIENTS FOR THE THREE MODELS AND THE ALTERNATIVE TO THE RECIPROCAL MODEL

Model (Dependent Variable)	R^2 Change due to CAUSAL Var. (x 100)	R^2 Change due to AGE (x 100)	Reestimated Betas AGE (b_1)	CAUSAL Var. (b_2)
Cognitive (LD)	8.8%*	7.7%*	.77*	.24 –
Linguistic (CD)	15.8%*	0.0%	.10	.90*
Reciprocal Presymbolic (LD)	16.4%*	0.1%	.49	.51 –
Symbolic (CD)	18.1%*	0.5%	.08	.93*
Alternative Presymbolic (CD)	11.6%*	4.2%+	.51 –	.49
Symbolic (LD)	7.0%*	23.7%*	.79*	.21

*Significant (p < .01)
+Significant (p < .025)
–Significant (p < .05)

reciprocal model or LD → CD in presymbolic and CD → LD in symbolic samples). The results of these analyses are presented in Table 1.

FINDINGS

(1) *The cognitive, linguistic, and reciprocal models are found to be initially viable in that each adequately accounts for change in the dependent variable with a minimal amount of error.* Specifically, each of the three models is able to describe a statistically significant[8] portion of change in the effect variable as a function of change in age and the causal variable (R^2 X100=90.3%, 82.3% and 86.1%/62.3%, respectively). Further, this functional determination of the various dependent variables is accomplished with a tolerable level of error. The conservative requirement that model estimates vary half as much as the variance of the dependent variable was met in each of the three instances (SEE = .32, .43, and .26/.41, respectively).

(2) *The evidence does not support the cognitive model across the entire sample of children.* It was observed that the addition of CD to the functional determination of LD variation by AGE alone (AGE → LD) produced a statistically significant increase in the amount of LD change accounted for by the model (8.8%) consistent with the cognitive position. But the adequacy of the cognitive model becomes suspect when we notice that AGE also significantly increases the determination of LD variance (7.7%) beyond what is given by a functional dependence on CD alone (CD → LD). If LD is causally dependent on CD, then not only should knowledge of CD significantly *improve* one's ability to account for LD changes (it does), but also such knowledge should be *sufficient* to account for the variation in LD that is observed (it is not). The hypothesized relationship that changes in CD causally result in changes in LD is not empirically borne out in the observation that variation in LD is not adequately explained by CD, but requires knowledge of AGE.

This suspicion about the cognitive position is reenforced by an examination of the regression coefficients for AGE and CD from the model. As originally estimated, the contributions of AGE (.48) and CD (.52) to variation in language development were about the same with each contribution being statistically significant. Application of Huang's reestimation method for sorting out the unique contributions of each, however, reveals that AGE (.77) is more important than CD (.24) in determining LD change.

The empirical evidence that LD change is determined as well by AGE as it is by CD casts serious doubt on the adequacy of this position. It is inconsistent to claim that language development is causally dependent on cognitive development and then find that children's language development can be better understood as a function of their age than it can as a function of their level of cognitive development.

(3) *The evidence does support the linguistic model across the entire sample of children.* The functional dependence of CD on AGE alone (AGE → CD) permits the determination of 66.76% of the change in CD. When LD is added to the model, however, this determination rises to 82.57%, a statistically significant increase of 15.81%. By comparison, the proportion of CD variation that is given by a functional dependence on LD alone (LD → CD) is found to be 82.56%. The addition of AGE to this function (LD, AGE → CD) contributes almost nothing (.01%). This is the pattern of results consistent with the hypothesized causality that was not found for the cognitive model. These findings support the claims of the linguistic position that LD alone is a significant contributing factor to observed variation in CD, and that explanation of CD change crucially requires knowledge of LD (knowledge of AGE, for example, is not needed). The values and significance of the model's regression coefficients are likewise consistent with the linguistic position.

(4) *In the* presymbolic *group of children, the data are consistent with the reciprocal model (CD → LD) while failing to support the linguistic model.* Addition of cognitive development to the linear function (AGE → LD) allows one to account for a

statistically significant 16.41% of additional variation in LD. The comparable contribution of AGE to the variance of LD beyond that which is functionally determined by cognitive development (CD → LD) is a nonsignificant .07%. By contrast, the linguistic model (information listed under "Alternative" to reciprocal model in Table 1) is not so clearly substantiated. While knowledge of language development significantly improves the proportion of CD variance accounted for by age (by 11.55%), change in CD among presymbolic children is not adequately explained by a functional dependence on LD alone (LD→CD). Though the addition of age improves the determination of CD variation by an amount less than that attributable to LD, the R^2 change of 4.17% is statistically significant at the .025 level. That is to say that while the effect of LD on CD variation may be greater than the effect of age, both explain a significant portion of CD change beyond what is attributable to the other. This finding does not support the causal role of language development posited by the linguistic position.

Comparative interpretation of the beta estimates associated with the models provides additional support for the reciprocal position while failing to support the linguistic model on the presymbolic sample. As originally estimated, the coefficient for CD (.88) is a significant determiner of LD change, while the age beta (.06) is not. This supports the claim of LD's causal dependence on CD from the reciprocal position. The causal claim of the linguistic position, however, is seriously questioned as the coefficients for both LD (.62) and AGE (.37) are found to be significant to the functional determination of CD variation (but at the .01 and .025 levels, respectively). The regression coefficient reestimates also exhibit support for favoring the reciprocal model over the linguistic one, but in a less than overwhelming manner. Consistent with the reciprocal position, cognitive development (.51) is found to make a significant contribution to accounting for change in language development while age (.49) does not (at the .05 level). Inconsistent with the linguistic model, age (.51) is significant to the determination of variation in cognitive development, but the contribution of linguistic development (.49) is nonsignificant (at .05). It must be noted though that the differences between these values are very small and should be taken as most tentative indicators.

But this limited evidence, when coupled with the more clear pattern of results from the R^2 change/semipartial correlation analyses (as well as the somewhat qualified indications of the original beta estimates), leads me to accept the relationship given by the reciprocal position (CD → LD) for the presymbolic group. Given the qualifications on these results, the evidence is consistent that change in language development is significantly and sufficiently determined by knowledge of cognitive development. The alternative relationship (the linguistic position, LD → CD) is not supported by the data in that age is found to account significantly for cognitive development variation beyond what can be attributed to a dependence on language development. The initial claim of the reciprocal position is then supported.

(5) *In the* symbolic *group of children, the data are consistent with the reciprocal model (LD → CD) while failing to support the cognitive model.* This second part of the reciprocal model is quickly confirmed. As this part of the reciprocal position makes the identical claim of the linguistic model, it is not surprising that the data give unambiguous support for this relationship in the symbolic group. Adding LD to the function (AGE → CD) produces a significant increase in CD change explained (18.12%), while the comparable addition of AGE to (LD → CD) yields a small (.49%) and nonsignificant increase. The alternative relationship (cognitive model) for the symbolic sample is correspondingly rejected because, while CD produces a significant increase in determining LD change (6.96%), AGE significantly improves the prediction of LD variation from CD by over three times as much (23.80%). Likewise, the reestimated regression coefficients reveal that only LD makes a significant contribution to CD change (.93 compared to .08 for age). By contrast, the cognitive model yields a significant coefficient only for AGE (.79), while the hypothesized causal variable contribution (.21 for CD) is not significant. The evidence clearly sup-

ports the reciprocal view of the relationship (LD → CD) for the symbolic group.

Independent assessment of the three models produces empirical support for the linguistic and reciprocal positions. But the evidence consistent with the linguistic position is highly qualified by the findings from the reciprocal model. In particular, the evidence favoring the causal role of cognitive development in determining language development variation for the presymbolic group, coupled with the failure to obtain comparable evidence supporting the causal claim of the linguistic position for those children, is the basis for accepting the reciprocal position as the model of relationship that accounts for the observations. It is not difficult, accordingly, to view the independent support for the linguistic position as an artifact of the analysis. It is first noted that the symbolic group (where the linguistic relationship LD → CD obtains as predicted by the reciprocal model) is somewhat larger than its presymbolic counterpart (21 to 16). Furthermore, the comparatively weak, albeit significant, effect of the causal variable in the presymbolic sample ($b_2(CD) = .51$) is apparently insufficient to balance the robust effects of the causal variable in the symbolic sample ($b_2 (LD) = .93$). When the two samples are combined to assess the linguistic position, these less robust effects (presymbolic group) do not counter the strong effects in the symbolic group, let alone override the effects of a larger sample which initially bias the analysis in favor of the linguistic model.

CONCLUSION

The purpose of this study has been to determine, based on evidence, which of several theoretically motivated models best describes the general relationship between language and thought in developing children. Consistent with regression analyses of data, the determination was made that the general relationship is a changing or reciprocal one. Specifically, younger children seem to exhibit a causal dependence of language development on levels of growing cognition roughly to a period when symbolic media become the general means for representing experience. After this period, the relationship becomes reversed and increased development of language produces growth to higher cognitive levels. Of course, the size of the samples observed imposes a certain tentativeness on this determination. The consistency and relative stability of the empirical relationship in these comparatively small samples, however, is encouraging. The point is that a determination of the general relationship between children's thought and language can best be made, I believe, from the joint perspective of theoretical and empirical specification.

Two implications of these findings particularly interest me. First, the pivotal point in the reciprocal model in the general onset of symbols used to represent experiences in the world. Though Bruner has made a very careful analysis of the shift from iconic to symbolic representational media, rigorous observational scrutiny of the qualitative changes in both cognitive and linguistic structures at this "point" is needed. The study of human development necessarily involves what Werner (1976:86) calls "the polar conceptualization of continuity and discontinuity." While at a quantitative level, development may be described as an increase in differentiation that is continuous and gradual, it must also be understood as successive changes from one qualitative state to another. It is the role of developmental research to link quantitative continuity with qualitative discontinuity. The reciprocal position supported by the present study identifies a general and obvious period in a child's development where qualitative change and quantitative growth are crucially linked. The generation of reliable means for distinguishing presymbolic and symbolic children seems to me a needed first step to permit such scrutiny.

Second, these findings are particularly relevant to communication scholars in so far as an understanding of language and thought in children appears to require the intermediate and crucial role of symbolic ability. Developmental studies in communication might profitably focus on the nature of this symbolic ability directly.

NOTES

1. Some scholars have argued that pathologies in the development of one process will not affect growth in the other, thereby implying a dissociation between language and cognitive development. See, for example, Furth (1971). These studies confirm that growth in the nonimpaired process does occur (however delayed). It should be clear, however, that such studies describe an exceptional kind of growth when compared to the general case.

2. A good description of these experiments appears in Luria, 1969:145-148.

3. One caveat to this perspective needs noting. Patricia Greenfield has found evidence that the employment of language for increased cognitive growth is likely to be a function of the formal training implicit in the culture. Her evidence for several cultures does indicate, however, that such intellectual training seems to be characteristic of American-educated children (among others). See Greenfield and Bruner (1966); and Greenfield (1966).

4. A detailed description of the five component measures of "cognitive development" and the four measures comprising "language development," as well as the unidimensional results of the separate factor analyses of these two sets of measures, is to be found in Elliott (1978).

5. CD and LD scores were standardized to permit comparative assessment of the models.

6. The model's coefficient of determination (R^2) and standard error of estimate (SEE) are indicants of this overall viability.

7. For a description of this test and my rationale for using it, see Elliott (1978:56-57, 89-90).

8. $p < .01$ is used throughout the chapter unless otherwise indicated.

REFERENCES

AVERROES (1954). Tahafut al-tahafut (The incoherence of the incoherence). London: Luzac.

BERLYNE, D. (1970). "Soviet research on intellectual processes in children." In Society for Research in Child Development (eds.), Cognitive development in children. Chicago: University of Chicago Press.

BLOOM, L. (1970). Language development: Form and function in emerging grammars. Cambridge, Mass.: M.I.T. Press.

BRADAC, J., and ELLIOTT, N. (1975). "Verbal behavior and drive: A theory in crisis." Paper presented at the meeting of the Midwest Modern Language Association, Chicago.

BROWN, R. (1973). A first language: The early stages. Cambridge, Mass.: Harvard University Press.

———, CAZDEN, C., and BELLUGI, U. (1970). "The child's grammar from I to III." In Psycholinguistics: Selected Papers by Roger Brown. New York: Free Press.

BRUNER, J. (1964). "The course of cognitive development." American Psychologist, 19:1.

——— et al. (1966). Studies in cognitive growth. New York: Wiley.

BRUNER, J., and OLVER, R. (1970). "Development of equivalence transformations in children." In Cognitive development in children. Chicago: University of Chicago Press.

CHOMSKY, C. (1969). The acquisition of syntax in children from 5 to 10. Cambridge, Mass.: M.I.T. Press.

ELLIOTT, N. (1978). "The general relationship between language and cognition in the developing child." Unpublished Ph.D. dissertation, University of Iowa.

FLAVELL, J.H. (1963). The developmental psychology of Jean Piaget. Princeton, N.J.: Van Nostrand.

FURTH, H.G. (1971). "Linguistic deficiency and thinking: Research with deaf subjects 1964-1969." Psychological Bulletin, 76:58-72.

FURTH, H. and YOUNISS, J. (1975) "Congenital deafness and the development of thinking." In E. Lenneberg and E. Lenneberg (eds.), Foundations of language development: A multidisciplinary approach, Volume 1. New York: Academic Press.

GREENFIELD, P. (1966). "On culture and conversation." Pp. 225-256 in J. Bruner (ed.), Studies in cognitive growth. New York: Wiley.

———, and BRUNER, J. (1966). "Culture and cognitive growth." International Journal of Psychology, 1:105.

HUANG, D. (1970). Regression and econometrics methods. New York: Wiley.

KERLINGER, F.N., and PEDHAZUR, E.J. (1973). Multiple regression in behavioral research. New York: Holt, Rinehart, and Winston.

LURIA, A.R. (1961). "The role of speech in the formation of mental processes." In J. Tizard (ed.), The role of speech in the regulation of normal and abnormal behavior. New York: Liveright.

——— (1969). "Speech development and the formation of mental processes." In M. Cole and I. Maltzman (eds.), A handbook of contemporary Soviet psychology. New York: Basic Books.

———, and YUDOVICH, F. (1956). Speech and the development of mental processes in the child. New York: Penguin.

MCNEILL, D., and MCNEILL, N. (1968). "What does a child mean when he says 'no?'." In E. Sale (ed.), Proceedings of the conference on language and language behavior. New York: Appleton-Century-Crofts.

MOSHER, F.A., and HORNSBY, J.R. (1966). "On asking questions." In J. Bruner et al. (eds.), Studies in cognitive growth. New York: Wiley.

MULLER, P. (1969). The tasks of childhood. New York: McGraw-Hill.

OLSON, D. (1966). "On conceptual strategies." In J. Bruner et al. (eds.), Studies in cognitive growth. New York: Wiley.

OLVER, R., and HORNSBY, J. (1966). "On equivalence." In J. Bruner et al. (eds.), Studies in cognitive growth. New York: Wiley.

PARISI, D., and ANTINUCCI, F. (1970). "Lexical competence." In G.B. Flores d'Arcais and W. J. M. Levelt (eds.), Advances in psycholinguistics. Amsterdam: North-Holland.

PIAGET, J., and INHELDER, B. (1948). The child's conception of space. New York: W.W. Norton.

SAPIR, E. (1921). Language. New York: Harcourt, Brace and World.

SCHAFF, A. (1973). Language and cognition. New York: McGraw-Hill.

SINCLAIR, H. (1975). "The role of cognitive structures in language acquisition." In

E. Lenneberg and E. Lenneberg (eds.), Foundations of language development: A multidisciplinary approach, Volume 1. New York: Academic Press.

SLOBIN, D. (1972). "Cognitive prerequisites for the development of grammar." In C. Ferguson and D. Slobin (eds.), Studies of child language development. New York: Holt.

――― (1974). Psycholinguistics. Glenview, Ill.: Scott, Foresman.

THURSTONE, L. (1946). "Note on a reanalysis of Davis' reading tests." Psychometrika, 11:185-188.

VYGOTSKY, L. (1962). Thought and language. Cambridge, Mass.: M.I.T. Press.

WERNER, H. (1976). "The concept of development from a comparative and organixmic point of view." The Process of Child Development. New York: New American Library.

Chapter 8

COMING OF AGE IN THE GLOBAL VILLAGE: TELEVISION AND ADOLESCENCE

Ronald J. Faber, Jane D. Brown, Jack M. McLeod

JULIE IS A JUNIOR IN HIGH SCHOOL. She is planning to take the college entrance examinations in a couple of weeks and has been studying hard in preparation for them. She becomes nervous, however, and grows increasingly unsure of her ability to score high enough to get into college. Her mother Ann, her sister Barbara, and the building superintendent Schneider are looking through college catalogues suggesting schools and potential majors for Julie. However, for Julie this only increases her fear of failing and she finally threatens them that maybe she won't go to college at all. This threat leads to an argument over the advantages and disadvantages of a college education. During the argument Julie accuses her mother of trying to run her life. She says she hasn't had time to decide what she wants to do for herself. Eventually both Julie and her mother give in a little and Julie decides to take the exams to avoid closing any options, yet does not make a commitment that she will go to college as her mother desires.

Each week, about 40 million television viewers tune in to view an episode of "One Day at a Time," from which this storyline was taken. Each week they witness the interpersonal drama (and comedy) of a three-person household made up of a young divorced woman and her two adolescent daughters. This show, and numerous other top rated programs like it, frequently focuses on the difficult and painful problems people face in their own lives. These shows, designed primarily as entertainment, have dramatized such serious problems as death, running away from home, falling in love for the first time, and coping with the stigma of a physical handicap. Do all viewers "take away" the same information and perceptions from this viewing experience? What is it they learn from watching such shows?

In this chapter we will argue that different viewers learn different things from such portrayals of life issues. We will develop a model of assessing mass media effects which suggests that the critical factor lies not just in how the program focuses on the problem, but rather in where the individual viewer is in relation to the problem. For example, an adolescent watching the episode of "One Day at a Time" just described may focus on how Julie deals with resolving the dilemma of future educational and career choices. The adolescent might also learn more about the specific kinds of educational options Julie is considering, as well as the arguments in favor of or against going to college. On the other hand, a mother of adolescent children would probably be more interested in the dilemma Julie's mother faces: how to persuade her daughter to take the tests and not limit her future options. However, another mother whose children are grown up and is considering what to do with the rest of her life may be most sensitive to the arguments for going to college or going to work even though they are discussed by an adolescent in the television presentation. A younger viewer might be expected to find Julie's problem interesting in that it points to issues they will soon have to grapple with themselves. Perhaps yet another viewer is currently involved in an argument with his or her own parents about an entirely different topic. This viewer might be most sensitive to Julie's discussion tactics as an example of strategies that might be used with his or her own parents.

These differences in perspective or issue salience brought with the viewer to the specific content will affect what that viewer takes away from his or her exposure. A number of other factors will intervene in the process of learning from television portrayals about life issues. Some of these factors will be discussed as important to an understanding of individual differences in media effects. A viewer who has had little personal experience with a range of occupations, for example, may more readily accept the television portrayal of various occupations, while a viewer who has had personal experience with persons in the occupation will compare the television portrayal with his or her prior understanding of the occupation. An individual's ability to think abstractly or to understand the underlying roles being portrayed will also affect what is learned from the presentation. The direction and pattern of influence of other socialization agents will also influence how an individual perceives specific media portrayals.

Before describing in more detail how these factors are interrelated, we will examine the issue of central concern here: how the resolution of developmental tasks may be related to media exposure. It is our intent here to develop a research model which may account for individual differences in mass media effects. The basis of the model is that we cannot assume that the media audience is similarly motivated to attend to the same attributes of particular presentations. The audience differs on a number of factors, but a critical difference is their current set of life issues. These life issues or tasks may be linked to various stages of human development. We argue that, if we can assess the salience of these life tasks at any one point in time, we will be able to predict which aspects of the media presentation will be attended to and will affect subsequent levels of knowledge, values, and behaviors of that individual.

Although any life stage can be examined similarly, we will focus here on the adolescent life stage for three reasons. First, a number of adolescent researchers and theorists (Havighurst, 1972; Erikson, 1968) have clearly specified certain developmental tasks which most adolescents are faced with between the ages of 12 and 22. These tasks include such things as choosing an occupation and other future roles, learning how to interact with the opposite sex, developing a sex-role identity, and achieving independence from the family. Second, adolescence is a period of increased activity oriented toward gathering information about the future. Such activity should increase the importance of television as an important source of information. Third, adolescents are generally in the final stage of cognitive development, unlike younger children whose thought processes are still progressing. Thus, the behavior of adolescents is less a function of what they *can* do and more a matter of what they *actually* do. They are also a more active audience than younger children because they have more control over how their individual needs for information will be satisfied. Thus, we might expect adolescents to understand more complex portrayals and perhaps even seek out such portrayals since they are relevant to their own lives.

THE RESEARCH MODEL

DEVELOPMENTAL TASK RESOLUTION STRATEGIES

The central elements of the research model described here are what we have called internal constraints. These are factors which are generated within the individual and are directly related to the specific tasks of the life stage. As the individual grows older and faces critical life decisions, he or she may adopt different strategies for dealing with the resolution of these life conflicts, e.g., what job to choose, what sort of political ideology to adhere to. The strategies a person develops for coping with these decisions vary along two dimensions. First, persons differ in the degree to which they have made a commitment to or personal investment in particular alternatives (choosing to be a doctor rather than a lawyer or nurse). Second, individuals differ in the degree to which this commitment (or lack of commitment) is based on active exploration of the range of alternatives. These dimensions are derived from Erikson's

(1968) argument that firm commitments which are preceded by periods of crisis or consideration of alternative options are necessary conditions of successful decision-making regarding life tasks. Marcia (1966) has based a program of research on Erikson's theory. He has labeled these two dimensions of decision-making "commitment" and "crisis." By dichotomizing the dimensions, he has developed a four-fold typology which may be thought of as four different strategies of life task/conflict resolution (see Figure 1). Presence or absence of crisis and the extent of commitment in any life task serves to define the decision strategy.

The *achievement* strategy is one in which the individual has experienced a crisis period and has invested in or commited him or herself to a particular choice. The *moratorium* strategy refers to those individuals who are currently engaged in decision-making, but have not yet been able to make a commitment. Individuals who adopt a *foreclosure* strategy have not experienced a crisis but have firm, often parentally or externally imposed or determined commitments. Those with a *diffusion* strategy have almost no strategy at all. The diffusion individual is not currently involved in trying to make a decision and has not made a commitment to any alternative, unlike the foreclosure who has made a commitment, but, similarly, has not experienced crisis.

Figure 1: Developmental Task Resolution Strategies adapted from Marcia's (1966) Conceptualization of Erikson's Criteria for Successful Adolescent Development

		Degree of Crisis	
		Has had or currently in period of crisis	Has not had period of crisis
Degree of Commitment	Has made commitment	Achievement	Foreclosure
	Has not made commitment	Moratorium	Diffusion

An individual may be characterized by different strategies depending on what life task is being examined. For instance, an adolescent may have successfully made a commitment to being a lawyer after many days of looking at alternative occupational choices. The person would be labeled as in an achievement strategy—having made a commitment after experiencing a crisis. At the same time, he or she may have adopted a diffusion strategy for dealing with the problem of autonomy from his or her parents. The adolescent is either comfortable in the current situation or not yet ready to cope with the anxiety of examining alternatives.

Marcia (1976) has found that decision-making strategies may also change in a rather logical sequence culminating in the achievement strategy. In a longitudinal study he found some evidence for a progression from the diffusion or foreclosure strategy to the achievement strategy through moratorium. Thus, as an adolescent moves into a period of actively seeking alternatives from which to choose (crisis) and begins to make tentative commitments (commitment), he or she moves out of the passive strategy of diffusion into moratorium. As the individual begins to firm up those commitments and narrow them down to particular, finite choices, he or she moves into the achievement strategy. The individual who begins with a foreclosure strategy (at adolescence, generally simply accepting the parents' commitments) might be pushed into a moratorium strategy by the critical change toward seeking alternatives. He or she might then conceivably get frightened by too many alternatives and either resort to the diffusion strategy or retreat back to the original foreclosure strategy. He or she could also, however, cope with the moratorium strategy of exploration of alternatives and move in the direction of adopting an achievement strategy.

ADOLESCENT DEVELOPMENTAL TASKS

A review of the literature on adolescent development indicates that these crises or tasks which an adolescent may be dealing with can be condensed and synthesized into five distinct areas. These tasks, in the chronological order that they are usually encountered during adolescence, are: (1) accepting changes in one's body and developing a positive body image; (2) developing more completely defined sex roles and learning about cross-sex relationships; (3) beginning to achieve economic and emotional independence (freedom from authority); (4) preparing for future occupational and family roles; and (5) developing civic competence. It is our belief that television, while not the sole socializing agent, can contribute to the way an individual resolves each of these tasks. Furthermore, we feel that Marcia's categories of decision strategies can be applied to each of the tasks to help determine what information from television will be most important to an adolescent using different decision strategies.

Body Image

The beginning of adolescence is usually defined by the onset of puberty and the development of changes in body shape (Campbell, 1969; Douvan and Gould, 1966). For girls, physical changes generally start around 10 years of age and last until 12 1/2. For boys, the growth spurt usually starts about two years later than for girls. Thus, boys generally start to develop around 12 and these changes continue until approximately 14 1/2 (Matteson, 1975; Tanner, 1964; Douvan and Gould, 1966).

These physical changes in early adolescence have been shown to affect also adolescents' attitudes toward themselves and their peers. Adolescents are highly self-conscious about their looks. Frazier and Lisonbee (1971) found that 50% of male and 82% of female adolescents were concerned about some aspect of their facial appearance. Jones and Bayley (1950) found that two-thirds of the adolescents they interviewed expressed a desire to change some component of their physique.

Physical attractiveness also seems to be an important factor in acceptance by peers during early adolescence. Research has shown that most young adolescents rate physical attractiveness as more important than similarity of ideas in choosing friends of either sex (Gronlund and Anderson, 1957; Cavior and Dokecki, 1973). These physical and attitudinal changes combine to form the first major task of adolescence—the development of a positive body image.

Entertainment television may play an important role in helping adolescents work through this task. Preadolescents and those people first entering adolescence have neither resolved nor thought much about their own concept of beauty or attractiveness. In Marcia's terms, these adolescents may be labeled as in diffusion in regard to their body image. For these people, television may serve as an informational device for learning what society's standards of beauty and attractiveness are. Television provides many examples of the ideal male and female bodies (for example, "Charlie's Angels"—a show starring three beautiful women detectives who solve cases at the direction of their unseen boss Charlie, "The Six Million Dollar Man" and the "Bionic Woman"—both shows starring physically attractive persons who have superior bionic powers which they use to solve crimes and avert disasters). These characters, representing the extreme stereotypes of masculine and feminine beauty, are often placed in action-adventure programs. Thus, not only are these characters beautiful, but they also display excellent control over their bodies.

Situation comedies may also be useful to adolescents who are concerned with learning society's values of beauty. Situation comedies are more likely to provide both ideal and nonideal types. For example, "Happy Days," a comedy set in the 1950s and centered around a middle-class American family, shows both the ideal (Fonzie) and the average (Richie, Potsie, and Ralph). "Welcome Back Kotter," a show about a high school teacher's relationship with his class of ne'er-do-wells, provides an even greater range of examples from Vinnie Barbarino (the ideal type) to Arnold Horshack. Thus, adolescents in diffusion may learn both the ideals and the range of acceptable body types from television.

Adolescents who are already concerned with their appearance, but who have not yet decided on how they can make the most of what they have, can be described as being in moratorium. These adolescents already know what society's values are and are concerned with living up to these values or learning to accept themselves as they are. For these adolescents, television may serve to provide a different type of information. These teenagers may pay particular attention to specific attributes of a wide range of characters. For example, the hair styles of the women on "Charlie's Angels," the "Bionic Woman," and other characters may be compared and contrasted by these adolescents to determine which they think are the best styles and/or which would most suit them. The same thing may also be done for other attributes of attractiveness such as make-up, clothes, physical builds, and walking styles. Thus, adolescents in moratorium are likely to use television to compare specific options they have open to them and to help decide which specific characteristics will most benefit themselves.

Foreclosure and achievement adolescents have already determined how they plan to resolve this task. For these young people, television may be useful only insofar as it presents characters who exhibit the particular style the adolescent has chosen for him or herself. These characters may be attended to in order to learn more detailed information. For example, an adolescent who views himself as very similar to Vinnie Barbarino may adopt some of Vinnie's mannerisms or copy his walk. These adolescents may pick up some of the more subtle information about body image, such as the importance of self-confidence in attractiveness, from a specific character. However, characters who do not fit with the adolescent's own self image are likely to be ignored or ridiculed, especially among foreclosure adolescents.

Sex Roles

Although evidence shows that much sex-role learning has already occurred before adolescence, this is the stage during which increased awareness of the biological determinants of sex differentiated behavior and increased interaction with age mates of both sexes leads to increased pressure to conform to sex "appropriate" behaviors. Nonstereotypical sex role behaviors are frequently accepted prior to adolescence on the ground that "this is just a stage which the individual will grow out of." If the person still wants to pursue these nontraditional behaviors into adolescence, however, they will often face ridicule from peers. This may be especially true for boys because they generally seek support from the full peer group while girls typically seek out a few close friends for support.

We assume that foreclosure is the most typical strategy for the sex role task in adolescence. Learning from parents, peers, and the media all combine to push the average adolescent toward sex-stereotyped roles before the adolescent or preadolescent has made any attempt to consider alternative forms. These adolescents will probably reject or ridicule television portrayals of nontraditional behaviors. While the vast majority of television content reinforces stereotyped behaviors, adolescents who are considering alternative roles may find their greatest (if not their only) source of support from those few, sensitively handled, nonstereotypical portrayals in the media.

Recent research on the concept of androgyny, or the blending of roles based on gender, suggests that sex roles are not a unidimensional construct. Individuals adopt patterns of behavior which are typically associated with their own gender along with attributes which have been traditionally associated with the opposite sex. Societal norms are slowly shifting toward greater acceptance of androgynous behaviors by both males and females. It appears that a greater degree of sensitivity in men and assertiveness in women, for example, is now acceptable.

These changes in societal norms may be encountered in the media before they are found among peers or parents. It is also now more acceptable for men to cry in some situations and for women to be less helpless and more athletic. Even a character who embodies the macho male toughness as much as the Fonz is now able to cry when his best friend is seriously injured. Action-adventure programs with female leads such as "Charlie's Angels" and "Wonder Woman" show women as competent and successful in difficult and dangerous situations. Women's sports have also gained greater respectability and wider television coverage. These programs may encourage women to continue in sports when they previously may have been discouraged by those around them. Television is even showing that women can compete with men in sports with programs like "Challenge of the Sexes" in which both male and female television stars compete in a variety of sports events. These shows may provide support for those adolescents currently considering what their options are as well as change the expectations and norms for younger viewers.

Another area of sex role learning which occurs during pre- and early adolescence is in regard to cross-sex relationships. Dunphy (1963), using participant observation, found that peer groups move from unisex groups to heterosexual cliques during adolescence. Those adolescents who are still in unisex peer groups and have not yet begun to date may be characterized as in diffusion on this task. These adolescents are aware that they will begin to date at some point and may be engaged in anticipatory socialization to prepare for this occurrence. Matteson (1975) has proposed that cross-sex behaviors are learned via the media before adolescence. During adolescence, when sexual feelings begin to emerge, adolescents may express these feelings in the ways they have seen them portrayed on television and in films.

What an adolescent will attend to during cross-sex encounters on television may differ depending on the adolescent's own prior experiences. Preadolescents who have not started to date may be most concerned with how their same sex characters are expected to act, what one does on a date, or what the sexual expectations are. Adolescents closer to beginning to date may be more concerned with specific strategies for getting dates. Entertainment television may provide examples for these adolescents. For example, strategies for asking someone out on a date have been explored in "James at 15" (the story of a young boy's adolescence), "Happy Days," and "Welcome Back Kotter." The appropriateness of girls asking boys for dates has been discussed on "Laverne and Shirley" (two young working-class women on their own in the 1950s), and "One Day at a Time." More subtle (and traditional) ways for girls to attract boys have been portrayed on "One Day at a Time," "Laverne and Shirley," "Three's Company" (two single women who have a male roomate), and "Rhoda" (single, now divorced woman on her own in New York City). Ways for women to turn down dates they do not want have also been shown on several of these shows. These portrayals may be the only way for adolescents to learn these strategies other than by trial and error. This may be especially true among males where one may feel compelled to pretend to have more experience than one does in order to obtain status within the peer group.

Television can also provide useful information to those adolescents who have already begun dating. These adolescents may use entertainment television programs to reinforce the behaviors they have already learned. Gerson (1966) found that while adolescents' use of media for norm acquisition about dating behavior is more common (42.4% report doing this sometimes or more frequently), media use for reinforcement was also fairly common (35.2%). Not surprisingly, nondaters in Gerson's study used media almost solely for acquiring norms and strategies, while those adolescents already dating reported greater usage of media for reinforcement.

Another way in which television's portrayal of cross-sex interactions can help adolescents involved in dating is by allowing them a glimpse of what life is like for the opposite sex. Girls who watch "Happy Days" or "James at 16" (the same adolescent boy one year older), for example, may be able to gain a greater understanding of the fears boys may experience in getting up the courage to ask a girl out. Similarly, boys watching shows like "One Day at a Time" may gain greater insights into adolescent girls' fears and expectations. Research studies have found that adolescent males stress eroticism over romanticism while adolescent females stress romanticism first (Ehrmann, 1959). Entertainment television may enlighten viewers of each sex about the values of the opposite sex. One episode of "One Day at a Time" recently centered around an adolescent girl's decision over which type of boy was more important to her; an attractive and popular boy who was interested in her only as a sex object versus a less physically desirable boy who was more sincere and cared for her as a person. Shows like this may help adolescents recognize these values and priorities in themselves and those around them.

Independence

Another task of adolescence is to begin to achieve emotional and economic independence from one's family. Three factors combine to make this task somewhat easier. First, strong peer groups exist during this period. During adolescence, the values of the peer group may for the first time begin to conflict with those of the family, thus giving the adolescent an alternative viewpoint (Bowerman and Kinch, 1959). Second, the adolescent is given greater opportunity to spend time outside of the home, making family relations less crucial. This also acts to prepare the adolescent for the future emotional break from home. However, studies have generally shown that adolescents use peer group norms for less important decisions such as clothing styles and music tastes, while the family's influence is still stronger for more important and long range decisions (Kandel and Lesser, 1969; Brittain, 1969). The final contributing factor is the acquisition of part-time or summer employment. These jobs make the first dent in the adolescent's economic dependence on the family.

Television may act as an anticipatory socialization agent for this task. Initially, adolescents in diffusion may be attracted to strong, independent characters who appear to have control over their own lives and successfully defy authority figures. However, as this task gains salience for adolescents and they become more concerned with actually making a break from their parents (greater crisis), the type of portrayal which is most likely to influence them changes. At this stage adolescents may attend to young adult characters on television who have or are in the process of making a break from their families. Shows like "Laverne and Shirley," "Busting Loose," and "Three's Company" show young adults out on their own for the first time, and the problems they experience.

Some programs have portrayed the difficulties in leaving home and shown the more negative aspects of life on one's own within individual episodes. The "Walton's" (a show which portrays an extended family in rural Virginia during the Depression) showed the difficulties of the oldest son's attempt to break from home to go to college. An episode of "Happy Days" depicted Richie leaving home to live with his older brother so that he could have more freedom. "One Day at a Time" ran a four-part episode where Julie ran off to live with her boyfriend. In the last two examples, the episodes ended with the major characters returning home after discovering the problems of life on their own. This may be functional in keeping those viewers who are not yet prepared from making the break from home too soon, or it can be dysfunctional in reducing the adolescent's confidence in his or her own ability to "make it" away from the family. Either way, these shows can alert the adolescent to potential problems in making the separation, as well as provide those adolescents who have already decided with specific strategies for making the break from home.

Autonomy in decision-making is also a recurrent theme on many family dramas and situation comedies. These presentations may alert the diffusion and some foreclosure adolescents to the impending task of making a separation from parental influence. For adolescents with other decision strategies, these programs may provide specific arguments and strategies they can use to gain greater decisional autonomy from their parents. However, these shows may provide the greatest benefit to those adolescents who watch them with their parents. These programs may lead to discussions of autonomy within the context of the viewer's own family. These discussions can be brought up in a less threatening and argumentative atmosphere than might have occurred without the televised presentation. These programs and/or the ensuing discussions may also serve to alert parents to the fact that their children are growing up.

Future Roles

During adolescence the individual is expected to begin preparing for the roles he or she will take on in adulthood. One of the most important future roles the adolescent will assume is the occupational role. While some search and thought about occupations occurs in childhood, there are usually large increases on both the crisis and commitment dimensions during later adolescence in regard to occupations (Ginzberg et al., 1951).

The process of occupational choice can be divided into three distinct stages. In the first stage, the individual searches through all of the possible options. Television presentations can affect this stage of the process in two ways. Normally adolescents cannot view or even know about all the potential occupations available in a modern industrial society. Technology and societal fads can invent new jobs overnight. Many potential occupations remain unknown to the majority of the population. The media can expose some of these possibilities to the adolescent. McLuhan first suggested such a sequence when he described television as serving as a global village, showing people the options they cannot come into contact with in their own lives. Even though television has been criticized for portraying only a limited range of occupations, this range may still be broader, or at least different from, those occupations the adolescent comes in contact with in his or her own environment.

Current programs on television are also beginning to present a wider range of occupational alternatives than have existed in the past. Previously, entertainment television has been characterized as presenting only a few possibilities (primarily doctors, lawyers, and police officers) primarily at the upper end of the occupational status categories (DeFleur, 1964). While these occupations are still prevalent, there is now a wider range of characters in less prestigious occupations such as garage mechanic (Fonzie), maintenance man (Schnieder on "One Day at a Time"), waitress ("Alice"), and factory workers ("Laverne and Shirley"). The middle range of occupational status positions is also represented by characters such as Archie Bunker (bar owner on "All in the Family"), Howard Cunningham on "Happy Days" and Walter on "Maude" (store owners), the characters on the "Mary Tyler Moore" show and "Lou Grant" (television and newspaper reporters, editors, and producers), Rhoda and Julie on "One Day at a Time" (designers), and Ann

Romano on "One Day at a Time," Julia and Maria on "On Our Own," and J.J. on "Good Times" (various jobs in advertising). This list represents only major characters on long running series. The number of occupations represented by characters appearing on just one episode of a program is even greater. At this stage of occupational decision, where the adolescent is merely looking at the possible options, these one-shot appearances are just as important as characters in recurring roles.

The way in which an occupation is presented may also affect whether or not it will be considered as an option. Traditional portrayals, in terms of sex appropriateness, may cause an adolescent to close out options, while nontraditional portrayals may increase the possibilities a person will consider. For example, the depiction of Jack on "Three's Company" as studying to be a chef, or of Angie Dickinson as a polic officer in the show "Police Woman," may lead adolescents to consider sex-stereotyped jobs as open to both sexes. Additionally, if an occupation is consistently shown as being dull or undesirable, it is not likely to get much consideration. DeFleur and DeFleur (1967), for example, found that children (6-13 years old) appear able to learn the prestige of various occupations from television. High television viewers were much closer to matching the status ratings parents and experts gave for occupations highly visable on television than less frequent viewers. However, at this first stage of occupational choice, the individual is more interested in what occupations are available rather than focusing on the merits of any particular job.

The second stage of occupational choice involves narrowing down all of the potential choices to those which are most desirable. Media presentations can affect this decision process. Adolescents are generally in the formal stage of logical operations. According to Piaget, one aspect of formal operations is the ability to think in terms of abstract, hypothetical reasoning (Piaget, 1972). The individual can now integrate different pieces of information in new ways. Therefore, adolescents should be able to extract different portrayals of an occupation and mentally put them together to provide increased knowledge of the differing rewards and requirements of each job. The degree to which the individual perceives televised portrayals of these occupations as realistic will obviously play an important part in determining whether this televised information is used to narrow the possibilities. If occupational portrayals are viewed as realistic, this should result in the elimination of some of the possibilities and the enhancement of others.

The last stage in the occupational decision-making process is to narrow the alternatives even further until a final decision is made. This is the process of moving from moratorium to achievement. This requires more specific information about the rewards, routines, and requisites of each occupation, as well as an awareness of the individual's own goals and values. Because televised portrayals rarely go into extensive depth in presenting occupations, it is unlikely that television will have a very large impact at this stage. However, it is possible that some televised portrayals may aid adolescents at this stage as well as those adolescents who have already made an occupational decision (foreclosure and achievement). For these people, subtle variations in their considerations may be influential.

The brother of one of our colleagues provides an example of how these subtle considerations may work. This particular adolescent had already decided that he wanted to become a chef. Upon watching an episode of "Love Boat," a comedy about short-term relationships evolving on short ocean cruises, he realized for the first time that chefs would be needed on ocean liners. Thus, he could combine his choice of vocation with his enjoyment of boats by seeking this type of employment. This possibility may never have occurred to him without his viewing of this program. This additional information may not seem very important to us, but could prove crucial to his future happiness.

Civic Competence

The final task of adolescence is the development of civic competence, a minimally informed participation in the affairs of the community. While this area, like most of the others already discussed, has its foundations in childhood, change continues through late adolescence when the legal age of voting becomes imminent and community issues become more perti- nent. Not only are these changes manifested by the accumula- tion of specific pieces of political knowledge, but later adoles- cence shows a difference in the frames of reference used to evaluate political action. Our political socialization research, utilizing the category system of Adelson and O'Neil (1966), found that 16 year olds compared to those three years younger saw problems of community conflict in rather different terms: they were more likely to consider future implications rather than just the present situation; they used impersonal as well as personal standards; they viewed the whole problem beyond its parts; they concentrated on the positive aspects of the situation rather than simply the negative facets; and they more often invoked a force of principle in analyzing conflict. All these attributes should affect the intake of television content.

Along with the growth in civic competence, older adolescents also begin to use the public affairs content of the media more (Jennings and Niemi, 1974; McLeod and Brown, 1976). There is also a growing awareness that the media may play an important role in developing political competence. Public affairs media use has been linked to the learning of specific information by adolescents during election campaigns (Chaffee et al., 1970), and our research also suggests that use of this type of content may develop more mature political frames of reference as well.

Information about politics and our legal system can also be gathered by watching entertainment television. Certainly the fact that most adolescents know that a person being arrested must be read their rights is a direct result of watching police programs on television. Most adolescents have never been in court yet they can pick up some information about the work- ings of the judicial system from shows like the "Tony Randall Show" where the main character plays a judge. However, enter- tainment television programs may be dysfunctional in this area by providing a distorted view of the judicial system for the sake of dramatic presentation.

Civic competence also includes developing one's own morals and values. Erikson, Marcia, and Kohlberg all discuss the period of adolescence as an important point in developing these values.

Kohlberg's work (1976) in moral development shows that as a person moves through the moral judgment stages there is a change in who they consider when making a moral decision. There is a movement from an egocentric orientation to a consideration of relevant others, to a societal orientation, and finally to a prior-to-society orientation.

At the beginning of adolescence individuals are usually at stages two or three in Kohlberg's hierarchy. These stages are concerned with what relevant other people will think of the individual. At stage three, for example, people determine what is morally right on the basis of what friends and peers will think. Stage four is the beginning of a societal orientation. Here, morality is based on what the law says is right. At the end of adolescence some people may reach stage five. This stage is based on a social contract philosophy. Rules and laws are seen as necessary for a smooth running society, but they are also seen as arbitrary and changeable. There is an awareness that certain principles may be more important then specific laws. This is the first stage of the prior-to-society orientation.

Kohlberg has found that most American adults never go beyond stages three or four. Additionally, the longer a person remains at a given stage the less likely he or she is to go beyond that stage. Thus, if people are going to reach the more principled levels (stages five and six), they generally do so at the end of adolescence or early adulthood.

Entertainment television presentations of the reasoning behind the action in decision-making situations can help or hinder social development. Kohlberg and Turiel state that stage growth occurs when a person begins to see the flaws in his or her own reasoning. This causes cognitive disequilibrium, which eventually produces stage change. Lorimer (1971) has shown that exposure to films can produce these changes. He used two experimental conditions. In one, subjects were taught how to reason through dilemmas and were given opportunities to try. The second group saw the movie "Fail-Safe" and two weeks later held an informal discussion about it. A control group was also used. In a 10-day posttest the instruction group showed the greatest amount of stage increase. However, on a 50-day posttest most of these subjects reverted back to their original stage. The film group, on the other hand, had a smaller increase on the 10-day posttest, but showed even greater increase on the 50-day posttest. Puzzled by these results, Lorimer reinterviewed several of the subjects. They indicated that the training group considered the instruction like school work—something to be memorized, regurgitated, and then forgotten. Subjects who saw the movie, however, were confronted with alternative forms of reasoning which they compared to their own decisions. This lead to actual disequilibrium which, in turn, lead to true stage growth. Therefore, it seems that some television presentations, coupled with interpersonal communication, can lead to stage change. However, given the current television content and the time constraints for presenting decisions in depth, it seems probable that stage growth beyond the conventional level (stages three and four) is more likely to be inhibited than enhanced. Nonetheless, the present trend toward mini-series like "Roots" and "Rich Man, Poor Man" and more feature-length televised movies may allow for greater depth in presentations which could contain the type of content necessary to stimulate stage growth.

Aside from an overall moral orientation, specific values are also undergoing examination during adolescence. These specific values appear in many individual episodes of the current television shows. "One Day at a Time," "What's Happening" (three adolescent black boys), and "Happy Days" have explored the issue of cheating in school. Lying or keeping silent to protect a friend has been dealt with on "James at 15," "One Day at a Time," and "Good Times" (a show depicting the life of an urban black family). Doing or not doing things which are against one's personal values for the sake of acceptance by peers has frequently been shown on shows like "James at 15," "Good Times," and "Eight is Enough" (a family of eight children and their parents). These are just a few of the possible examples. These programs may help adolescents to think about and clarify their own values and ethics, and eventually help them to achieve their own sense of morality.

EXTERNAL CONSTRAINTS

Until this point we have argued that the stage of resolution and the content of the task currently being resolved by individuals will affect what kinds of effects television presentations will have on their audiences. We have generally assumed that, except for the stage of resolution of the specific task, adolescents are similar in how they will perceive television shows. But even adolescents in similar resolution stages probably do not perceive the same portrayals similarly. At least three kinds of factors intervene or serve as constraints on the linkage between developmental task resolution and the effect of exposure to television. Adolescents differ in terms of prior relevant experience with the content matter, cognitive and social abilities, and social-cultural norms. We have labeled these factors external constraints because they are external to the task resolution process. We will describe each set of external constraints in turn.

Experiential constraints

Varying amounts and diversity of personal experience provide individuals with more or less information with which to evaluate media portrayals in relation to their own perceptions of social reality. These evaluations will play a part in determining the extent to which an individual uses media to help resolve the various life cycle tasks. Pingree (1978), for example, found that when children were told that actresses in television commercials actually hold jobs they represented in the commercials, the children showed less stereotypical attitudes than other children exposed to the same commercials.

Amount of experience is an important variable since we hypothesize that television will have a greater effect when individuals do not have personal experiences to use as a yardstick to measure the accuracy of the television portrayal. Noble (1976) describes television as a necessary extension for learning for modern man. In village societies all potential options are available for observation within a person's everyday encounters. However, due to the complexity of modern industrial societies, many alternatives now lie outside an individual's normal experiences. Thus, television may help to provide information about these unobservable possibilities. We would expect, for example, that urban adolescents who have had relatively little opportunity to be exposed to occupations located primarily in rural areas, such as farming or taking care of animals, would attend to portrayals of such activities in a less judgmental way than rural adolescents who have had the opportunity to observe such activities first-hand.

Cognitive and Social Ability Constraints

Adolescents differ developmentally in terms of both cognitive and social skills. We have already discussed briefly how cognitive variables may limit what adolescents can take away from media exposure. These cognitive variables are important during adolescence in at least two ways. First, adolescents who have achieved a higher level of reasoning (formal operations), and thus the ability to think abstractly, would be expected to be able to take parts of different portrayals across different shows and mentally manipulate and integrate them in different applications in their own lives. Adolescents who have not achieved this more abstract reasoning ability would be less likely to be able to assimilate diverse portrayals and thus in a qualitative sense would be learning quite different things from their exposure to television. We would expect, for example, that adolescents who have not achieved formal operations would be less likely to move into the moratorium or achievement stages of task resolution since they lack the ability to integrate different pieces of information into a coherent pattern. Pre-formal-operations adolescents might be expected to accept more readily the full role portrayal rather than only certain aspects or attributes of the portrayed role.

Second, cognitive variables are important in that they serve as a constraint on an adolescent's orientation toward the future. Concrete operational individuals have been found to be primarily limited to a "here and now" orientation, rooted in the present. The development of formal operations, on the other hand, allows the person to move beyond the present to a more future planning orientation. With the onset of formal operations, the adolescent is able to project him or herself into the future and speculate what different roles might be like. Until this time television portrayals may not seem relevant except in a very specific, short-term sense. However, in relation to some of the tasks, such as body image and interpersonal relations, the ability for future projection may not be as important as with some of the other tasks such as the development of civic competence and the selection of occupational roles, which require consideration of future, relatively unpredictable situations.

Social skills or role-taking ability may also act as a constraint on learning from the media. Generally, role-taking, or the ability to put oneself mentally in the place of the other, has been found to change with age (Selman, 1971; Flavell et al., 1968). To comprehend fully the demands and constraints on a television character, that viewer must be able to place him or herself in the character's position. This sort of comprehension is not possible until higher stages of role-taking ability have been reached. Generally, the study of role-taking has been concerned with the understanding of only one relevant constraint on another's viewpoint. However, the process of role-taking can also involve understanding multiple roles which have conflicting demands. The few studies which have investigated conflicting role presentations have found that the ability to cope with the conflicting information changes during adolescence. Gollin (1958), for example, studying how children of different ages resolve inconsistencies in role portrayals (i.e., the character is helpful in one situation and nasty in another), found that younger children (10 1/2 year olds) focused on only one of the behaviors in describing the character. Viewers who were 13 1/2 years old mentioned both the good and bad aspects of the behaviors, but still used only one of them in describing the character's personality. Subjects who were 16 1/2 years old, however, were able to discuss both behaviors and to attribute motivations to account for both of them. These results have implications for both inerpersonal interactions and for what an adolescent can and will comprehend in media presentations.

Persons with higher levels of role-taking ability may also be more likely to comprehend the difference between attributes of an individual character and the attributes of the role that character occupies. This is a crucial aspect of gathering accurate information about sex, occupational, and familial roles. For example, one must be able to discriminate between attributes which are due to Kojak's personality and those which are general attributes of all police officers. This ability to separate attributes allows the viewer to determine more appropriately how he or she might "fit in" to a given role. For example, in making choices about occupational roles, the adolescent must be able to match his or her own values, abilities, interests, desires, and so forth with attributes of the occupation such as the potential rewards, the requirements for entrance to the occupational category, and the various routines of the job. Without higher levels of role-taking ability, this process of objective comparison is not possible.

Societal and Cultural Constraints

Factors in the adolescent's environment may also influence to what extent media are used in task resolution and which aspects of media presentations are found relevant. Previous research on such variables as social class, family communication patterns, and degree of peer group integration has found that these factors influence both the pattern of media use and the kinds of effects exposure has on the individual.

For example, a large number of studies have found a positive relationship between an adolescent's social class standing and his or her occupational aspirations and expectations (Leifer and Lesser, 1976; Wylie, 1963). Social class has also been found to be related to patterns of media use. Greenberg and Dominick (1969) found that blacks and adolescents from lower social class backgrounds watch more television than adolescents from higher social strata. Lower income adolescents have also been found to perceive television as being more like real life than adolescents from higher income families.

A series of studies (summarized in McLeod and Chaffee, 1972) have shown that the patterns of communication emphasized in the family influence the adolescent's subsequent usage of the mass media. These studies have shown, for example, that adolescents who have been constrained by the need to maintain harmony in interpersonal communication situations are the heaviest users of television and spend the most time with entertainment rather than public affairs-oriented content on television. This suggests that adolescents learn patterns of communication from the interpersonal situation which they may then generalize to the mass communication situation as well. It also suggests that they may approach the mass communication situation with compensatory motives. For example, adolescents in families that emphasize the maintainence of harmony and discourage the exploration of controversial issues have been found to use entertainment television as a source of aggression. Here then, they may be able to find an outlet for those repressed desires they are not allowed to express in their family environment. Thus, we might expect that adolescents who approach the viewing situation with different motives as well as different communication expectations will attend to different aspects of the media content and will learn different things from the exposure.

The cultural context of the adolescent can influence the relationship between media exposure and task resolution in still another way. Television, or the media environment, is only one of a variety of sources of information about the larger social environment. As adolescents grapple with the tasks of their life stage, they are influenced not only by their parents, their teachers, and perhaps their church, but also by their age mates. Although most research on the influence of peers during adolescence suggests that parents retain their status as the more influential socialization agent, other research suggests that regardless of influence, simply the process of being involved with the peer group is an important part of adolescence. Johnstone (1974) found, for example, that adolescents who aspired

Figure 2: Model of Life-Span Developmental Approach to Mass Media Uses and Effects

External Constraints	→	Internal Constraints	→	Media Constraints	→	Media Uses	→	Effects
A. *Experiential*		Developmental Task Resolution Strategy		Media Content		Attributes of Content Attended To and Used In:		A. Knowledge
B. *Cognitive and Social Abilities*				(Breadth and depth of portrayal of relevant task)				B. Values
C. *Societal and Cultural*		a. Diffusion				a. Direct Learning		C. Behaviors
		b. Foreclosure				b. Stimulation of Fantasies		Regarding Developmental Tasks of Life Stage
		c. Moratorium				c. Stimulation for Interpersonal Discussion/ Consideration		(in Adolescence:)
		d. Achievement						a. Body Image
								b. Sex role
								c. Independence
								d. Future roles
								e. Civic Competence

to be accepted as members of specific peer groups, but were not fully integrated with the chosen group, were the heaviest viewers of television. Horrocks (1965:20) writes: "In addition to providing emotional bulwarks for the adolescent in the form of security, prestige and so on, the peer group has the further function of acting as a proving ground—a place to test oneself, to try things out, and to learn to cope with others."

Perhaps when the adolescent does not have the "security" of the peer group in which to test these things out, he or she may turn to another kind of proving ground—that of the world of television. Perhaps with television the adolescent may find learning about interpersonal relationships less threatening than in the peer group, which may ridicule or ostracize the adolescent for deviant "testing out" behaviors. Thus, we would expect to find greater use of the media for learning about things which are threatening or taboo in the peer group, as well as greater use of the media by adolescents who are not well-assimilated in the peer group with which they desire to be associated. Although somewhat less likely, adolescents may also use television as a third standard of comparison when the values proposed by their parents and friends are in conflict.

In sum, a number of other factors operate as constraints on the relationship between the adolescent and his or her use of television in the resolution of life tasks. We have discussed some which we consider most relevant. As more research is conducted on the use of television by adolescents other constraints will certainly emerge. At this point, however, these are some of the other factors which should be taken into account. The full research model we have been describing here is diagrammed in Figure 2.

MEDIA CONSTRAINTS

We have discussed the first two sets of constraints (internal and external) diagrammed in the model. A third set of constraints, those within the media content per se, remain. Obviously, media can be a factor in adolescent development only if portrayals relevant to life tasks are available. In our previous discussion we have provided anecdotal evidence which suggests that, at least on prime time entertainment television of recent seasons, issues centered on adolescent tasks have been portrayed. Existing content analyses of television unfortunately do not provide us with adequate information regarding the extent and diversity of such portrayals. We do not know, for example, how often and in what way issues relevant to the resolution of the task of achieving independence from the family are presented. However, we do know that, although a variety of occupations are portrayed on television, television characters are most likely to be in professional occupations and women are underrepresented in occupational roles of any kind (DeFleur, 1964). We also know that a great deal of television content is devoted to the analysis of interpersonal relationships as well as the discussion of public affairs, which suggests that television is a potential source of learning about such tasks as developing a sex role and civic competence, but also that such portrayals may be highly stereotypical or inaccurate, thus serving to limit options.

We also know, however, that television has begun to explore more taboo subjects (masturbation on "Mary Hartman, Mary Hartman"), alternative lifestyles (homosexual marriage, also on "Mary Hartman;" transsexualism on "Medical Center"), and nontraditional occupations (female lawyers and police officers). These presentations may broaden the range of options perceived by adolescents. In fact the media may play its most important role in presenting information about nontraditional lifestyles and options because these may be the most threatening topics for an adolescent to bring up in interpersonal communication. Their only source of information about these possibilities may be media presentations.

Television presentations may be an important factor in the resolution of life tasks for still another reason. Television presents a strong visual image of the outcomes of different problems and resolution strategies. Janis (forthcoming) and Abelson (1976) argue that when a person has a particularly strong visual image of an upcoming event or outcome, it will exert an inordinately strong influence on their decision-making regarding that event. This visual image is called a script. Janis believes that people can easily develop personal scripts from television, because the vivid visual image is presented there for the individual. Repetition of a specific image can add to its likelihood of being adopted as a personal script. If television can facilitate the development of personal scripts, and these scripts do influence decision-making, then media content may be of central importance in resolving many of our developmental tasks.

MEDIA USES

The three types of constraints just discussed are expected to influence media usage. Media uses are defined here as the specific content attended to and recalled, as well as the ways in which such content is used in the process of resolving specific life tasks. We have hypothesized three ways in which television content can be used in the process of task resolution.

First, television content may be used for direct learning of information relevant to the task. Adolescents may learn directly from media presentations about societal norms and ideals of female beauty, for example, from watching televised beauty pageants or commercials for beauty products. Direct learning is likely to be most important to people who feel that their considerations about a task are likely to be ridiculed or rejected in an interpersonal communication situation. For example, adolescents who mature physically earlier than their age mates may feel embarrassed about discussing the changes in their bodies with parents or peers. Similarly, an adolescent who is considering a nontraditional sex role or occupation which does not conform to peer or parental expectations may be highly fearful of discussing these topics. Therefore, much of their learning about such topics may come from the media, which is a less threatening source of information.

Second, the media can affect the resolution of life tasks through the stimulation of fantasies. Singer (1973) has found that day-dreaming is most frequent during adolescence. Adolescent fantasies tend to focus on romance, sex, achievement, and the future. Adults, on the other hand, tend to fantasize about more concrete, real life situations (e.g., where to spend a vacation, job promotions. Because adolescents are day-dreaming about future possibilities, media content relevant to the tasks of their life stage may act as a springboard for these fantasies.

Third, media content may serve as a stimulus for interpersonal discussion and consideration of options relevant to the issues of adolescence. Television has been found to be a topic of conversation in interpersonal communication between adolescents and their parents and friends (Foley, 1968; Lyle and Hoffman, 1972). Television presentations may help to raise subjects which might otherwise be hard to bring up. It may also be less threatening to discuss these issues in terms of the television character rather than as directly relevant to one's own self.

MEDIA EFFECTS

Finally, the model predicts that each of the constraint sets as well as the uses made of the media content (generation of fantasies, interpersonal communication, direct learning) will affect knowledge, values, and behaviors regarding each of the life tasks. We hypothesize that adolescents will gain information about the task area, will learn and apply new values, and finally will exhibit patterns of behavior based, at least in part, on observation of media presentations. Changes in knowledge should occur all during the task-resolution process. Changes in basic values and behaviors are more likely to occur at the point of reaching stable achievement on the task, although some exhibition of different behaviors may occur during periods of experimentation with various options (e.g., wearing make-up for a period of time to see what it looks like because women on television wear make-up).

RESEARCH IMPLICATIONS

We have presented a rather speculative look at how the mass media in general and television content in particular may affect how individuals resolve issues related to their stage in the life cycle. The focus has been on the adolescent life stage as an example of how this model may be applied. We believe this model provides a useful framework for a better understanding of the effects of the mass media on individuals.

First, the model is audience-centric rather than content-centric. Although it allows for the constraints imposed by specific kinds of media content, it forces us to place greater emphasis on the constraints with which the individual comes to the media content. In this sense it is not unlike the model of media effects called uses and gratifications (Blumler and Katz, 1974). However, this model has the advantage of not assuming rationally motivated media use, a fundamental problem of the traditional uses and gratifications approach. Unlike the classical uses and gratifications approach, we are assuming that, once individuals are exposed to the media content, they will attend to and be affected by attributes of that content which are relevant to the issues they are dealing with at the time of the exposure. We are not asserting that individuals will seek out content that will aid them in the resolution of these tasks, as the uses and gratifications approach would suggest. Although such behavior may occur, it is not a critical piece of the process we are describing here. Effects may be focused or heightened by age-related constraints with or without the conscious awareness or rational motivation of the audience member. Hence, we as researchers do not have to rely on our respondents' descriptions of why they selected a specific kind of media presentation. Rather, this model suggests that we can predict which attributes will be attended to in whatever content an individual is exposed to. The important variables here then are the stage of resolution of the task and the specification of which tasks are especially salient at the time of exposure to the media. Thus, the model serves as a method of categorizing and specifying what sorts of content we would expect to have effects on the viewer. It also provides the researcher with a method for predicting what kinds of topic areas we might expect to find media exposure related to.

For example, if viewers were exposed to the episode of "One Day at a Time" described at the beginning of this chapter, we would expect very different patterns of effects depending on the salience of life tasks and the stage of resolution of those tasks regardless of whether the person would have voluntarily chosen to watch this particular episode. We would expect, for instance, that adolescents' recall would be primarily centered on the adolescent task being discussed—choosing future roles. Exactly which attributes are recalled would also depend on to what extent the individual viewer has resolved this particular task. Adults exposed to that program would be expected to center more on the problem Ann faces in the episode—coping with children. Elderly persons dealing with the tasks of adjusting to a lifestyle without children in residence may attend to the patterns of interaction between the two adolescents or between them and their mother. In short, the model predicts that the effects of exposure to media content might be quite unrelated to the central focus of the plot. The greatest advantage of the model is that it suggests which aspects of the total media package will be most relevant to individual audience members.

The model also takes into account other factors which are likely to influence the effect of media presentations on individuals. Social class position and other external constraints, for example, may mediate the impact of exposure. The working class adolescent may see the struggles of television's privileged youngsters' attempts to plan for college in a rather different light than will an affluent middle class adolescent. While the latter may use the televised material as information for future decision-making, the non-college-bound youth may regard it as irrelevant and be affected largely through an accretion of dissatisfaction with middle class goals and values. By examining such factors as social structural location, previous experience with the content area, cognitive and social abilities, and the direction and pattern of influence from other socialization agents, we can begin to account more precisely for individual differences in the outcome of exposure to various kinds of media content.

Throughout the chapter we have suggested various points at which more research is needed. Our perspective on the model is that a great deal of research needs to be conducted within each of the components of the model before an examination of linkages between the components is possible. For example, we need to conduct more complex content analyses of existing media content in terms of their relevance to developmental life tasks. We also need to develop approaches to the measurement of task resolution strategies as well as more reliable measures of cognitive and social abilities.

A test of the linkages in the larger model implies a longitudinal data gathering strategy supplemented with experimental studies. For example, in longitudinal studies we could examine changes in media learning as the individual moves from one resolution strategy to another in regard to a particular life task. Experimentally we might manipulate the salience of specific tasks and measure the degree of recall of information peripheral to the central focus of the media stimulus, but relevant to the salient task.

A variety of methods and research strategies may be needed to elaborate the mediating effects of life-stage tasks. In the end, we are likely to see a rather complicated depiction of the effects of the mass media. While television may bring McLuhan's "global village" to the far corners of the world, it is likely that the impact of a common set of media stimuli may be very different across the life cycle and in different cultures of the world.

REFERENCES

ABELSON, R. (1976). "Script processing in attitude formation and decision making." In J. Carroll and A. Payne (eds.), Cognition and social behavior. Hillsdale, N.J.: Lawrence Erlbaum.

ADELSON, J. and O'NEIL, R. (1966). "Growth of political ideas in adolescence: The sense of community." Journal of Personality and Social Psychology, 4:295-306.

BLUMLER, J. and KATZ, E. (ed.) (1974). The uses of mass communications: Current perspectives on gratifications research. Beverly Hills, Cal.: Sage.

BOWERMAN, C., and KINCH, J. (1959). "Changes in family and peer orientation of children between the fourth and tenth grade." Social Forces, 37:206-211.

BRITTAIN, C. (1969). "Adolescent choices and parent-peer cross-pressures." In R. Grinder (ed.), Studies in adolescence. Toronto: Macmillan.

CAMPBELL, E. (1969). "Adolescent socialization." In D. Goslin (ed.), Handbook of socialization theory and research. Chicago: Rand-McNally.

CAVIOR, N., and DOKECKI, P.R. (1973). "Physical attractiveness, perceived attitude similarity, and academic achievement as contributors to interpersonal attraction among adolecents." Developmental Psychology, 9:44-54.

CHAFFEE, S., WARD, S., and TIPTON, L. (1970). "Mass communication and political socialization." Journalism Quarterly, 47:647-659, 666.

DEFLEUR, M. (1964). "Occupational roles as portrayed on television." Public Opinion Quarterly, 28:57-74.

——— and DEFLEUR, L. (1967). "The relative contribution of television as a learning source for children's occupational knowledge." American Sociological Review, 32(5):777-789.

DOUVAN, E., and GOULD, M. (1966). "Modal patterns in American adolescence." In M. Hoffman and L. Hoffman (eds.), Review of Child Developmental Research, Vol. II. New York: Russell Sage Foundation.

DUNPHY, D. (1963). "The social structure of urban adolescent peer groups." Sociometry, 26:230-246.

EHRMANN, W.W. (1959). Premarital dating behavior. New York: Holt, Rinehart and Winston.

ERIKSON, E.H. (1968). Identity: Youth and crisis. New York: Norton.

FLAVELL, J., BOTKIN, P., FRY, C., WRIGHT, J., and JARVIS, P. (1968). The development of role-taking and communication skills in children. New York: Wiley.

FOLEY, J. (1968). "A functional analysis of television viewing." Unpublished Ph.D. dissertation, University of Iowa.

FRAZIER, A., and LISONBEE, L.K. (1971). "Adolescent concerns with physique." In R. Muuss (ed.), Adolescent behavior and society: A book of readings. New York: Random House.

GERSON, W. (1966). "Mass media socialization behavior: Negro-white differences." Social Forces, 45:40-50.

GINZBERG, E., GINSBURG, S.W., AXELRAD, S., and HERMA, J.L. (1951). Occupational choice: An approach to a general theory. New York: Columbia University Press.

GOLLIN, E. (1958). "Organizational characteristics of social judgment: A developmental investigation." Journal of Personality, 26:139-154.

GREENBERG, B., and DOMINICK, J. (1969). "Racial and social class differences in teen-ager's use of television." Journal of Broadcasting, 12:331-344.

GRONLUND, N., and ANDERSON, L. (1957). "Personality characteristics of socially accepted, socially neglected and socially rejected junior high school pupils." Educational Administration and Supervision, 43:329-338.

HAVIGHURST, R. (1972). Developmental tasks and education. New York: Longmans, Green.

HORROCKS, J. (1965). "Adolescent attitudes and goals." In M. Sherif and C. Sherif (eds.), Problems of youth. Chicago: Aldine.

JANIS, I. (forthcoming). "The influence of television on personal decision making." In S. Withey and R. Abeles (eds.), Television and social behavior. Hillsdale, N.J.: Lawrence Erlbaum.

JENNINGS, M., and MIEMI, R. (1974). The political character of adolescence: The influence of families and schools. Princeton, N.J.: Princeton University Press.

JOHNSTONE, J. (1974). "Social integration and mass media use among adolescents: A case study." In J. Blumler and E. Katz (eds.), The uses of mass communications: Current perspectives on gratifications research. Beverly Hills, Cal.: Sage.

JONES, M.C., and BAYLEY, N. (1950). "Physical maturing among boys as related to behavior." Journal of Educational Psychology, 41:129-148.

KANDEL, D., and LESSER, G. (1969). "Parental and peer influence on educational plans of adolescents." American Sociological Review, 34:212-222.

KOHLBERG, L. (1976). "Stages and moralization: The cognitive-developmental approach." In T. Lickona (ed.), Moral development and behavior: Theory, research and social issues. New York: Holt, Rinehart and Winston.

LEIFER, A., and LESSER, G. (1976). The development of career awareness in young children. Washington, D.C.: National Institute of Education Papers in Education and Work: Number one, H.E.W.

LORIMER, R. (1971). "Change in development of moral judgments in adolescence: The effect of a structured exposition versus a film and discussion." Canadian Journal of Behavioral Science, 3(1):1-10.

LYLE, J., and HOFFMAN, H. (1972). "Children's use of television and other media." In E. Rubinstein, G. Comstock, and J. Murray (eds.), Television and social behavior, Vol. IV, Television in day-to-day life: Patterns of use. Washington, D.C.: U.S. Government Printing Office.

MARCIA, J. (1966). "Development and validation of ego identity status." Journal of Personality and Social Psychology, 3:551-558.

--- (1976). "Identity six years after: A follow-up study." Journal of Youth and Adolescence, 5:145-160.

MATTESON, D. (1975). Adolescence today: Sex roles and the search for identity. Homewood, Ill.: Dorsey.

MCLEOD, J., and BROWN, J. (1976). "The family environment and adolescent television use." In R. Brown (eds.), Children and television. Beverly Hills, Cal.: Sage.

MCLEOD, J., and CHAFFEE, S.H. (1972). "The construction of social reality." In J. Tedeschi (ed.), The social influence process. Chicago: Aldine-Atherton.

NOBLE, G. (1976). Children in front of the small screen. Beverly Hills, Cal.: Sage.

PIAGET, J. (1972). "Intellectual evolution from adolescence to adulthood." Human Development, 15:1-12.

PINGREE, S. (1978). "The effects of nonsexist television commercials and perceptions of reality on children's attitudes about women." Psychology of Women Quarterly, 2:262-277.

SELMAN, R. (1971). "Taking another's perspective: Role-taking development in early childhood." Child Development, 42:1721-1734.

SINGER, J. (1973). The child's world of make-believe. New York: Academic Press.

TANNER, J.M. (1964). "The adolescent growth-spurt and developmental age." In G.T. Harrison, J.S. Weiner, J.M. Tanner, and N.A. Barnicot (eds.), Human biology: An introduction to human evolution, variation, and growth. Oxford: Clarendon.

WYLIE, R. (1963). "Children's estimates of their schoolwork ability as a function of sex, race, and socioeconomic level." Journal of Personality, 31:203-224.

Chapter 9

THE YOUNG CHILD AS CONSUMER

Ellen Wartella, Daniel B. Wackman, Scott Ward,
Jacob Shamir, Alison Alexander

GOVERNMENT REGULATORS, CONSUMER ADVOCATES, major children's advertisers, and consumer educators all are interested in discovering how children acquire and use information about consumer products, especially that contained in advertising to which they are exposed. Similarly, as communication researchers, we have focused attention on children's reactions to advertising stimuli in an attempt to examine how children of different ages process television information and the kinds of particular processing demands advertising places on the child viewers. In this chapter we will discuss some new directions our research is taking in attempting to meld pressing public policy, marketing, and educational questions with broader theoretical and methodological issues in studying children's consumer information processing activities. Specifically, we will examine young children's consumer activities in two areas: first, how they represent, i.e., select, interpret, and make sense of

AUTHORS' NOTE: The research reported here was supported by Grant No. APR 76-20770 from the National Science Foundation.

advertising information; and second, how they utilize product choice strategies.

The notions presented here are an extension and elaboration of our previous work on children's consumer information processing (Ward et al., 1977). The basic model of information processing outlined in this previous research relied heavily on Piaget's theory of cognitive development to suggest major dimensions along which children younger and older than middle childhood vary. Perhaps best known of these dimensions is that of perceptual boundedness: younger children's tendency to focus on the perceptual and surface characteristics of products and advertisements (Wartella and Ettema, 1974; Ward and Wackman, 1973). We have viewed these dimensions of cognitive growth and the general cognitive abilities available to children as "rules for processing information" at various levels of cognitive development (Kohlberg, 1969).

This initial conceptual model followed rather strictly Piaget's theory and was useful in isolating the general distinctions among grade school children's knowledge about TV advertising and products. For instance, between kindergarten and sixth grade, children acquire greater understanding of the purpose of advertising; they tend to select both more and varied kinds of information when recalling a television commercial and describing a product; and they gradually use multiple attributes when comparing brands of a product group (Ward et al., 1977: Chaps. 3-4).

Piaget's theory is often interpreted as essentially a theory of deficits, i.e., children of a certain cognitive stage are seen as being unable to perform mental operations more characteristic of another stage. Piaget has contributed to this emphasis by making a number of predictions concerning children's inability to perform various cognitive tasks until reaching a certain age. These predictions are not always supported by the data (Case, 1974).

This deficit-oriented emphasis has had a profound influence on cognitive development research. Our own research has developed with this kind of deficit emphasis. Indeed, the notion of centration which we have used, describes how young kindergarten children tend to focus on less than all of the available information when either attending to an advertisement or making a consumer choice (Ward et al., 1977).

More recently, however, various cognitive developmental theorists and researchers have been shifting their research emphasis from concentrating on cognitive deficits of young children to examination of the conditions under which younger children's performance can be facilitated. For instance, in memory development research, Flavell's (1970) distinction between mediational and production deficiencies illustrates this shift quite well. A child is said to have a mediational deficiency for a particular cognitive operation if his execution of it does not facilitate recall. This is similar to a cognitive deficit. On the other hand, a child is said to have a production deficiency if he fails to produce a cognitive strategy on his own for reasons other than lack of ability or skillfulness. Thus, instead of focusing on younger children's inability to perform certain operations, i.e., searching for mediational deficiencies, increasingly researchers are focusing on *conditions facilitating the performance of the operations,* i.e., searching for production deficiencies (Flavell, 1977). Crucial in the research perspective is researcher attention to the informational demands of the experimental tasks utilized (Pascual-Leone, 1970). For instance, it has been found that young children are able to perform rather sophisticated cognitive operations when conditions are "right," but under normal conditions they do not perform these operations (Case, 1974; Brown, 1975a). Thus, in terms of their typical spontaneous behavior, young children may have rather low level cognitive response patterns. Under other circumstances, children, even kindergarteners, may perform at higher levels.

These studies suggest then that in research on children's consumer activities, two crucial conceptual clarifications must be made: first, the information processing demands of the processing tasks should be clearly delineated; and second, the conditions which facilitate optimal performance in a task should be examined. These two distinctions have informed and guided our current research in the two areas of how children understand television advertising and how children make product choices. In the remainder of this chapter, elaboration of these distinctions in the context of studying young children's consumer activities will be made: first, in the area of how children represent, i.e., select, interpret, and understand, television advertising; and second, in presenting a new approach to examining young children's product choice strategies.

CONSUMER TASKS: WATCHING TELEVISION ADVERTISING AND CHOOSING PRODUCTS

In our previous research we examined children's information processing transituationally: i.e., the same mental processes intervening between the input of a stimulus and the child's output of a response were assumed to occur both in the television viewing situation and in product choice situations. Consequently, we tended to focus on information processing activities which were similar in both task situations. For example, information selection from an advertisement was operationally defined as recall of elements in a commercial, and information selection about products was operationally defined as the kind of attributes children focus on when they are asked to consider buying a new product (Ward et al., 1977). For purposes of describing general characteristics of children's thought about the consumer environment, this conceptual and methodological approach proved useful.

However, as Dawes (1975) points out, any model of information processing is necessarily circumscribed by the task being modeled. In particular, problem-solving tasks might best be viewed as conceptually distinct from non-problem-solving tasks (Berlyne, 1970). While many of the same mental activities are involved in both situations, the task posed for the child information processor is probably much different. Similarly, television watching and choosing products are probably very different tasks for the young child since a major distinction between the television viewing situation and the product choice situation is the degree to which each task is problem-oriented, wherein the child is seeking information to reach some solution or decision, such as a product choice.

It would seem reasonable to assume that in most instances when young, grade-school children sit down in front of a TV set and watch a commercial, there is little "intention" to seek information to use in a purchase decision. This assumption is based on the evidence of relatively low comprehension of the purpose of advertising as a source of new product information across a wide range of products (Ward et al., 1977).[1] Such directed and planful use of television advertising probably occurs only rarely, and most likely at particular times during the year, such as Christmas time when children are seeking gift ideas (Caron and Ward, 1975). On the other hand, when children are asked to "choose" a cereal at the store or are given money to spend on a product of their choice, the information processing task at hand involves directed thinking activities and intentional use of information to solve a problem, i.e., to "buy" the product that "best" satisfies the child's needs or desires.

This is not to say that children do not use information which they have learned from television viewing influences product requests at Christmas time (Robertson and Rossiter, 1977). This suggests that viewing TV advertising may directly affect product choice by influencing the child to buy a particular product, i.e., by raising the salience of product X above all other brands of a product group. Alternatively, TV advertising may influence the child's strategy for approaching a product decision by suggesting certain attributes of brands in a product class to be considered, i.e., suggesting that the child buy the brand of a product that has the *most* of attribute X (Wright and Barbour, 1975).

However, the crucial point is that television advertising most likely enters product decision-making tasks sometime after viewing the television advertisement even if during TV commercial viewing, the child's desires for a product is raised. This suggests that we should examine children's memory of what they have seen and heard from television commercials, because it is what they have stored and retrieved from memory which will influence their processing activities at the time of product decision-making, while models of problem-solving activities might be most useful for examining children's product choice strategies. First, let us consider a conceptualization of young children's memory for a television advertisement, and findings from a study utilizing this conceptualization.

CONCEPTUALIZING MEMORY OF CHILDREN'S ADVERTISEMENTS

In examining how children represent advertising information in their memory, we have relied on a view of memory which distinguishes between two types of memory: episodic memory or memory for a specific event which occurred at a specific time and place; and semantic memory, or the accumulated knowledge one has acquired about the world (Brown, 1975b). Piaget and Inhelder (1973) refer to the former as "memory in the strict sense" and the latter as "memory in the wider sense." Episodic memory involves memory for directly experienced occurrences, the actual input or verbatim recollection of experience and "for discrete perceptual instances that are distinct and separable from the larger unit in which they occur" (Brown, 1975b:136). Thus, episodic memory is usually what is referred to as verbatim memory for a television commercial or program, because it involves remembering the elements of the television commercial. On the other hand, Brown (1975b) notes that semantic memory involves "memory for meaningful systems of units in context." Such memory is constructive and holistic and it is memory for the gist of the narrative or story, such as the overall "message" a viewer constructs from a TV commercial.

Further, as Brown (1975b) points out, no particular interaction with an environmental stimulus is totally one type of memory experience or the other for a child; aspects of both episodic and semantic memory are involved whenever a child interacts with the environment. Children's semantic memory system, in the broadest sense their acquired knowledge about the world and their attendant cognitive abilities, skills, and language, helps determine what they will "remember" about any specific episode or occurrence, i.e., it influences children's episodic memory: "What the head knows has an enormous effect on what the head learns and remembers" (Flavell, 1977:189).

This perspective maintains that memory is a constructive process. Memory "involves an imaginative reconstruction or construction built on extant knowledge" (Brown, 1975b). Both at the point of storing and retrieving information from memory, the subject is constructing and reconstructing an internal representation of that information to be remembered (Paris, 1975).

One result of this constructive aspect of memory is that children attempt to integrate information they remember to comprehend the "gist" of the stimuli presented (Paris, 1975). Children integrate semantic information to construct a holistic meaning of that information. They go beyond the information given to integrate ideas and form inferences. Further, as Paris (1975) points out, children's integration of information is sometimes at the expense of correct recognition of information they had actually seen or heard.

The perspective on memory outlined above has a very basic implication for research on children's information processing of television advertisements: as researchers, we should examine more than children's verbatim or episodic memory for particular elements of commercials, such as brand name or product attributes mentioned. Examination must be made of the kinds of inferences and connections children make when integrating the advertised information into their semantic memory system, i.e., what overall message do the children take away from the commercial? Even in the absence of children's faithful and accurate retrieval of specific elements from an advertised message, these children may still "remember" some constructed or integrated meaning from the message. It may be this "constructed meaning" from the message which children recollect from the advertisement during product decision-making situations.

How best can researchers measure children's memory for the television advertisement? What measurement procedures should be used to avoid interpreting a production deficit, i.e., poor retrieval of information which is stored in memory rather than a true mediational deficit (i.e., no memory for the information)?

Particularly, the issue becomes quite thorny when young children such as kindergarteners are the subjects of investigation.

Measurement of children's memory for television advertising information has typically employed open-ended recall measures (Rossiter, 1975; Rubin, 1972; Ward et al., 1977). Furthermore, researchers have focused primarily on verbal memory to the neglect of visual memory (Rossiter, 1975). Although the particular modality used to code information in memory is still open to debate (Bransford and McCarrell, 1974; Brown, 1975; Piaget and Inhelder, 1973), it seems reasonable to allow for the possibility of multiple forms of representation—visual, verbal, and imaginal. As Rossiter (1975) has suggested, multiple memory codes should be measured.

The issue of how best to measure retrieval of information from memory may deserve more attention than previous research on advertising and children has acknowledged. Particularly, more attention should be paid to the distinctions between recall and recognition memory. While researchers may tend to think of recall and recognition questions as measurement tools, recall and recognition activities also constitute types of retrieval activities for the subject being interviewed. Moreover, recall and recognition memory place different task demands on the subject for actively retrieving information from memory.

Recognition involves external memory cues for the child, such that there is already something present in immediate experience to assist the retrieval process. There are no such external cues present in recall memory. In recall, the subject has to do more of the retrieval job himself; "Recall is the more difficult process as it demands regeneration in the absence of the stimulus" (Brown, 1975:111). Piaget (1968) and Brown (1975) have proposed that there is a developmental progression in the development of these retrieval activities, such that recognition memory develops earlier in the child than does recall memory. Several studies provide evidence that recognition is a more efficient memorial process than recall for children younger than middle childhood (Brown, 1975; Ritter et al., 1973; Kobasigawa, 1974). This research literature suggests that both recognition and recall measures should be used to examine young children's memory for television advertising information. It may be the case that previous research has underestimated what young children are remembering from television. In the next section of this chapter, we will consider some research findings on children's memory for television advertisements utilizing the conceptual and methodological distinctions in memory development identified here.

RESEARCH FINDINGS ON CHILDREN'S MEMORY FOR TELEVISION ADVERTISEMENTS

In the past two years, we have been engaged in a series of experiments designed to examine kindergarten and third grade children's information processing of several specially produced commercials for hypothetical brands of candy and game products. In one study in Columbus, Ohio, 76 kindergarteners and 84 third graders were shown in small groups a one-half four videotaped cartoon show in which commercials for two hypothetical chocolate covered raisin candy products, Yummies and Gobbles, were included. The children came from a middle class suburban school district and were tested in their schools.

The commercials shown the children varied along two dimensions. One of the dimensions varied the type of appeal made in the ad: product appeals stressed the ingredients and health attributes of the product; social appeals stressed personal benefits or attributes the child would incur from using the product, such as making friends. A second dimension manipulated the mode of presentation of these appeals: the information was presented either audio-visually, just visually, or just audially. Thus, both the number and kind of product attributes mentioned in the commercials and the overall intended message of the commercials which the child viewed were manipulated. Each child had three exposures to a product attribute appeal for one brand and three exposures to a social acceptability commercial for another brand of the candy.

A post-viewing interview was designed to tap those aspects of memory which we have discussed, i.e., children's episodic and semantic memory for the advertising information. The general question strategy used in assessing children's memory for specific elements of the commercials began each type of question about a commercial or product attribute with a recall measure (e.g., "What product did the commercial show you?"). If the child was unable to retrieve completely the commercial information, a multiple choice recognition item was then asked (e.g., "Was it: (a) a raisin candy, (b) a chocolate covered raisin, or (c) a chocolate covered peanut?"). Thus, through a revolving sequence of recall and visual and verbal recognition measures, we attempted to maximize our ability to assess what the young children remembered both about the product advertised and the narrative message presented in the commercial.

In addition, we attempted to assess how young children might go beyond the information given in the television commercial, i.e., to assess their semantic memory for the commercial. For instance, two measures we utilized were to ask the child first, "What does this commercial want you to know about Yummies/Gobbles?" and second, "What does this commercial want you to do?" Thus, we were interested in examining the kinds of connections and inferences the children might make between the commercial information and their own consumer behavior.

Let us consider the data regarding the children's overall impression from the commercials first. For purposes of this chapter, the data from the Columbus study will be presented in terms of children's memory for the two types of commercial appeals: product attribute appeal (PA) commercials, and social acceptability appeal (SA) commercials.

The most striking finding regarding the question "What does this commercial want you to know?" is the children's difficulty in answering it: more than half of the kindergarteners for both PA and SA commercials did not respond to this question, as opposed to about 10% of the third grade children. Similarly, for the question "What does this commercial want you to do?" 40% of the kindergarteners did not respond when discussing product attribute commercials and 47% did not respond when discussing social acceptability commercials. On the other hand, a negligible percentage of third graders did not respond to this item—about 5%.

When children did answer the question, the most frequent response for both age groups (between one-quarter and one-half of the children across appeal type) was to mention a specific product attribute of commercial element. A second major category or response was a general affective response, e.g., "This commercial wants you to like the product."

Lastly, when children did answer the question regarding what the commercial wanted them to do, about four-fifths of the third graders for both PA and SA commercials responded "buy the product." About 50% of the kindergarteners for PA commercials and two-thirds of the kindergarteners for SA commercials also said this. The next most frequent type of response for both age groups was that "The commercial wants you to try them or eat them."

The impression these data make are that nearly half of the kindergarten children are not taking away much of the "gist" of the commercials, at least not as evidenced by the way in which we attempted to measure semantic or wholistic memory for the commercials. The message children do articulate is that the commercial wants you to like and buy the product advertised.

While it may be argued that the children may just not be retrieving or remembering much of the commercial after only three exposures, examination of the data on children's memory for discrete product elements indicates that this is not really the case, although as previous research has shown, third graders do recollect more of the discrete information in the commercial than do the kindergarteners. For instance, when you examine children's accuracy in either recalling or recognizing particular attributes mentioned about the products in the commercials, such as "What's a Yummie/Gobble?" or "How many candies are there in a box?" about half the kindergarteners and about three-quarters of the third graders accurately recollect more than three of the six different product elements measured for each appeal type.

Moreover, of interest here is that, if only recall measures of children's memory were taken, we would be underestimating the kindergarteners performance. For instance, Table 1 presents the percentage of kindergarten and third grade children accurately recollecting product attribute information from both the product attribute appeal and social acceptability appeal commercials. The data differentiate between those children accurately and completely recalling the information and those accurately recognizing the correct answers. As this table indicates,

Table 1: KINDERGARTENER AND THIRD GRADER RECALL AND RECOGNITION OF PRODUCT ATTRIBUTE INFORMATION FROM PRODUCT ATTRIBUTE APPEAL (PA) COMMERCIALS AND SOCIAL ACCEPTABILITY APPEAL (SA) COMMERCIALS

	SA Commercial		PA Commercial	
	K	*3*	*K*	*3*
1. What is a Yummie/Gobble?				
Recall	28%	74%	36%	83%
Recognition	35%	11%	25%	7%
No complete retrieval	37%	15%	39%	10%
	N = 71	N = 82	N = 72	N = 80
2. How many raisins are in a single Yummie/Gobble?				
Recall	38%	80%	44%	78%
Recognition	22%	9%	15%	7%
No complete retrieval	37%	15%	39%	10%
	N = 69	N = 81	N = 72	N = 80
3. How many Yummie/Gobbles in a box?				
Recall	0%	11%	1%	13%
Recognition	27%	38%	27%	41%
No complete retrieval	73%	51%	72%	46%
	N = 71	N = 82	N = 71	N = 79
4. How is a Yummie/Gobble made?*				
Recall			29%	62%
Recognition			24%	14%
No complete retrieval			47%	24%
			N = 71	N = 79

*Note: This questions was not asked about SA commercials

third graders show better memory overall of the advertised product than do kindergarteners, particularly when recall measures are employed. However, when recognition measures are used, the percentage of kindergarteners remembering the commercial product elements improves considerably.

Thus, again, to assess accurately young children's optimal performance in remembering the advertised information, it is crucial to assess their memory through use of more than recall measures. Otherwise, we might underestimate the young children's learning from the advertisement.

These data are provided to illustrate the importance of the conceptual distinctions we have made in our continuing research program. We are continuing to analyze our experimental data with regard to more accurately assessing young children's optimal performance in recollecting television advertising.

Furthermore, the conceptual clarifications of adequate task analysis and assessment of optimal performance on tasks are addressed in a new approach to studying children's consumer choice decision-making. In our current research we are attempting to distinguish and clarify those processes involved in choice situations, the kinds of choice strategies children use. Below, in considerable detail, we will consider a new approach to studying how young children engage in consumer choice strategies in an experimental setting. The procedure to be discussed was part of the overall series of experiments examining young children's consumer information processing.

CONCEPTUALIZING CHILDREN'S PRODUCT CHOICE DECISIONS

In order to conceptualize how children utilize information in reaching product choices, the kinds of decision strategies they use, and the consistency of their use of particular strategies, we began our analysis of product choice tasks by examining the adult literature on consumer decision-making. Specifically, we relied heavily on multiattribute models of product choices (Wilkie and Pessemier, 1973; Holbrook and Hulbert, 1975; and Hansen, 1976). Such research has typically utilized a preference rating approach to measuring choice strategies. Measures of adults judgments of the importance of a product attribute or a value dimension are combined with measures of the extent to which subjects believe different brands possess the attribute or fulfill a particular value. Then, by applying various averaging or adding rules which represent specific data combination processes, predictions are made concerning the subject's preference scores for the different brands. The specific process used is then validated against measures of overall brand preference. In this adult research, the data combination processes are usually assumed to be equivalent to choice strategies.

However, there are two major dimensions characterizing any data combination process. First is the amount of information used. Some data combination processes use all of the available information, e.g., those defined as a weighted averaging compensatory model, while others may use only minimal information, at least in some circumstances, e.g., those defined as lexicographic or sequential elimination models.

Second, and more importantly, is *how* information is used. Some models, such as compensatory models, involve object comparisons, i.e., all information about each individual option is combined together to develop a series of overall evaluations of the options before the options are compared to each other. Other strategies, such as lexicographic and sequential-elimination models, involve essentially attribute comparisons, i.e., options are compared on the basis of information about a single attribute or a series of attributes, taken one at a time. This distinction is similar to that used in analyses of consumers' information behavior, i.e., interdimensional search or intradimensional search strategies (Payne, 1976). We wanted to clearly distinguish these two dimensions, given our expectations of how young children make product choices.

We expected children's use of product choice strategies to reflect the kinds of differences we have found in our earlier research on use of product information. First, young children are likely to use less information in making choices and, furthermore, are less likely to use more abstract information, such as attribute importance information (Ward et al., 1977). Second, children younger than middle childhood appear to have great difficulty performing the cognitive operation of compensation, i.e., recognition that one action or dimension in a perceptual task can counterbalance another action or dimension (Flavell, 1977), whereas older children are able to do so more easily, at least as evidenced by performance on various conservation tasks. Expressed in quasi-mathematical terms, this would suggest that young children cannot perform averaging operations very easily. Therefore, they may have substantial difficulty using various compensatory choice strategies.

However, several recent studies have indicated that young children do average when developing preference ratings of consumer products and people (Butzin and Anderson, 1973; Hendrick et al., 1975). In both studies subjects were asked to integrate two items of information. However, when kindergarteners were asked to integrate more information, they did not use a consistent averaging strategy (Capon and Kuhn, 1978). Findings from these studies perhaps indicate that young children may experience a production deficiency in performing an averaging operation when the informational task is expanded beyond a small number of "bits."

Third, kindergarten and third grade children also differ in performing ordering operations. Kindergarteners can order objects, but they appear to lack an overall plan or guiding principle when they do so (Inhelder and Piaget, 1964). On the other hand, third graders appear to construct orderings on the basis of a plan or consistent principle. Differences in performance of this operation suggest that younger children are likely to have more difficulty in using strategies which involve hierarchical ordering of attributes, such as a lexicographic strategy.

Thus, our general expectations regarding children's use of choice strategies were that older, third grade children should use choice strategies which utilize more and more abstract information than those used by younger, kindergarten children, and older children should use consistent choice strategies as compared to younger children. We were also interested in examining the range of different kinds of decision strategies kindergarten and third grade children use.

MEASURING CHILDREN'S PRODUCT CHOICE STRATEGIES

A rather elaborate measurement procedure was developed to assess children's strategy use. It manipulated two aspects of product information: the importance of attributes and the amount of the attributes included in a particular candy. Five candy attributes were used—chocolate, caramel, raisins, peanuts, and licorice. Each attribute was differentiated from the other visually in two ways: shape and color.

Attribute importance information was manipulated by telling the child to imagine that she or he was to choose a present for a friend who likes chocolate very much and raisins and peanuts somewhat less. Information about the importance of the two other attributes—caramel, an even more important attribute than chocolate, and licorice, an unimportant attribute—was introduced in a similar fashion later in the interview. Visual reminders in the form of smiling faces for amount of liking were displayed on cards before the child throughout the measurement process.

Importance information was assigned to the subject's hypothetical friend (John/Mary in order to minimize the effect of the subject's own attribute preference on his choices. Furthermore, importance "weights" were assigned in order to create an ordering such that chocolate would be seen as only slightly more important than raisins and peanuts. This was done in order to provide a relatively sensitive test of a sophisticated compensatory model—a weighted adding strategy. Similarly, licorice was assigned much less importance than the other attributes in order to provide a robust test of a low information model—what we call an amount strategy.

Amounts of attributes which the hypothetical candies contain were manipulated by showing a card to the child. Generally, five pieces of the attribute were used to indicate a large amount of an attribute and two indicated a small amount. Each candy contained anywhere from one to three attributes. Subjects were asked to choose a candy for their friend from among the two or three candies displayed on each card. These were

Figure 1

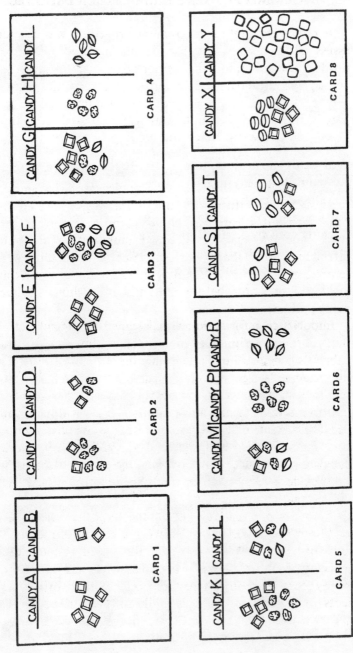

verbally described by the experimenter. For example, in describing Card #2, the experimenter read:

> Candy C has a little chocolate (E points at chocolate in Candy C) and a lot of raisins (E points at raisins in Candy C).
>
> Candy D has a little chocolate (E points at chocolate in Candy D) and a few raisins (E points at raisins in Candy D).
>
> Which one do you think John/Mary will like better—this one (E points to Candy C) or this one (E points to Candy D)?

Subjects were provided the set of choices represented by the eight cards shown in Figure 1. The first card was a warm-up for the child, but the remaining seven cards all contributed to our measure of choice strategies.

To measure various strategies, we constructed the specific set of cards used by first identifying a number of plausible choice strategies (Wright, 1975). The strategies we identified were the following, ordered in terms of the amount and kind of information used:

1. Amount—choice based on total number of items contained in candy; no differentiation of attributes.

2. Best Single Attribute—choice based only on the amount of the single most important attribute contained in the candy.

3. Variety—choice based on the number of attributes a candy contains; total amount of candy and amount of each attribute are irrelevant.

4. Lexicographic—choice based on the amount of the most important attribute, but if the options are tied on this attribute, choice is based on the amount of the second most important attribute.

5. Weighted Adding—choice based on the sum of the products of the importance weights and amounts of all the attributes contained by each candy; choose the option with the highest score. (This assumes a subject applies a metric similar to the one we manipulated.)

We then developed a series of cards which would do two things: (1) indicate the consistent use of each strategy in terms of a pattern of choices; (2) distinguish each strategy from every other one by at least one choice, and sometimes two.

For example, the lexicographic strategy involved the following series of choices on cards two through eight: C, E, G, K, M, T, and X. The weighted adding strategy involved the following series of choices: C, F, G, K, M, T, and X. As we can see, these two patterns were the same except for the choice on Card 3: subjects using a lexicographic strategy would choose Candy E to maximize the most important attribute, chocolate; subjects using a weighted adding strategy would choose Candy F to maximize the overall value of the candy.

This measure enables us to identify which specific strategy each subject uses *on the basis of his choices alone.* It has other features as well, however. It is designed so that lower information strategies would not always provide a choice. For example, on two cards—numbers 6 and 7—an amount strategy will not provide a clear choice. Therefore, subjects who prefer this strategy must shift to another strategy at this point. Subjects who prefer to use a best single attribute strategy cannot make a clear choice at Card 2. Subjects using a variety strategy cannot make a clear choice at Cards 2 or 7.

In classifying subjects in terms of the strategy they used, we did *not* demand complete consistency for all relevant choices. Rather, we classified those subjects as users of a strategy if their pattern of choice was consistent with the designated pattern with no more than one exception. Thus, classifying a subject as a user of a specific strategy indicated the subject's choices were entirely consistent with the strategy or deviated only one time.

One further aspect of our methodology should be noted. After a subject made each choice, he was asked why he made the choice he did.

CHILDREN'S USE OF PRODUCT CHOICE STRATEGIES

Fifty-four kindergarteners and 165 third graders were tested using the above product choice measure. All came from middle class suburban schools: the kindergarteners from Columbus, Ohio, and third graders from Ohio and St. Paul, Minnesota. As we expected, more third graders were classified as strategy users (i.e., they had a highly consistent choice pattern), 94% compared to 83% of the kindergarteners (χ^2 - 6.5, df. 1, p = .01). However, more important than the difference is the finding that such a large percentage of *both* age groups exhibit consistent patterns.

However, as Table 2 indicates, there are major differences between the kindergarteners and third graders in their use of choice strategies. Fully 70% of the kindergarteners use an amount strategy involving no attribute information, compared to 18% of the Ohio third graders and 6% of the Minnesota third graders. On the other end of the scale, only one of the kindergarteners used a strategy which involves attributes ordered by importance, compared to 25% of the Ohio and 26% of the Minnesota third graders. Twenty-eight percent of the kindergarteners did take attribute importance into account to some extent by using either a best single attribute or variety strategy; however, much larger percentages of third graders did so—57% of the Ohio and 68% of the Minnesota third graders. Validation for our classification of children as users of specific strategies comes from the children's verbal descriptions of their reasons for each choice. These descriptions were coded in terms of the same five strategies. For each group, we compared the percentage of children who were consistent strategy users and who verbalized this strategy frequently (i.e., three or more times).[2]

Examining kindergarteners, we find that 74% of the children classified as amount users also verbalized this strategy fre-

Table 2: CHILDREN'S CHOICE STRATEGIES BY AGE

Choice Strategies	Ohio Kindergarteners %	Ohio Third Graders %	Minnesota Third Graders %
Amount	70	18	6
Best single attribute	22	29	41
Variety	6	28	27
Lexicographic	2	22	21
Weighted adding	0	3	5
	100	100	100
Sample size	54	65	100

quently, compared to only 28% of the other kindergarteners (χ^2 = 12.3, df. 1, p < .001). Similarly, two-thirds of the kindergarteners classified as best single attribute users expressed this strategy frequently compared to 18% of the other kindergarteners (χ^2 = 9.5, df. 1, p < .001). Comparisons for the third graders show similar results.

Both the choice pattern and verbalization measures strongly support our expectations that older children are much more likely to use attribute importance information in making choices than are younger children. Indeed, much of the data suggests that most kindergarteners simply do not use this kind of information. Let us examine this more closely, however, by looking at the strategies that amount-strategy kindergarteners shift to when their preferred strategy does not provide a choice.

Up until Card 6, amount users could consistently apply their simple strategy because on each card this strategy provided a clear choice. However, on Card 6, each of the options contained six items (there was no product which had more of an attribute). Among the kindergarteners, only 37% shifted to a strategy involving the use of the given attribute importance information, as indexed by their verbal description.

These results would appear to suggest that a large number of kindergarteners had a mediating deficiency—a cognitive deficit— preventing them from incorporating attribute importance information in their choice strategies. However, as we shall see by examining their choice strategies on Card 7, this is probably not the case.

Before the children were presented with Card 7, new attribute information was introduced and the experimenter reviewed the subject's understanding of the attribute importance information introduced previously. *All* subjects correctly answered the questions indicating that they were aware of the attribute importance information without being reminded. Then the experimenter said:

> Now imagine that your friend John/Mary likes caramel even more than chocolate, so s/he likes caramel most of all. You see there is a very big smile on the caramel face: s/he likes caramel even more than chocolate.

Essentially, what is being done here is solidly reinforcing the salience of attribute importance information. We are, in effect, creating a condition which makes it easier for the child to recognize the relevance of this information so that when his preferred strategy does not provide a choice, the cues help him shift to another strategy. Thus, when amount users face the equal amounts of candy in Card 7, it is likely that they will apply a best single attribute strategy—unless they have a cognitive deficit. The results clearly indicate that the great majority of kindergarteners do *not* have a cognitive deficit preventing them from using attribute importance information. In fact, 35 of the 38 kindergarten amount users expressed a best single attribute strategy in Card 7.

However, the fragile nature of these kindergarteners' use of this strategy is indicated by their choices and verbalizations in Card 8. Before this card was presented to the subjects, they were told that licorice was the candy least favored by their friend. But Card 8 contained a major discrepancy in terms of the total number of items, with 22 pieces of licorice compared to 10 items of chocolate (5) and caramel (5). In their choice on Card 8, 21 of the 38 amount users chose the licorice candy, totally ignoring the attribute importance information and verbally 20 of the kindergarteners indicated they were using an amount strategy.

These children were responding heavily to the perceptual features of the choice situation, but it is important to note that this is *not* just a methodological effect. A great deal of evidence suggests that the younger child is highly susceptible to perceptual aspects of his environment, perhaps relying too heavily on these aspects in many situations. In the research setting we utilized, many kindergarteners clearly responded to the number of items, a dominating perceptual feature. In real consumption situations, they are equally likely to respond to perceptual features, such as the size of the box, presence of a premium in the product, and so forth.

The pattern of responses of the amount strategy kindergarteners in Cards 6, 7, and 8 suggests that their use of a limited information strategy is not due to mediational deficiency—a cognitive deficit. Rather it is due to a production deficiency which can be counteracted, as their strategy in responding to Card 7 indicates.

Besides examining shifts in strategy made by subjects whose preferred strategy provided no clear choice on a particular card, we were also able to examine certain features of higher information strategy users, i.e., children who used a lexicographic or weighted adding strategy. In these analyses we were interested in the extent to which the subjects indicated they had used their preferred strategy in their verbalizations or had used another strategy instead.

We found that those choices involving more complex information were handled differently from choices with simpler information arrays. For example, Card 5 involved a relatively complex information array. In this choice 71% of the high information users provided verbal descriptions of their strategy which were coded as high information strategies (lexicographic or weighted adding). On the other hand, for Cards 6 and 8, which involved less complex information arrays, more than half of the high information users indicated utilization of lower information strategies through their verbal descriptions.

These results suggest that high information strategy users may be just as sensitive to situational factors as children who prefer to use strategies involving lower levels of information. It may be the case, for example, that when a choice situation is relatively simple and does not require the use of elaborate information integration, high information strategy users will indeed utilize a simpler strategy, such as best single attribute or variety, which will yield the same choice as a more complex strategy. On the other hand, when faced with more complex information, they move easily to a higher information strategy.

We think the research reported here raises a number of both substantive and methodological issues worth discussing. Recent research on young children's use of information in evaluating products has yielded contrasting results. Butzin and Anderson's (1973) study indicated that kindergarteners consistently used an averaging process in forming judgments when two items of information were involved. On the other hand, Capon and Kuhn

(1978) found evidence of considerable inconsistency in kindergarteners' approach to evaluating a set of options where four dimensions of information were involved. Their results indicated that perhaps kindergarteners use a "shifting single dimension strategy" in developing a set of evaluations, similar to a basic ordering principle identified by Inhelder and Piaget (1964).

In the present study, we found that the great majority of kindergarteners (83%) used a consistent strategy in making a series of choices. This is despite the fact that our information environment was *more* complex than Capon and Kuhn's, at least on the surface. Every card involved at least two attribute dimensions, for which both attribute importance and attribute amount information was relevant. Thus, each choice may have involved eight or more items of relevant information, compared to only four in the Capon and Kuhn study.

However, it is probably the case that our kindergarten subjects coded the information in such a way as to simplify it considerably. In particular, as indicated by the large numbers who used an amount strategy, many may have simply coded one aspect of information—the total number of items in each candy—and ignored all other aspects of the information. Thus, by simplifying the information environment to a single dimension, they were able to apply a consistent choice principle with ease.

Similarly, others who used a best single attribute strategy also may have simplified the information environment by focusing only on the number of items in a specific subclass, i.e., the most important single attribute—chocolate or, later, caramel. For these subjects, too, simplifying the information environment may have made it easy to apply their preferred strategy with high consistency.

It may be the case that young children are always able to apply evaluation or choice strategies consistently when they are able to code—or recode—the information presented such as to simplify it considerably. On the other hand, they may not be able to use a strategy consistently, when they cannot do this.

We believe the methodological approach utilized here has a number of advantages. Perhaps one of its chief advantages is that it can be very helpful in developing conceptualizations of a process. For example, analysis of the variety strategy indicated that performance of this strategy involved the following operations: (1) ignoring the total amount of each candy; (2) ignoring the amounts involved in subclasses of each candy, such as amount of chocolate, raisins, or peanuts; (3) focusing on and counting the number of subclasses contained in each candy; and (4) choosing the one with the most subclasses.

When we combined this "task analysis" with some developmental principles, it suggested to us that few of the kindergarteners would be likely to use the variety strategy because it required that a dominant perceptual cue—the number of items—be ignored. Thus, thinking about the strategies for the purpose of developing our measure of choices was very useful for conceptual and hypothesis development. As Newell and Simon (1972) and Dawes (1975) point out, this kind of task analysis is essential in conceptualizing human information processing generally.

Other, more methodologically oriented strengths of the choice pattern procedure include the following: (1) it places minimal reliance on verbal behavior though verbal aspects of the measurement can be useful for providing validation of the choice pattern as well as other information regarding subject's strategies; (2) it provides an opportunity to assess consumer choice strategies in terms of a sequence of choices, and, at the same time, to examine the impact of specific situational factors on consumer choices; and (3) the procedure allows subjects the freedom to combine information in any way they choose, the key methodological requirement for measuring consumers' choice strategies, as we see it.

A major drawback of the procedure, however, is that it does not duplicate real shopping situations, so that inferences to child consumers' in-store behavior are suspect. However, it may be possible to modify the procedure to make it more realistic. This, of course, would result in losing some control of the information environment.

A CONCLUDING NOTE

In this chapter we have attempted to outline some new approaches to examining the young child as consumer. We feel that the information processing approach we have utilized in our past research has been informed by considering two important conceptual clarifications: first, adequate analysis of the information processing task posed in various consumer situations whether it be watching television advertising or making product choices; and second, attempting to assess through various measurement strategies children's optimal performance in task situations. Of crucial concern is that the researcher attempt to assess whether the child is *unable* to perform a task, i.e., has a cognitive deficit, or whether the child can perform the task under certain circumstances, i.e., has a production deficiency.

In the area of examining children's memory for television advertising, we believe that the two above-noted distinctions have led us to better estimate young children's recollections of advertising information. In addition, they have provided us with a totally new direction for examining children's product choice behavior. We believe that our conceptual distinctions between the TV viewing situation and product choice situations will better help us analyze precisely how advertising information may impact on consumer choices. For the moment, our concern is with adequate assessment of the young child's performance in these two situations. In future, we will be examining in greater detail how the one impacts on the other.

NOTES

1. For instance, among kindergarten, third, and sixth grade subjects surveyed, only 4%, 15%, and 38% respectively, indicated that they recognized the selling motive when they responded to the question: Why are commercials shown on television? (Ward et al., 1977:60, Table 4-4). Further, when these same children were asked to name sources of new product information for toys, clothes, and snack foods, fewer than one-third of the kindergarteners, and only about one-half of the third and sixth graders mentioned TV commercials (1977:57, Table 4.2).

2. The number three was chosen as the cut-off point for two reasons. First, since some strategies could not be used to make some choices because both options were equal according to the strategy, we thought that a verbal indication by a subject that

he had used a strategy on one-half of the choices or more was sufficient to indicate high usage. Second, *no* child verbally expressed two different strategies three times each. Consequently, by using three as a cut-off point, no child would be classified as a user of two separate strategies in terms of the measure of verbal expression.

REFERENCES

BERLYNE, D.E. (1970). "Children's reasoning and thinking." In P.H. Mussen (ed.), Carmichael's manual of child psychology. New York: Wiley.
BRANSFORD, J.D., and MCCARRELL, N.S. (1974). "A sketch of a cognitive approach to comprehension: Some thoughts about what it means to comprehend." In W.B. Weimer and D.S. Palermo (eds.), Cognition and symbolic proceses. New York: Winston.
BROWN, A.L. (1975a). "The development of memory." In H.W. Reese (ed.), Advances in child development and behavior, 10. New York: Academic Press.
——— (1975b). "Recognition, reconstruction and recall of narrative sequences by preoperational children." Child Development, 46:156-166.
BUTZIN, C.A., and ANDERSON, N.H. (1973). "Functional measurement of children's judgments." Child Development, 44:529-537.
CAPON, N., and KUHN, D. (1978). "The development of consumer information processing strategies." Unpublished manuscript, Harvard University.
CARON, A., and WARD, S. (1975). "Gift decisions by kids and parents." Journal of Advertising Research, 15:15-20.
CASE, R. (1974). "Structure and stricture: Some functional limitations on the course of cognitive growth." Cognitive Psychology, 6:544-574.
CELLERIER, G. (1972). "Information processing activities in recent experiments in cognitive learning—Empirical studies." In S. Farnham-Diggory (ed.), Information processing in children. New York: Academic Press.
DAWES, R.M. (1975). "The mind, the model and the task." Pp. 119-130 in F. Restle, R.M. Shifrin, N.J. Castellan, H.R. Lindman, and D.P. Pisoni (eds.), Cognitive theory, Vol. 1. New York: Wiley.
FLAVELL, J.H. (1970). "Developmental studies of mediated memory." In Advances in child development and behavior, Vol. 5. New York: Academic Press.
——— (1971). "First discussant's comment: What is memory development the development of?" Human Development, 14:272-278.
——— (1977). Cognitive development. Englewood Cliffs, N.J.: Prentice-Hall.
HANSEN, F. (1976). "Psychological theories of consumer choice." Journal of Consumer Research, 3:117-142.
HENDRICK, C., FRANTZ, C.M., and HOVING, K.L. (1975). "How do children form impressions of persons? They average." Memory and Cognition, 3:325-328.
HOLBROOK, M.B., and HULBERT, J.M. (1975). "Multi-attribute attitude modles: A comparative analysis." In M.J. Schlinger (ed.), Advances in consumer research, Vol. 2. Chicago: Association for Consumer Research.

INHELDER, B., and PIAGET, J. (1964). The early growth of logic in the child. New York: Norton.

KOBASIGAWA, A. (1974). "Utilization of retrieval cues by children in recall." Child Development, 45:127-134.

KOHLBERG, L. (1969). "The cognitive-developmental approach to socialization." Pp. 347-480 in D. Goslin (ed.), Handbook of socialization theory and research. Chicago: Rand-McNally.

LIEBERT, D.E., SPRAFKIN, J.N., LEIBERT, R.M., and RUBENSTEIN, E.A. (1977). "Effects of television commercial disclaimers on the product expectations of children." Journal of Communication, 27:118-124.

NEWELL, A., and SIMON, H.H. (1972). Human problem-solving. Englewood Cliffs, N.J.: Prentice-Hall.

PARIS, S.G. (1975). "Integration and inference in children's comprehension and memory." In F. Restle, R.M. Shiffrin, N.J. Castellan, H.R. Lindman, and D.P. Pisoni (eds.), Cognitive theory, Vol. 1. New York: Wiley.

PASCUAL-LEONE, J. (1970). "A mathematical model for the transition rule in Piaget's developmental stages." Acta Psychologica, 63:301-345.

——— and SMITH, J. (1969). "The encoding and decoding of symbols by children: A new experimental paradigm and a neo-Piagetian Model." Journal of Experimental Child Psychology, 8:328-355.

PAYNE, J.W. (1976). "Heuristic search processes in decision-making." Pp. 321-327 in B.B. Anderson (ed.), Advances in consumer research, Vol. 3. Cincinnati: Association for Consumer Research.

PIAGET, J. (1968). On the development of identity and memory. Worcester, Mass: Clark University Press and Barre.

——— and INHELDER, B. (1973). Memory and Intelligence. New York: Basic Books.

RITTER, K., KAPROVE, B.H., FITCH, J.P. and FLAVELL, J.H. (1973). "The development of retrieval strategies in young children." Cognitive Psychology, 5:310-321.

ROBERTSON, T.S., and ROSSITER, J.R. (1977). "Children's responsiveness to commercials." Journal of Communication, 27:101-106.

ROSSITER, J.R. (1975). "Visual and verbal memory in children's product information utilization." In B.B. Anderson (ed.), Advances in consumer research, Vol. 3. Cincinnati: Association for Consumer Research.

RUBIN, R.S. (1972). "An exploratory investigation of children's responses to commercial content of television advertising in relation to their stages of cognitive development." Unpublished Ph.D. dissertation, University of Massachusetts.

WACKMAN, D.B., and WARD, S. (1975). "The development of consumer information processing skills: Contributions of cognitive development theory." In B.B. Anderson (ed.), Advances in consumer research, Vol. 3. Cincinnati: Association for Consumer Research.

WARD, S. and WACKMAN, D.B. (1973). "Children's information processing of television advertising." Pp. 119-145 in P. Clark (ed.), New Models for Communication Research. Beverly Hills, Cal.: Sage.

——— and WARTELLA, E. (1977). How children learn to buy: The development of consumer information processing skills. Beverly Hills, Cal.: Sage.

WARTELLA, E., and ETTEMA, J.S. (1974). "A cognitive developmental study of children's attention to television comercials." Communication Research, 1:46-69.

WILKIE, W.L., and PESSEMIER, E.A. (1973). "Issues in marketing's use of multi-attribute attitude models." Journal of Marketing Research, 10:428-441.

WRIGHT, P. (1975). "Consumer choice strategies: Simplifying vs. optimizing." Journal of Marketing Research, 12:60-67.

––– and BARBOUR, F. (1975)." "The relevance of decision process models in structuring persuasive messages." Communication Research, 2:246-259.

ABOUT THE CONTRIBUTORS

ABOUT THE CONTRIBUTORS

ALISON ALEXANDER is a doctoral candidate in the Department of Communication, Ohio State University. Her research interest focuses on the development of communicative competence from the mass media and in interpersonal communication settings.

JANE D. BROWN is Assistant Professor in the School of Journalism at the University of North Carolina (Chapel Hill). She received her Ph.D. in Mass Communications at the University of Wisconsin (Madison). Her major research interests include media and socialization, media and development across the life span and media portrayals of the elderly.

W. ANDREW COLLINS is Associate Professor in the Institute of Child Development at the University of Minnesota. A 1971 Ph.D. of Stanford University, he has been involved in research on cognitive developmental aspects of television effects and is also interested in the development of interpersonal skills and perceptions.

JESSE G. DELIA is Professor and Head of the Department of Speech Communication and a Research Professor in the Institute of Communications Research at the University of Illinois at Urbana-Champaign.

NORMAN ELLIOTT received a Ph.D. from the Communication Research Division of the Speech and Dramatic Art Department, University of Iowa, in 1978. His dissertation study, which is the basis for the essay in this volume, was awarded the Speech

Communication Association Dissertation Award for 1978. His research on a variety of aspects of language behavior has included reports in *Human Communication Research* and *Journal of Communication Disorders,* as well as papers presented to the Chicago Linguistic Society, Speech Communication Association, and elsewhere. Elliott is currently an Assistant Professor of Communication at the Ohio State University.

RONALD J. FABER is a Ph.D. candidate in the School of Journalism and Mass Communication at the University of Wisconsin (Madison). His research interests include life-span development and media use, cognitive development, and children and television advertising.

WILLIAM HUSSON is a doctoral student in communication at Rensselaer Polytechnic Institute. His interests center on the information processing and cognitive development of children.

ROBERT KRULL is Associate Professor and Director of the Communication Research Laboratory at Rensselaer Polytechnic Institute. He is interested in the appeals and effects of television.

JACK M. McLEOD is Professor of Journalism and Mass Communication and Chairman of the Mass Communications Research Center at the University of Wisconsin (Madison). He received his Ph.D. in social psychology from the University of Michigan. His work has included the political socialization of adolescents and comparative political effects of communication among young and older voters.

BARBARA J. O'KEEFE is an Assistant Professor in the Department of Speech Communication, Theatre, and Journalism at Wayne State University.

BYRON REEVES is an assistant professor of Journalism and Mass Communication at the University of Wisconsin-Madison. He received his Ph.D. in communication from the Department of Communication, Michigan State University. His research interests are concentrated in the general area of media and children with specific interest in children's perceived reality of television, children's perceptions of television characters, children and television news, and television and sex-role development.

GAVRIEL SALOMON is an Associate Professor of Educational Psychology and Communication at the Hebrew University of Jerusalem and was until recently Head of the Educational Psychology Program there. He has recently spent two years at Stanford University writing a book on *Media, Cognition and Learning,* and another book, to be published in Israel, on *Communication and Education.* He has received his Ph.D. in educational psychology and communication at Stanford University. He is presently interested in research on communication patterns in organization.

JACOB SHAMIR is a doctoral candidate in the School of Journalism and Mass Communication, University of Minnesota. His major research focus is on consumer behavior and the development of consumer training programs for grade school children.

DANIEL B. WACKMAN is Professor and Director of the Communication Research Division, School of Journalism and Mass Communication, University of Minnesota. His research focuses on the role of communication—both interpersonal and mass communication—in childhood and adult socialization. He has recently coauthored the books *Alive and Aware: Improving Communication in Relationships* and *How Children Learn To Buy.*

SCOTT WARD is Associate Professor of Business Administration at Harvard University and Senior Research Associate at the Marketing Science Institute, a nonprofit research organization affiliated with the Business School. He is coauthor of the book *How Children Learn To Buy.* His current research interests are in understanding consumer behavior processes in family units, focusing on how parents and offspring interact and influence purchase decisions, and in understanding how major purchases occur in families through the life cycle.

ELLEN WARTELLA is an Assistant Professor in the Department of Communication, Ohio State University. Her research focuses on the application of cognitive development theory to children's perception and comprehension of television programming and advertising. She is coauthor of the book *How Children Learn To Buy*.